ATHEISTS IN AMERICA

Edited by

MELANIE E. BREWSTER

ATHEISTS
IN AMERICA

Columbia University Press / New York

Columbia University Press
Publishers Since 1893
New York   Chichester, West Sussex
cup.columbia.edu

Library of Congress Cataloging-in-Publication Data
Atheists in America / edited by Melanie E. Brewster
        pages   cm.
   Includes bibliographical references.
    ISBN 978-0-231-16358-3 (cloth : alk. paper) — ISBN 978-0-231-53700-1 (e-book)
   1. Atheists—United States—Biography. 2. Atheism—United States.
I. Brewster, Melanie E., editor of compilation.

   BL2747.3.A845   2014
   811'.80973—dc23

                                                2013040430

Columbia University Press books are printed on permanent and durable
acid-free paper.
This book is printed on paper with recycled content.
Printed in the United States of America

c 10 9 8 7 6 5 4 3 2 1

COVER DESIGN: Catherine Casalino
COVER IMAGE: © Shutterstock/alexkar08

References to websites (URLs) were accurate at the time of writing.
Neither the author nor Columbia University Press is responsible for URLs
that may have expired or changed since the manuscript was prepared.

CONTENTS

CONTENTS

PART 3

TWO CLOSETS?
Identifying as Both LGBTQ and Atheist

91

PART 4

AIN'T NO MOUNTAIN HIGH ENOUGH
Navigating Romantic Relationships as an Atheist

117

14. ON LOVE AND CREDULITY

Matt Hart

PART 5

——

FAMILY LIFE AND ATHEIST PARENTING

15. DINNER WITH GRANDMA

Ronnelle Adams

16. PARENTING AUTHENTICALLY IN AN INTERFAITH MARRIAGE

Kevin J. Zimmerman

17. HAVING A BABY MADE ME AN ATHEIST

Amy Watkins

18. BORN SECULAR

Adrienne Filargo Fagan

PART 6

——

THE SEARCH FOR CONNECTION

Coming Out to Friends and Questing for Community

CONTENTS

CONTENTS

ACKNOWLEDGMENTS

I AM DEEPLY grateful to the friends, family, and colleagues who encouraged me to write this book. I would particularly like to thank my parents for their undying love, even when I officially joined *the dark side*. And finally, a big thank you to James Mouritsen for his critical eye and fervent advocacy of the Oxford comma.

ATHEISTS IN AMERICA

INTRODUCTION
THE OTHER CLOSET

An Introduction to Atheism and Coming Out Processes

WHAT WE "KNOW" ABOUT ATHEISM

"Unbelief is the greatest of sins." Though most people are largely oblivious to his writings, the spirit of St. Thomas Aquinas's words seems to have permeated the collective psyche of the American public. Almost daily, political officials and conservative news networks remind us of the "attack on Christianity" by secularists and, subsequently, the perils of losing sight of our foundation as a religious nation. However, atheists themselves have also become increasingly vocal. Controversial authors such as Daniel Dennett, Victor Stenger, Richard Dawkins, Michael Shermer, Sam Harris, Dan Barker, and the late Christopher Hitchens have all contributed to the surge of pop-atheism books published in the past five to ten years. And, in looking at book sales for these authors, it seems clear that consumers were hungry for the content they offered. At the time, the popularity of the books seemed to baffle journalists, with one candidly expressing that "secularism is suddenly hip, at least in the publishing world" and positing that the phenomenon was a backlash against the perceived rise in religious fundamentalism and crazes for pop-spirituality books.[1] Perhaps the clearest example of success is Dawkins's *The God Delusion*; released in 2006, by 2010 the English version sold over two million copies[2] and remained on the *New York Times* nonfiction bestseller list for fifty-one weeks.[3] In the book, Dawkins persuasively argues that God or any supernatural creator is unlikely to exist and therefore that personal belief in God is upheld only by persistent belief in the face of strong contradictory evidence, the textbook definition of delusion. Collectively, the tone of these books is assertively oppositional toward religion, claiming the alleged intellectual and moral high ground of nonbelief.

The rise of this movement within the secular community has been termed "New Atheism" and is marked by "a more militant, in-your-face kind of atheism."[4] The founding New Atheist authors were some of the first people truly to bring atheist discourse *out of the closet* and into mainstream discourse—indeed, they are renowned scientists, journalists, professors, and thinkers, undeniably successful and intelligent. Deftly described by Seth Andrews, an infamous atheist blogger and radio personality, these men challenged stereotypes about *who* atheists were:

> In the minds of the faithful (at least here in the American Southwest), the atheist is the poster child for darkness and chaos, a rebellious, rudderless, angry, sad, pathetic malcontent who is ill-equipped to understand the God-originated concepts of joy, love, goodness, truth, family, life and death. The atheist poisons the well. The atheist is a molester of minds that children should be shielded from. The atheist lurks in the shadows of upright society, a counter-culture anomaly, a freak.[5]

In their books, lectures, and debates the founders of New Atheism generally appear composed, thoughtful, informed, and even humorous or playful—certainly not disfigured creatures of the night. With unapologetic tones, unabashed defiance, and sometimes mocking sarcasm, their words deftly undermine thousands of years of religious belief and indoctrination. But the approach of those in the New Atheist movement has not been uniformly embraced by larger atheist communities, who sometimes view such books as combative, ridiculing, counterproductive, and evangelizing.[6]

For many people, painting all religious institutions as, in Christopher Hitchens's words, "enemies with gnarled hands who would drag us back to the catacombs and reeking altars" is unnecessarily filled with hubris and machismo.[7] Reactions to the New Atheist movement also highlight the imbalance of demographic representation (in terms of voice and numbers) within the community.[8] Specifically, some individuals perceive atheist communities as exclusive clubs (for men who are white and upper middle class) that do not openly welcome women or other minority group members. Barry Kosmin, director of the Institute for the Study of Secularism in Society and Culture and Research at Trinity College, describes that hard-secularist positions are increasingly held by men; illustratively, the Freedom from Religion Foundation (a positive atheist group) reports that 79 percent of their members are men. Kosmin states that "a lot of women are turned off by what they call the 'warlords of atheism' and what they interpret to be very aggressive attitudes held by Christopher Hitchens and Richard Dawkins and people like that."[9] Thus, many individuals may agree with atheist beliefs, but they do not support the dogmatic mobilization efforts and violent animus of the male leaders of New Atheist movements. Throughout *Atheists in America*, voices of atheist individuals who represent a diverse array of racial groups, socioeconomic classes, and genders are presented; their relationships to the broader atheist community and outspokenness about religion vary greatly, highlighting that New Atheists are not the rising (or sole) faces of the secular in America.

CONSPICUOUSLY UNDERSTUDIED

At this point, you may be wondering how academics, specifically social scientists, have weighed in on atheism. If you are hearing crickets, this should give you some indication of the state of thoughtful and empirically valid atheist literature within academia. An EBSCOhost search (a major search engine for academic publications) of peer-reviewed religiosity and spirituality-related (R/S) articles related to the social sciences from the last decade will yield roughly 480,000 articles. Parallel searches with atheist-related keywords will yield about 1,200 articles. Though academic literature on R/S beliefs is vast and growing, few studies include meaningful discussion of nonbelievers and atheist individuals, and the few articles that include atheism do not address nonbelief as a valid diversity issue.[10]

One major theme within recent R/S research is to explore the links of belief with the promotion of well-being, including mental health, cancer, HIV, heart conditions, and many other physical ailments.[11] However, Frederick Kier and Donna Davenport note that "if one subscribes unthinkingly to the theory that those who are religious are healthy, it is not a far stretch for one to flip this logic into a theory that those who are unreligious are unhealthy, sick, or otherwise impaired."[12] As only a handful of studies have begun to explore the well-being of nonreligious individuals, society as a whole may take on this potentially damaging view of atheists.

The conspicuous gap in academic research regarding atheism may be linked to scholars' focusing their attention on topics that are "more publishable"—in short, those that are politically correct and unlikely to draw controversy. Within the currently religious and conservative sociopolitical climate of the United States, atheism is a contentious topic.[13] However, the fundamental hesitancy of researchers to address atheist issues in the social sciences is growing increasingly problematic. Some estimates suggest that there are between 500 and 750 million atheists, agnostics, and nonbelievers worldwide. In the United States, the number of atheist-identified people are rising;[14] 4 to 15 percent of individuals in the United States identify as atheist,[15] which translates to a minority group comparable in size to LGBTQ (roughly 4 to 10 percent),[16] African American, and Asian American populations in the United States (roughly 13 percent and 5 percent, respectively).[17] In both numbers and decibel level of protests, atheists are rapidly becoming a minority group that demands scholarly attention.

ATHEISM: IDENTITY, RELIGION, OR PHILOSOPHY?

It should be noted that estimates of the rates of atheist identification are notoriously unclear as the "precise definition of 'atheism' is both a vexed and vexatious issue."[18] There remains no clear consensus on who atheists are and what they believe (or, rather, don't believe). Recent literature presents non-belief as a spectrum that ranges from strong atheism to weak atheism.[19] Specifically, "a principled and informed decision to reject belief in God" or gods would be considered strong atheism[20] whereas someone who lacks a strong belief in or is unsure of the existence of God/gods (an agnostic) would be consider a weak atheist.[21]

Beyond a lack of consensus about *what* atheists believe, debates about what it *means* to call oneself an atheist are rampant. Is atheism an identity in the same way that being a woman, a Methodist, or an Asian American is an identity? Is atheism a part of one's core self or simply a signifier of what a person does *not* believe? And what about the differences among New Atheists, humanists, and people who just want to wax poetic about social justice and secularism without a label?

NEW ATHEISTS

Most historians trace the birth of the New Atheist movement to September 11, 2001, and the acts of terror that day. While nonbelievers and secular humanists had been present in the media for years, they typically operated on the defensive (e.g., fighting for rights when infringed upon) and not the offensive (e.g., openly attacking and challenging the sanity of religious belief). Dale McGowan describes how many atheists felt a collective sense of exasperation with the notions that the only acceptable "American" response to religious-based terrorist attacks was for citizens to pray, strengthen faith-based initiatives, and "crusade" against those who committed the crime. Using religious belief to fight crimes that were motivated by religion felt counterintuitive, but what felt even more upsetting to atheists was blaming the terrorism on the "secularization" of America. Enraged, Richard Dawkins released an essay four days after the attack to "make the case that religion was an 'elephant in the room' that everybody was too polite to talk about, and that religion wasn't just incidentally involved but had played an essential, indispensible part in the tragedy—the tragedy that literally *couldn't have happened without it.*"[22] He went on to clarify that he was motivated by a deep sense of anger and grief that, within the United

States, we maintained a "hands off knocking religion" respectfulness and even encouraged mourners from incompatible religious backgrounds to pray together without facing the devastation and murder enacted *through* faith on 9/11.

Dawkins was later joined by the writers and thinkers Sam Harris, Daniel Dennett, and Christopher Hitchens, to form the (tongue-in-cheek) Four Horsemen of New Atheism. Victor Stenger, a physicist and proponent of New Atheism writes:

> Perhaps the most unique position of New Atheism is that faith, which is belief without supportive evidence, should not be given the respect, even deference, it obtains in modern society. Faith is always foolish and leads to the many evils of society. The theist argument that science and reason are also based in faith is specious. Faith is belief in the absence of supportive evidence. Science is belief in the presence of supportive evidence.[23]

This view, shared by Stenger and other New Atheists, has been dubbed "scientism" by some critics of the movement (e.g., Massimo Pigliucci) and described as an "unrealistic fixation" on empirical facts and data to dictate morals and serve as an antidote to supernatural beliefs. In this light, science becomes a replacement faith that is forcefully defended with the same dogma and zeal as religion. In his book *The New Atheism*, Stenger provides an interesting rebuttal to such criticisms.

According to New Atheists, people around the world need to be released from the spell of religion and start living thoughtful and authentic lives. The Four Horsemen and others point to events such as parents' belief in faith healing leading to the death of their kids (e.g., the recent case of seven-month-old Brandon Schaibe, who got a minor rash and died because his parents refused to treat him with antibiotics and instead prayed)[24] and question how society reached a point where this level of "tolerance" of unscientific and dangerous beliefs became acceptable. The New Atheists have organized rallies, coming out campaigns, and aggressive billboard advertisements and, for the first time in atheist history, have actively sought to recruit fellow nonbelievers to "leave the closet" and join in the fight to immunize humanity against the God virus.[25]

(SECULAR) HUMANISTS

While the term "humanism" may have a relatively brief history, the tradition dates back to the ancient Greeks. It died down during the height of Christianity and was revived during the Renaissance. Humanism is not a religious orientation but instead an ethical lens from which a person is responsible for choosing her own destiny while living considerately toward others. A primary goal of humanism is to be intentional and thoughtful when enacting values and goals. By definition, humanism is disinterested in issues of the supernatural or an afterlife. As eloquently stated by the philosopher A. C. Grayling: "Humanism is the concern to draw the best from, and make the best of, human life in the span of a human lifetime, in the real world, and in sensible accord with the facts of humanity that are shaped and constrained by the world. This entails that humanism rejects religious claims about the source of morality and value."[26]

In contrast to New Atheists, humanists do not take an oppositional stance against religion; rather, they often choose to downplay differences between believers and nonbelievers, working for the greater good for all of humankind. In 2007, the Harvard Humanist Chaplaincy hosted an event called "The New Humanism" (a direct riff off of New Atheism) to set goals and give a name to the growing population within the secular community that was discontent with the aggressive approach of the Four Horsemen. New Humanism aims to be sympathetic and tolerant while acknowledging the human condition; illustratively, a primary mantra within the movement is *do good and be good . . . without god*. A flurry of New Humanist books have been published since 2007, some of which have been met with disdain by New Atheists for seeming apologetic, eager to please, or Pollyannaish. Some of this discontentment may be in reaction to the impulse that some atheists have to go "above and beyond" (in terms of community service, helpfulness, and kindness) in order to convince believers that they are not only moral but super-moral. Such pressure to be a model minority is not foreign within identity discourses.[27] However, according to New Atheists, all atheists have a responsibility to speak out against religion, not simply "do good" and let religion continue to "do bad."

There is a longstanding tradition of African American humanist thought that has tended to be more realistic and critical of human nature. From this perspective, humanism is not just about "doing good" but also about being aware of the power some groups have to inflict harm. Anthony Pinn posits that black *nontheist humanism* puts history, social justice, and responsibility at the forefront of its identity, as it recognizes both the potential and limits of humanity—the ability to do both great harm and great good. He writes:

> African American nontheistic humanist ethics involves proper action and behavior in the context of concrete and historically arranged life. As such, it concerns a wrestling over both language and materiality. In wrestling over language, African American humanist ethics exposes the fragility of discursive constructions that oppress—exposing them as nonessential structures of meaning that can be challenged. With respect to materiality, this ethical platform concerns itself with the promotion of more fulfilling and free modalities of our occupation of space and time. This ethical system recognizes that the battle takes place from within systems that we resist, but also support as embodied selves.[28]

Finally, some nonbelievers have made it their focus to centralize humanistic values within politics and government. The social philosopher Austin Dacey argues for a revival of secular liberalism—which is not a religion but an intellectual and political movement that puts freedom of individuals before God or government and seeks sources of meaning, morality, and community outside of organized religion. He laments that both *secular* and *liberal* have become dirty words in the United States, and thus, the few individuals who push back against religiosity in government are labeled as militant or fundamentalist atheists.[29] Dacey purports that beliefs (religious, atheist, or blasphemous) should not be relegated to the private sphere but instead held up to conscious thought and public appraisal to assess their strengths, weaknesses, and relevance. Through this open conversation and appraisal, the understanding and creation of greater good may be born. He writes:

> Secular ethics begins with the reality of love, the desire for the good of the other for the sake of the other. Our good or well-being is not just what we happen to want, but what we would want if we knew what we were doing. . . . Conscience is what unites thinking persons and free peoples across ethnic, national, and creedal lines, and in its unfolding through public conversation, our moral lives are measured out. Conscience cannot be found in duty to God, for it is conscience that must judge where one's duty lies, and so the faithful cannot hold a monopoly on morality.[30]

Though distinct in some ways, an overarching theme of New Atheism, humanism, and other forms of secular ethics is that people are capable of living full, content, and socially just lives without the guiding hand of God or the proscriptive tenets of religious faith. For some, atheism may be a cherished personal identity, readily disclosed and fought for. For others, it may be a lens through which to view the world or simply a philosophical stance about morality and politics.

SO, JUST WHO ARE THE ATHEISTS?

DEMOGRAPHICS

In the United States, several demographic characteristics of atheists emerge: they tend to reside in the Northeast or West and are well educated, politically liberal or independent, and more likely to identify as men and Caucasian.[31] This means that studies find almost unanimously that atheist identification is less common for women and for people of color and that levels of religious involvement are higher for these groups.[32] Religiosity may provide solace from feelings of frustration and anxiety linked with a marginalized position in a society in which sexism and racism is rampant. Indeed, as discussed further in chapter 2, many studies have found that individuals from socially oppressed groups use their religious communities as systems of support in dealing with a "one down" position in the world.[33] Reports of the demographic composition of atheist populations routinely show that atheists tend to have privileged identity statuses in society (i.e., well-educated white men of higher socioeconomic status). Therefore, occupying these privileged positions may reflect the subsequent lack of a "need" to use religious beliefs, communities, or organizations as buffers against oppression.

However, reasons for demographic disparities among atheists may be more complex. Prominent African American humanist thinkers (e.g., Sikivu Hutchinson, Donald Barbera) critique leaders of the New Atheist movement for marginalizing atheist women and people of color. Indeed, the founding Four Horsemen (Dawkins, Dennett, Harris, Hitchens) are all older, privileged, white men. The feminist and atheist blogger Greta Christina presents a call to arms against the whitewashed sexism of the atheist movement:

> When we say things like, "Sure our movement is mostly white and male—but that's not our problem . . ." What we're really saying is, "White male atheists are the real atheists. White male atheists are the ones who count. The reason white men stay in religion, or have a hard time coming out as atheists—those are the real reasons, the ones we should be addressing. Women and people of color—they're special, extra, other. We shouldn't have to change our behavior to include them in the movement. This should be a One Size Fits All movement—a size that fits white men."[34]

Drawing from work by Hutchinson—acknowledging that organized religions have largely been "bulwarks" for institutionalized sexism, racism, and heterosexism—it seems evident that more women, people of color, and LGBTQ individuals would join atheist movements if they felt more represented and included in the dominant discourse. Illustratively, even as far back as 1852, Frederick Douglass criticized the hypocrisy and complicity of the faithful in the face of slavery during a fiery speech in New York:

> The church of this country is not only indifferent to the wrongs of the slave, it actually takes sides with the oppressors. It has made itself the bul-

wark of American slavery, and the shield of American slave hunters. Many of its most eloquent Divines, who stand as the very lights of the church, have shamelessly given the sanction of religion and the Bible to the whole slave system . . . and this horrible blasphemy is palmed off upon the world for Christianity! For my part, I would say, welcome infidelity! welcome atheism! welcome anything! in preference to the gospel, as preached by those Divines! They convert the very name of religion into an engine of tyranny, and barbarous cruelty, and serve to confirm more infidels, in this age, than all the infidel writings of Thomas Paine, Voltaire, and Boling-broke, put together, have done.[35]

Clearly, atheism is not an identity that historically, or presently, belongs to white men.

DECONVERSION

In attempting to explain *who* atheists are, it is also important to address what they are not. Unfortunately, there are no firm national statistics that capture the percentage of atheists who were "born without belief" (or, for whatever reason, for whom religion did not stick during their upbringing) versus those who "deconverted" from a religious belief system later in life. It is also unclear if atheists are typically apostates from some faiths more than others, though a small study by Hunsberger and Altemeyer did find that 63 percent of forty-six atheists sampled were originally Catholic.[36]

John D. Barbour describes religious deconversion as a metaphor for radical personal transformation; specifically, it is "the metaphor in Western culture for analogous experience of change involving radical doubt, moral revulsion from a way of life, emotional upheaval, and rejection of a com-munity."[37] While not necessarily as devastating or dramatic as described by Barbour, deconversion involves the complicated process of "becoming an ex" and leaving a role that you previously knew. Helen Rose Fuchs Ebaugh posited that there may be a number of stages to exiting religious roles, including experiencing doubts, seeking alternative beliefs, experiencing a turning point, and creating a new role as an ex.[38] It should be noted that there are many forms of deconversion, but the focus of this book is on *secularizing exits*, in which a person becomes a nonbeliever and nonreligious (as opposed to switching religions or becoming privately faithful but no longer attending formal services).[39] Research by Heinz Streib and his colleagues finds that a majority of individuals deconvert by early adulthood (around thirty) and—despite the frequent cinematographic portrayal of sudden deconversions caused by trauma or crisis (e.g., the father who angrily swears off God by his dying son's bedside)—almost all deconversions are painstakingly thoughtful and gradual.

As I explore further in chapter 1, reasons for deconversion vary across several general themes. In Hunsburger and Altemeyer's study of atheism, parents reported that they stopped taking their children to religious services for several reasons, most commonly "as I grew up, I saw a lot of hypocrisy in the people in my religion"; "church was boring. I wanted to do other things with my time"; and "in my youth, if you did not go to church, pray, etc. people thought there was something wrong with you. It's not like that anymore." However, it does not mean a family is atheist or agnostic if it stops participating in religious services. To flesh out the "roots" of deconversion more deeply, the researchers interviewed twenty active atheists from nonreligious backgrounds and twenty from religious upbringings. Those from nonreligious upbringings typically reported that faith was never really emphasized in their homes, so when they were exposed to scripture or religious people, the practices seemed bizarre and filled with contradiction. Individuals from religious upbringings explained that social causes—such as the treatment of women and LGBTQ people—or learning about the universe, science, and other cultures made their faith-based beliefs seem preposterous and impossible to maintain. Another of trigger for deconversion is a growing sense of skepticism or incredulity about the claims made within religious scriptures. With humor, Seth Andrews describes his reaction to rereading the story of Noah's Ark as an adult with a more objective lens:

> How did a 600-year-old man build a stadium-sized boat with only felled trees and pitch? How did Noah fit millions of animal species onto the

ark? What about the dinosaurs? How did Noah accommodate the specialized animal diets like bamboo shoots for the giant pandas, meat for the carnivores, plants for the herbivores, etc.? Where was the food stored and how was it kept from spoiling? How did eight ancient humans shovel tons of daily animal waste out of a 450-foot-long boat with a single window?[40]

Despite the rising doubt that many individuals begin to feel about their faiths, deconversion continues to be a slow and painstaking process for many people because of the guilt they feel for questioning their family's belief system and fear of what could potentially happen to them (shunned by family and friends, smited by God if he is real). Though what often shines through deconversion narratives, once the dust settles and atheists begin to feel firmer in their nonbelief, is feelings of freedom. In an impassioned 1889 lecture, "Why I Am Agnostic," Robert Green Ingersoll—the Illinois lawyer, Civil War veteran, and abolitionist—highlights the joys of religious deconversion: "When I became convinced that the Universe is natural and that all the ghosts and gods are myths, there entered into my brain, into my soul, into every drop of my blood, the sense, the feeling, the joy of freedom. The walls of my prison crumbled and fell, the dungeon was flooded with light, and all the bolts, and bars, and manacles became dust. I was no longer a servant, a serf or a slave."[41]

PERSONALITY

Finally, the few studies that have examined personality traits of atheist people tend to find that they are more open, nondogmatic, feminist, tolerant of ambiguity (Hunsberger and Altemeyer), independent (Argyle), and introverted (Bainbridge) compared to religious individuals.[42] Mostly, these studies suggest that atheist people are a less hazardous and deviant group than otherwise suspected. While scant, this available research suggests that atheists constitute a distinct portion of the U.S. population, and the experience of being a nonbeliever in a predominately Christian nation is likely laden with unique challenges.

MUCH ADO ABOUT NO BELIEF: ATTITUDES TOWARD ATHEISTS IN THE UNITED STATES

Among developed nations, the United States is the most religious.[43] Beliefs and practices enacted through religion or spirituality are frequently credited as uniting forces for people in the United States,[44] and in recent years, even the historic divisions among religious sects have been dissolving steadily, blurring boundaries of belief and communities of worship.[45] However, research suggests that this notable decrease in sectarianism and increase in overall tolerance of other religions is not extended to atheists. To put it mildly, attitudes toward atheists are wary and unaffirming. Survey data consistently find that atheists are regarded as "more troubling" than other groups of individuals on a long list of historically oppressed populations, including Muslim, African American, LGBTQ, and Jewish people.[46] Beyond this, national opinion polls from past and current decades consistently paint Americans as fearful or even disgusted by atheists.[47] As a clear example of this, a 2006 Gallup Poll found that 84 percent of Americans surveyed agreed that "America is not ready for an atheist president."[48] This phobia has been termed *atheophobia* and is defined as "the fear and loathing of atheists that permeate American culture."[49] Such attitudes that atheists are immoral, untrustworthy, or to be feared are ironic, given statistics on incarcerated populations in the United States. Upon entering prison, new inmates are asked for their religious affiliations; data suggest that most religious groups have about the same percentage of members in prison as in the general population, with one marked and hugely underrepresented group. As Dale McGowan humorously puts it:

> About five percent of Americans identify not just as nonreligious but specifically as atheist. But only 0.09 percent of the federal prison population identifies as atheist—50 times fewer than would be expected. . . . I don't think this is because the legal system has a crush on atheists. Neither do I think it means atheists are necessarily more virtuous. But at the very least, it should give pause to those who think they're *less* virtuous.[50]

The prevalence of these atheophobic and negative attitudes shapes the experiences of atheist people. Not surprisingly, atheist individuals report having experienced significant discrimination in schools, at their places of employment, within the legal system, and in many other settings.[51] However, recourse against discrimination is limited and often social suicide. As Dacey describes, there is a vast history of nonbelievers being punished for speaking out against religion or pointing out violations in the civil liberties of atheists perpetrated by faith-based groups.[52] This hypervigilance for and defense against "perceived blasphemers" by religious groups aims to silence atheists and send the message that all belief systems are respected *except* nonbelief. A recent example is the 2010 case of Jessica Ahlquist, who spoke out against the prominent display of the Lord's Prayer in a public Rhode Island high school. She explained that as an atheist, the banner made her feel that she didn't belong in the school and that it was a clear violation of the constitutional ban on teacher-led prayer in schools. Though in 2012 the court finally ruled that the prayer had to be removed, Jessica has already received violent threats, been refused service by local businesses, and had a state representative publicly call her an "evil little thing" on local radio.[53]

Antiatheist discrimination has persisted for centuries. The poet Percy Shelley was kicked out of Oxford University in 1811 for expressing atheist views, and Charles Bradlaugh was removed from his seat in Parliament for refusing to swear a religious oath. In the United States, the orator and former Illinois attorney general Robert Green Ingersoll was urged by the Republican Party to run for governor in the late 1800s but pressured to hide his agnosticism. When he refused to hide his beliefs, he was deemed unelectable.[54] Since Ingersoll's time, only two U.S. congressmembers, Pete Stark (a democratic member of the House of Representatives from 1973 to 2013) and Kyrsten Sinema (an Arizona representative from 2005 to 2011), have been out as atheists. Though freedom of religion and speech remain protected rights in the United States, constitutional provisions bar atheists from public office in seven states.[55] The constitution of the state of Mississippi (Article 14, Section 265) states: "No person who denies the existence of a Supreme Being shall hold any office in this state." Arkansas even has a law that bars atheists from testifying as witnesses in trials.[56] Findings like these suggest atheists are a marginalized minority group within the United States.

Though developed and validated with other marginalized groups, decades of scholarship on minority stress demonstrate that there are physical and psychological consequences linked with identifying as a member of a socially marginalized group.[57] In short, experiences of discrimination and stigma may lead to increased psychological distress and physical health problems. It follows that, similar to other stigmatized groups, the marginalization experienced by atheists may also translate to higher levels of identity-related stress. The prejudice and social stress associated with openly being atheist may pose a serious threat to an individual's well-being. Therefore, the hesitancy to include people who identify as atheist in the broader multicultural and social justice discourse is puzzling and troubling.[58]

WHAT'S THIS ABOUT CLOSETING?

In the autumn of 2011, a *New York Times* article began with the bold statement, "Ronnelle Adams came out to his mother twice, first about his homosexuality, and then about his atheism"[59]—a sure indication that viewing atheist identity as parallel to other marginalized identities had permeated mainstream identity discourse. Even more recently, following the devastating tornado that hit Oklahoma in May 2013, the mainstream media was flabbergasted by an unexpected coming out during an interview. Standing in the rubble of her home, the tornado victim and young mother Rebecca Vitsmun was asked by CNN's correspondent Wolf Blitzer if she "thanked the Lord" for her last-minute decision to leave town and avoid the tornado that would have surely killed her family. Rebecca, visibly flustered, replied "I . . . I . . . I'm actually an atheist . . . We are here and you know, I don't blame anybody for thanking the Lord." This simple disclosure went viral online and caused widespread, unbridled joy among the unbelieving community. The American Humanist Association donated $10,000 to Rebecca and her family to help with their recovery, and the executive director of AHA released the following statement: "Rebecca Vitsmun's courage to speak forthrightly about her atheism inspired humanists and others who are good without a god across the country to help her through this difficult time. . . . Natural disasters are a product of our environment, not supernatural forces, and we have a responsibility to help those affected by them."[60] As you can imagine, if Rebecca would have replied, "yes, we do thank the Lord because we're Baptist," the brief news clip would have gone unnoticed.

Perhaps the most touching outcome of this story was the outpouring of support from the atheist community. An Indiegogo fundraising campaign was started for Rebecca to help defray the significant costs of rebuilding her home; within seventeen hours the website had reached its fundraising goal of $50,000, and by the third day, over $100,000 had been raised.[61] Reactions to this interview highlight just how taboo and rare coming out as atheist remains in the United States and how thrilled (and generous) atheists become when they hear coming out stories.

Unsurprisingly, some academics, activists, and scholars have begun to draw commonalities between LGBTQ people and atheists, notably, that both may "closet" or choose to conceal their identities as members of stigmatized groups.[62] While using models of LGBTQ development to inform studies about atheist identity development may be a useful first step in furthering our understanding of the coming out process, we should be mindful of notable differences between the two groups. First, to move from a heterosexual identity to a gay or lesbian identity typically means the beginning of romantic relationships that are structured differently than previous relationships (e.g., having same-gender romantic partners as opposed to other-gender partners). Moving from religious to atheist may mean that one will stop going to church or praying, but nonbelief does not necessitate additive or visible behavioral changes. Requirements of being "out as atheist" do not include wearing a scarlet letter or snoring loudly in church. Further, copious bodies of research suggest that many LGBTQ people face near-daily threats of violence and discrimination because of their sexual orientations or gender identities.[63] While prejudice toward atheists certainly exists,[64] the intensity of such experience appears to be muted, comparatively.

However, similarities between the two groups do exist. As with LGBTQ identities, atheism is considered a marginalized identity, and to be nonreligious in most Western cultures relegates a person to a minority status associated with oppression and prejudice.[65] Discussed by Cimino and Smith, the practice of coming out as atheist has never been a matter of publicly identifying as a nonbeliever along a well-worn or legitimate path.[66] Instead, coming out involves emerging from invisibility to claim a personal and social identity that carries deeply laden stigma. There are remarkably few examples of openly atheist politicians, media figures, or celebrities—leaving nonbelieving individuals little opportunity to model their coming out process on the experiences of others. Recent calls from leaders in the New Atheist movement have encouraged atheist people to come out of the closet and be proudly identified as apostates.[67] A primary example of this is the Out Campaign website, sponsored by Richard Dawkins, which encourages atheists to disclose their identities. However, not all atheists are supportive of this zealous movement to drag each other out of the proverbial closet and join the war against believers.[68] As with coming out as LGBTQ, there are very real risks—job loss, trouble adopting children, child custody battles, and social exclusion—of outing oneself as atheist in some regions of the United States.[69] Atheist individuals should use caution and assess the safety of their environment before proudly proclaiming godlessness from the rooftops.[70]

As described by Thomas Linneman and Margaret Clendenen, there are some equivalent patterns in the coming out journeys for LGBTQ and atheist individuals.[71] Notably, as with minority sexual identities, an individual's atheism is not readily visible (as gender or racial minority status may be) and requires a formal disclosure by the atheist person to be recognized by others. Depending on the perceived open-mindedness or sociopolitical climate in which an atheist person resides, he may employ a variety of identity-management strategies. Though currently discussed within LGBTQ literature, these techniques may be used by nonbelievers, too. Extending the theoretical work of Scott Button, atheists may *counterfeit*, meaning actively construct a false religious identity by continuing to attend church, pray, wear a cross or Star of David, or engage in spiritual activities; *avoid*, or continuously self-edit and provide half-truths through leaving the room when topics related to faith arise, verbally dodging religious conversation, or saying vague statements such as "I'm not very religious"; or (3) *integrate*, wherein the atheist person is open about her identity and manages whatever reactions arise from this disclosure.[72]

Unfortunately, once a person reveals having an atheist (or LGBTQ) identity, other people are likely to react to these identities as if they are master statuses that dictate all aspects of the individual's behavior. As posited by Siner, coming into an atheist identity requires people to undergo simultaneous challenges to development: figuring out, first, how to define their own faith (or lack of faith) and, second, how to establish connections with a particular faith group.[73] Like LGBTQ identities, atheist identity development exists in both internal (personal, emotional, spiritual) contexts and external (social, community, familial) contexts. Specifically, Siner draws from earlier models of lesbian and gay identity development and overlays this framework to create a four-stage model for individuals who come out as atheist from religious backgrounds:

1. Awareness. Recognition that you are different from others if you are a nonbeliever and that other atheist people exist
2. Exploration: Figuring out what it means to be a nonbeliever; deciding if you would like membership in an atheist community
3. Deepening/Commitment: Learning more about and feeling more self-fulfilled by expressions of atheism; actively participating in atheist groups or communities
4. Internalization/Synthesis: Atheist beliefs begin to interact with all dimensions of identity; individuals identify as a member of the atheist community across all life contexts

This model of identity development was an important first step in exploring patterns of atheist identity development and coming out. However, additional exploration of how real-life coming out experiences of atheist people fit (or do not fit) this model is important. Additionally, it is important to note that some atheist people never have a formal coming out. In more liberal regions of the world where atheists are a less stigmatized social group, there may be no need for processes of self-discovery, exploration, or commitment to atheist activism. Finally, "coming out of the closet" and "becoming" atheist may not be relatable perspectives for all atheists. Specifically, some people may view their atheism as a philosophical position rather than a social identity. Some secular humanists likely view atheism as a lens from which to view the world, not a core belief system or replacement religion. Identity politics discourses (such as queer theory and critical race theory) highlight that concrete identities and labels can obscure and negate the fluidity of lived experiences for some individuals.

WHY KEEP READING?

While acknowledging the potential for major differences in coming out experiences, *Atheists in America* will shed light on shared themes in this process. Specifically, through a national call for submissions, this book garnered personal narratives from twenty-seven people from across the United States who identify as atheist. These authors represent a wide range of ages, races and ethnicities, sexual orientations, gender identities, and socioeconomic statuses. The contributors to this volume share poignant, witty, awkward, and sometimes heart-wrenching accounts of their experiences of being nonbelievers across various sectors of life. As such, the chapters (and narratives contained within each chapter) address the following topics: religious deconversion, culture, LGBTQ issues, romantic relationships, parenting and family concerns, friends and community, workplace dynamics, and aging.

Across chapters, several themes emerge in the narratives. First, many of the authors describe their process of coming into an atheist identity as gradual. Often, it occurred after years of internal strife, sadness, fear, and confusion. Several authors mention that they identified—as an informal stepping stone in their coming out—as unsure or agnostic before embracing atheism. For some, this was a version of Pascal's Wager (e.g., "I can't be fully atheist just in case God is real"); for others, it was meant to lessen the blow of their unbelief to religious friends, family, and colleagues. The pull of social justice issues was a strong pressure for many authors to deconvert. Disillusionment with their religions' stances on women's issues, LGBTQ rights, race, or politics started a cycle of self-examination that was hard to reverse. And, ironically, for many authors it was deep study of religious scripture that shaped their decisions to reject faith.

While the vast majority of authors did deconvert, a few contributors were raised in atheist families and never held religious beliefs. Interestingly—whether deconverted or "always atheist"—all narratives depict some form of hardship or struggle to navigate core life experiences (e.g., finding a romantic partner, raising kids, making friends) as a direct result of being atheist. Even though the authors themselves were settled in their nonbelief, the religious climate of the United States triggered interpersonal strife and awkwardness. The authors typically describe employing a wide variety of identity-management techniques (e.g., concealing or hiding their atheism, avoiding discussion of faith or religion) when interacting with others socially, out of fear of rejection or offending with their nonbelief. The narratives frequently capture a deep yearning for community, connection, and fellowship that is often out of reach for atheist people. Astoundingly, even in the most liberal cities in the country (e.g., New York) and in occupations perceived to be the most open-minded and progressive (e.g., university professor) authors *still* reported that they experienced stigma for being open about their atheism. The book, therefore, begins to debunk the myth that atheophobia is restricted only to the Bible Belt.

However, it would be remiss to paint these narratives solely as stories of marginalization, isolation, and loss. Overwhelmingly, the authors express sheer joy for being able to live authentically, openly, and as the sole masters of their destiny. While the road to coming out may have been challenging, it is clear that there are no regrets for any of the authors. Chris, a seventy-seven-year-old woman from the Gulf Coast, eloquently captures this spirit with her closing remark: "I am now in the last quarter of my existence. Looking back on a good and productive life, I'm glad I've lived it with integrity and without God." Taken together, *Atheists in America* is a collection of stories about nonconformists openly declaring themselves as unbelievers against the religious grain of the United States.

PART 1

LEAVING FAITH

Arriving at Atheist Identity from Religious Backgrounds

MANY UNSPOKEN NORMS exist in the United States, one of which is that individuals will have a belief system guided by a particular religious denomination. However, interesting interplays between religious beliefs and religious certainty exist. For example, roughly 90 percent of people express some sort of belief in a God/gods, but only 60 percent feel positive that God exists.[1] Thus, religious belief is treated as nearly compulsory as a cultural value—and to question or shed belief is atypical. The ubiquity of religiosity presents challenges to leaving faith. As found by Jesse Smith in his qualitative study of atheist identity formation, many participants felt like they had no choice in going to church or being faithful as a child.[2] Church was a large part of family life and a critical ritual for social and developmental processes (i.e., meeting other children through Sunday school). However, even when some participants stopped attending church later in their childhood, they still identified as believers. Taken together, these findings suggest that attending religious practices regularly and feeling certain of your beliefs are both unnecessary in considering oneself a believer.

For many people, deciding to be (or remaining) religious may involve a rational decision-making process where rewards and costs are weighed and considered. Notably, some of the perceived rewards of religiosity include having a system to cope with grief and loss, a moral compass, community support, and potential access to an afterlife.[3] And, bluntly, as captured by Pascal's Wager, atheism equals punishment after death if God exists. Indoctrination into many religions involves constant exposure to threats of pain, loneliness, and horror in the afterlife if one is not a true believer. This early imprinting of fear makes it hard for individuals to explore freely doubts they may have about their faith. As Seth Andrews, a former Christian, describes in his memoir:

> Fear is a powerful weapon. It keeps us in submission. It stops us from asking too many questions. As I grew from a student to adult in the years ahead, fear would mute my own innate curiosity and concerns about the foundation my life had been built on. I would be told continually how much God loved me, but the underlying threat of the Tribulation and Hell would keep me in lock-step with the rest of my religious family, friends and culture. One day the Son would come. And I didn't want to get left behind.[4]

As a result of this fear, many people who experience religious doubt tell themselves that their uncertainties are "just a phase" and will pass once they receive some sort of confirmation, sign, or divine spark. A crisis of spirit is just that, a crisis, and like other difficult times, it too will pass.

That said, what does it typically take to deconvert fully someone from being a believer to a nonbelieving atheist? Prevalence rates and patterns regarding apostasy among different religious groups are nearly nonexistent, though some themes that emerge in recent literature include leaving childhood homes, entering new social contexts, meeting people who you respect and enjoy who identify as atheist, and doubts surrounding the morality of certain religious creeds.[5] Most research suggests that this process is painstaking and deliberate. Through interviews with forty-six apostates, Hunsberger describes that becoming atheist is "strongly intellectual and rational, and seems to result from a slow, careful search for meaning and purpose."[6] Within the United States, deconversion is a process of individuation and reflection that often occurs during emerging adulthood (eighteen to twenty-five) or "the college years," when identity exploration may be at its peak and many people leave their family homes for the first time. The process often occurs in conjunction with a period of socialization, when personal identity and values are reexamined.

Plainly, incongruencies between the teachings of conservative religious organizations about women's rights, LGBTQ populations, and the personal beliefs of more liberal congregation members may also inspire some individuals to begin to question their religious beliefs. A key example of this tension was described by Zuckerman: "One man started to feel alienated from his religion when the words 'God Hates Fags' were spray-painted on a wall at the small Midwestern Christian college he was attending. Although not gay himself, such religious-inspired intolerance opened his eyes, causing him to look at the negative aspects of his religion, where before he had only seen the positive."[7]

For the vast majority of individuals who leave their faiths, the process of deconversion is gradual; however, in a few rare cases *sudden deconversions* can occur. Explored by Strieb and colleagues in their cross-cultural qualitative study, sudden deconversions are seen as breakthrough events laden with realization. A clear example of such an event was noted by one of the participants after he turned to God for guidance and realized no one was listening: "And there I [said] okay God, lead me, and . . . I think I will come to the right decision . . . And suddenly it was real, like a reality check, yup. It was like, wham, like as if, like as if you wake up from a trance, like . . . what are you doin' here? Yup, crazy . . . like someone had thrown a nail in this vase."[8]

The narratives of this chapter depict many of these same themes, across the experiences of four individuals who left Orthodox Jewish (Alvin), Evangelical Christian (Lynnette and Chris), and Latter-Day Saint (Cora) faiths. Within the first narrative, Alvin describes his experiences of bearing witness to and practicing rituals yet not being able to grasp the powerful feelings that others seemed to have in these same practices. However, he felt compelled to hold onto his religious beliefs for the sake of his mother and because he knew no alternative. At the end of his confirmation, he expected finally to feel the "spark" of Judaism that others experienced, but instead, he had a sudden deconversion when he felt no different following the ritual. On the other hand, Lynnette, Chris, and Cora each reported very gradual deconversions beginning after they were young adults and into their twenties. For Lynnette, deconversion was strongly linked to sexist views within the church and from her very religious father. She felt confused by mixed messages, such as God loved her as a woman but that women should never hold positions of political power and must be obedient to men. Like Alvin, she also described wanting to have a "special feeling" in her faith, but this feeling never came.

It should be noted that none of the authors describe leaving faith because they were "mad at God" or out of rebelliousness, anger, or boredom. Instead, each of the narratives describe shedding a belief system that was inherited by default from the author's family. The authors do not go on to describe voids that were left by shedding their views but instead express gratitude and freedom. In line with Pascal's Wager, both Chris and Cora described initial fear in leaving their religions. Chris described becoming agnostic as a "stepping stone" to atheism, believing that being unsure of his stance was less risky. In a poignant statement, he captures the fear described by much of the extant deconversion literature: "Living in a godless universe was terrifying for me because I had learned that God gave us meaning and without a god there was no meaning." And, weighing the social risks of leaving faith are epitomized by Cora's narrative; in this piece, she describes the hardships of becoming an apostate in the Latter-Day Saint religion, a tight-knit community, collectivist and insulated. Taken together, the narratives depict that leaving faith was informed by learning more (about science, politics, social issues), meeting an inspirational new person, or feeling conflict between personal beliefs (e.g., women's rights) and religious doctrines. Though the authors come from very different backgrounds, it remains clear that, uniformly, leaving faith can be a challenging undertaking.

1

HOW I GOT TO NONE OF
THE ABOVE

Alvin Burstein

Alvin, eighty-one, is a retired psychology professor and psychoanalyst.
He currently volunteers at the New Orleans–Birmingham Psychoana-
lytic Center, where he teaches and serves as librarian.

When I arrived at the Army Induction Center in 1954, I was required to fill
out a form so that my dog tags could be punched out. The information to
be included, beyond name and serial number, was religious orientation. The
choices were Catholic, Protestant, Jewish, or none. I chose the last.

A grizzled sergeant came up to me. "Burstein, aren't you Jewish?"

"No, my family is, but I'm not."

"If you're wounded, maybe dying on the battlefield, don't you want a chap-
lain to hold your hand, comfort you?"

"I would want someone to hold my hand, I guess, but I don't care who."

I have always thought of my mother as an observant Orthodox Jew, but
how do I know that? I was sent to Hebrew school for years, attending for
several hours after my public school classes. I don't remember how many days
each week the Hebrew school classes occurred, but I am pretty sure I didn't
volunteer for them. They were no fun at all. We learned only a few words of
Hebrew, paradoxical ones. The Hebrew word that sounds like "dawg" means
"fish," "hee" means "she," "hoo" means "he." Sometimes the teacher would hold

something up, say a book, "Mah zeh [what is this]?" If you said "Zeh ha safer [this is a book]," you would be rewarded with "Tov m'ode [very good]." But mostly we translated the Old Testament, sounding out the cryptic Hebrew letters one at a time and translating word by word. We learned no grammar and acquired no conversational skills. It is a dead language.

As even more evidence of my mother's orthodoxy: I know my mother cooked for the Jewish Community Center's summer camp, and I am pretty sure the meals had to be kosher. That meant keeping dairy products and meat products separate, making sure that meat came only from animals that chewed a cud, had split hooves, were killed in a ritually proper way, and had all traces of blood banished before cooking. Seafood was required to have scales. Chicken seemed to be easy.

I know my father and my maternal grandmother had orthodox services at their funerals, though I know, without knowing how I know, that my father, a thirty-second-degree Mason, wanted a Masonic funeral. And I know for sure that we had four sets of dishes, separate everyday sets for dairy foods and meat foods and a parallel sets for the Passover. I also remember my mother lighting the Sabbath candles, the *bench licht*. I believe it to be the only Orthodox Jewish religious ritual that is gender specific. It must be performed by a woman. Mom would cover her head with a cloth, chant a *barucha* (blessing), and wave her hands above the candles toward her face in an arcane gesture, as though she were wafting some spiritual essence to be smelled and savored. Although it seemed to me that many of the religious mandates she observed were performed as matters of routine, this one seemed imbued with meaning.

I remember, too, that the unmarried rabbi of the Orthodox synagogue just a few blocks from our house used to have Friday-night dinner with us. He would have driven from his house to the synagogue Friday morning. But because driving on the Sabbath was forbidden after sundown, he would walk to our home, have dinner, and spend the night with us. The next morning he would walk back to the synagogue, and after sundown Saturday, he could drive his car back to his own home.

One Friday evening, my mother was rushed and forgot to *bench licht* before the rabbi arrived. When he noticed, he walked hurriedly, head down, into his bedroom, closing the door until my mother, abashed, realized the problem and performed her ritual. He must have been listening at the door because as soon as she finished, he emerged. Without mention of the situation, he went to the Sabbath table, with its candles properly lit. There we joined him for the meal: braided challah bread, chicken soup, fish, maybe veal chops and flaky, oily strudel, redolent of cinnamon, apple, and raisin. After the meal, Rabbi Rakofsky would open a book and read aloud. It was an astonishing experience. No one had read poetry to me before. He read Poe, and the sonorous rhythms and rhymes of "The Raven" and "The Bells" fixed themselves in my memory.

He wore a vested suit and had a thin Clark Gable mustache. To my preadolescent eyes he epitomized wisdom and sophistication. I was devastated when he left town under a cloud of disgrace, for reasons I could not fathom, although I remember overhearing hushed comments about "hot pants." It is unusual for Orthodox rabbis to be unwed, and that may have accounted for congregational suspicions. Only recently has it occurred to me that the suspicions might have included my widowed mother, who also did some house cleaning for the rabbi.

In the years leading up to my bar mitzvah at thirteen, my Judaism took some twists and turns. I was furious at the people I thought persecuted my idealized rabbi. Although I felt an irrational excitement about the activities of the Jewish kibbutzim and of the Jewish underground fighting for the independence of Israel, I had an intellectual conviction that nationalism itself was a problematic concept. I regularly attended Orthodox Sabbath services, giving sermons in the Junior Congregation and playing Theodore Hertzl, a prominent Zionist, in a Hebrew school pageant. The congregation of our synagogue offered me a scholarship to a yeshiva, a Jewish seminary. I declined, partly out of fear of leaving home and partly because of my doubts about Orthodox Jewish beliefs.

Despite the doubts, I was observant because I thought that my mother might be responsible in some cosmic way if I broke the law before I became confirmed. After that, the responsibility would be mine. I remember specific grounds for my religious doubts: my father's wish for a Masonic funeral and my sense that not respecting that wish could not be right. In addition, I was troubled by the content of two of the many required daily prayers. The first was a prayer in which men said (in Hebrew, of course), "Blessed art thou, O Lord, King of the universe for having made me a man," while women said, "Blessed art thou, O Lord, King of the universe for having made me in accordance with your desire." Though Betty Friedan and feminism were some decades away, I found the notion of women as second-class citizens irrational. Another prayer praised God for choosing us (Jews) from all the nations. I thought the community in the synagogue, the old men dipping snuff and bobbing back and forth as they rattled off prayers, the women gossiping in the balcony, the smooth-shaven, self-important big shots that ran things, all pretty ordinary, not much of a divine selection.

Nevertheless, as the time approached for my confirmation, I spent a lot of time hanging around the rabbi's office at the synagogue. I thought there was a chance, albeit a small one, that he might have something of profound importance, an earthshaking truth, to impart. I didn't want to miss that precious moment. The weeks went by, and my laborious practice of chanting the Torah portion assigned to the week at my bar mitzvah came to an end without a call to the rabbi's office.

At the synagogue for the ceremony, I remember wearing my tallis (prayer shawl) and yarmulke (skull cap). The small black boxes, the teffillin, containing the sacred words "Hear, O Israel, the Lord thy God, the Lord is one" hand-written in Hebrew, were bound to my left arm and forehead. I was to carry the holy Torah from the ark, at the front, to the *bemah*, the platform in the center of the synagogue where the cantor sang and where the portion of the holy Torah for the week was to be chanted. I felt the slippery parchment of the scroll under the ornate velvet cover in my sweaty hands. I was terrified at the possibility I might drop the Torah and be visited with a terrible punishment, maybe fasting for a year, for the desecration. I made it to the *bemah* and managed my solo chant of the portion of the week without a major stumble. As the service concluded, I stood with the new rabbi at the front of the congregation. I was a pretty good speech writer, and my memorized comments went well. The rabbi began his response, and I had the hopeful thought, maybe now, maybe this is it. Maybe . . . but no. The best he had to offer was a string of banalities. No poetry and no kabbalist mysteries. Yearnings for epiphany, for ultimate truths, were not to be satisfied in the temple—or elsewhere.

So, in that moment and from that day forward, the case was closed; it was *none of the above* for me.

2

RELIGION AND THE F-WORD (FEMINISM)

Lynnette

Lynnette, twenty-one, lives in Chicago with her boyfriend. She is working toward a degree in art and design.

I've always hated the question, "when did you become a Christian?" because I don't remember ever becoming a Christian. I always was one. Sure, there might have been a time where my mother sat down with me and had me say a special prayer, as I remember her doing with my younger siblings, but I don't remember that time. "Becoming" a Christian always seems to imply some sort of choice in the matter, as if my parents had given me all the information and I thought about it for a while and decided that this was what I really wanted to do. That's not really how it works, though. I was taught Christianity the same way I was taught how to walk, talk, read, and write. Asking me when I became a Christian is like asking when I accepted the alphabet.

I am twenty-one years old. I was a Christian since before I could remember, and I held on to those beliefs for eighteen years. I began to have doubts during my senior year of high school, and I abandoned my beliefs by the end of that summer, right before I started college. It is a very common misunderstanding among Christians that people who leave the faith were never really sincere to begin with. That is simply not the case. I was as sincere as I could possibly be. I went to church every Sunday, and I was very involved with my church's youth group. I was commonly seen as one of the more mature people and someone who modeled Christian behavior very well. I believed in everything that the typical Evangelical Christian believes in, and I would defend it fiercely if anyone questioned me about it. But of course, what really matters most is that I had a personal relationship with Jesus Christ. I would talk to God all throughout the day and while I was falling asleep at night. It was comforting, and even though I knew I didn't actually hear anything, I knew he was there because of the comfort I felt when I was talking to him.

What's interesting for me when I look back is that until my last year of high school, I don't think I ever had any doubts that God was real. I remember one moment when I was about ten years old that I thought to myself, "Will I always be a Christian?" But as soon as that thought popped into my head, I quickly shook it out because I knew God was listening. It seemed like any time any hint of doubt came up, this was my immediate response. The fear of how God would punish me for my doubt kept me from ever doubting. But eventually this fear was overcome, and the doubt could not be held back.

Trying to tell this story is sort of like trying to tell someone a dream you had. You know how it happened in your mind, but for some reason when you're actually trying to lay it out in chronological order, it doesn't work. Since most of this story is about my thought process through this time, it won't make a lot of sense if I try to tell it in order. Instead, I'll focus on the different ways my thinking changed over a year-long period. The first thing I started thinking about was the relationship between women and Christianity. At the same time, I was also considering the possibility that the Bible might not be literal truth, as I'd always been taught. My dad died when I was twelve years old. Most of my memories of him are from when we were watching television or a movie, and then he'd stop it and start talking to us about the morality of what we just saw or heard. He took "parental guidance" very seriously. This would get us going on many topics, like evolution, abortion, politics, and more. During one of these talks, I remember that my dad was explaining why a woman should never be president. First, he explained that the story of Adam and Eve clearly shows that women are not fit for leadership because women are easily deceived. He said he didn't really think it was fair that Eve's sin made all women subordinate, but that is what God decided, so that's the way it is. Also, if a woman is running for president, more men will vote for her because they're attracted to her. When we reasoned that the same could be said of women voting for a male candidate, he responded by saying, "So women shouldn't vote."

My dad had much to say on the topic of gender roles. He, like many in the Christian community, believed that our gender is based off of the story of the Garden of Eden. Eve brought sin to humanity when she was deceived into eating the forbidden fruit. This meant that all women were easily deceived and therefore should never be the head of a household or church. After all, women make their decisions based off of emotion, but men make their decisions based off of logic. He actually told us that whenever a woman does something wrong, it is because she is deceived and doesn't understand what she is doing, but when a man does something wrong, it is always willful disobedience. He believed, as the Bible says, that a woman should be submissive to her husband and let him lead the house. I can understand why he believed this. His mother was a very controlling woman who continues to this day to boss around everyone she knows. I think he saw his mother as the reason that women should never take charge. She was the example of what a woman shouldn't do. Then, in contrast, there was my mother, who is a sweet, quiet, thoughtful woman who was content to cook and clean and take care of the children. He upheld her as the perfect example of womanhood. I think these two women had the biggest influence on his thoughts of gender. He was such a stubborn man that he would never be willing to change his mind, even for his daughters.

For years, I put all that I'd heard him say about women to the back of my mind. I didn't want to think about it. I knew my dad had never been a very good father, but I could at least be comforted that God was the perfect father. My dad didn't value me much as a woman, but God did. Then when I was in my teens, my church had a meeting, as they always do when they decide on new leadership positions. Usually, they introduce the person who has already been interviewed by the pastor and the elders, and then they ask for the congregation's approval. The congregation always approves because they trust the judgment of the pastor and the elders. But this time the meeting went on for over an hour. The reason was because this time, the person being appointed to minister of evangelism was a woman. My church already had women serving as elders, so it shouldn't have been a problem. They already ignored the verse about women not being allowed to speak in church. But it was just because it had "minister" in the title, which implied some sort of leadership, even though she would not be the head of the church. It seemed like the most trivial debate to me. The debate should have been about her qualifications, not about her gender. On the ride home, I voiced my frustration to my mom, but I was surprised to find that she disagreed with it as well. She explained, "Well, the Bible does say that a woman should not be in authority over a man."

I was completely shocked by all of this. In most of my experience with the church, it seemed that most people just ignored those verses. I had heard sexist beliefs from my dad but very rarely from other people. This event was what first made me start thinking about what I believed about the Bible. I started asking God tons of questions. I think it was easier for me to start with this instead of wondering outright whether or not God existed. It seemed pretty fair to just ask God to clarify a few things. But when I asked God what he meant, there was silence. With other questions, I would feel my emotions go one way or another, and I took that to mean that God was telling me something. Not this time; I felt no answer.

The more I started thinking about these issues, the more they started to depress me. I looked at the story of Adam and Eve and how Eve received most of the punishment, even though her crime was the same as Adam's. She just ate first, and that was somehow enough to make all women subservient to men. Then I thought about different stories in the Bible. The vast majority of the stories are about men. If there's ever a story where the woman finally gives birth after being infertile for so long, the child is always miraculously a boy. Then I remembered the story in Genesis 19. Two angels came to visit Lot in Sodom. While they were at his house, the men of the town surrounded them and told Lot to send out the men so they could rape them. Lot says, "No, my friends. Don't do this wicked thing. Look, I have two daughters who have never slept with a man. Let me bring them out to you, and you can do what you like with them." This goes unpunished, but when Lot and his family are escaping from Sodom, his wife looks back and is turned into a pillar of salt.

What kind of god kills a woman for looking back at her home but doesn't raise a finger when a father is willing to let his own daughters be gang-raped?

All my questions about the role of women in the Bible made me start thinking about the Bible's authority. I'd always been taught that it was literal truth, but I was finding it much more difficult to accept that. I started to see plainly that parts of the Bible could not possibly be the truth of an all-loving God. God suddenly seemed so harsh, much more like my real dad than the loving Father in heaven that I'd always imagined.

One day at my youth group, Mark, the youth group leader, told us that next week we would be having a Q&A about God and Christianity. I usually hated those days because I never learned anything. I already knew all of the answers or could at least guess them well enough, and I never had a question. This time I surprised myself; I actually had a question that I genuinely could not figure out for myself. It had been confusing me so much over the past few weeks. We all wrote our questions on note cards. I wrote something along the lines of, "Why was it seen as a good thing that Abraham obeyed God's orders to sacrifice Isaac? I was always under the impression that God would never ask someone to do something wrong, but he told Abraham to kill his son. I would worry about the sanity of anyone who was willing to kill another person because God told them to do it." This story had been bothering me so much because it just seemed so morally backward. Even if God spared Isaac, he still blessed Abraham for following a terrible order. The next week, we sat down as Mark read the questions he had received out loud and answered them based on scripture. I waited till the end of the meeting, but not one of the questions he read was mine. He chose to skip over a genuine, thoughtful question I had, and instead he answered all the questions like, "How far is too far?" and "Is listening to non-Christian music okay?" He answered the easy ones but didn't even attempt to answer mine.

I think it was at that point that I realized the Bible could not be inerrant. I knew the best answer I would get from anyone would be that we can't always understand God's ways. At this point, I'd had enough. I was sick of being valued less as a woman because of God's mysterious ways. I was sick of playing mind games to try and make sense of God's inconsistency. It felt like when you're looking at an optical illusion and you're confused because you can't see the hidden picture. Then suddenly you shift your eyes slightly and it all just clicks into place. It suddenly just made sense that the Bible was the way it was because it was written by men, men that had their own flaws and prejudices. Some parts of it just couldn't be true if it was supposedly written by a perfect, loving God.

Everything was starting to take shape logically in my mind, but I wasn't ready to let go of God just yet. That was more of a personal journey that couldn't just be reasoned away. I talked to God, after all. I felt his presence. How could that not be real? But if I was really honest with myself, I was always so frustrated by God's silence. It always seemed like God was there to comfort me but refused to talk to me or answer me.

Then one day, my mother sat me and my siblings down to talk with us. We were running out of money and could not afford to stay in this area. We would have to move over the summer. I was panicking. I was planning on going to school nearby and was counting on being able to live at home. I had no job and no savings; where was I supposed to go? That night I was praying about my situation. I was so scared and had no idea what to do. At the time, I had been dating someone for two and a half years. We both felt very much in love and we were convinced that we would get married someday. While I was praying and freaking out, for the first time in my life, I felt God telling me to do something very specific. God was telling me to marry my boyfriend when we graduated high school. This scared me to death. I kept asking God if that's what he meant, and I kept getting a very strong feeling that this was what I was supposed to do.

The next day I told my boyfriend about my family's situation and I tentatively explained what I felt God was telling me to do. I can't say I was surprised that he didn't agree with me. I knew he wanted to go through college first. He just kept saying that he didn't think it was a good idea and when he prayed about it, he didn't feel that God was telling him to marry me. Still, it just confused me so much that the one time I actually felt God telling me something specific, it wasn't the right choice. If God had been telling me to do this, he surely would have told my boyfriend the same thing.

Within a week, my mother had talked things out with family and decided that we would not be moving any time soon. With the fear and emotions lifted, I was able to think more rationally about what had happened. I saw clearly that my fear had guided my thinking. I had been so scared about what I would do and where I would go. The emotional part of me just wanted to know that someone would be there to help me out. I wanted that someone to be my boyfriend. I wanted to share a life together so that I wouldn't have to go through my financial problems by myself. I felt so stupid and humiliated. I am usually a very logical person, and I felt ashamed that I had seemed so foolish and naïve to my boyfriend.

This started my internal realization about what God really was. All my life, I had felt comfort when I talked to God, but I felt the same thing when I would hug a stuffed animal. I loved to sing and felt close to God when we were singing in church. But I had the same emotions when I was singing secular songs in my school choir. Talking to God was nothing more than talking to myself. Listening to God was nothing more than listening to my emotions and my knowledge of how God is described in the Bible. It is why I was "told" to get married while my boyfriend was told to wait; it was just our different feelings on the subject, nothing more. It is why people of any religion say that they feel their god's presence and use that as proof that what they believe is the true religion.

I remember how I used to pray to God about baptism. In our church, people would wait until they were older to be baptized as a personal decision. Though we didn't believe baptism was the same as salvation, it was something that we were supposed to do if we were Christians. I was afraid of having to go up in front of everyone, so baptism was the last thing in the world I wanted to do. I would talk to God about this, but since I already knew based on scripture that God wanted me to be baptized, I felt intense guilt for not following his commandment. In this sense, talking to God was like having a fake conversation with a person you know. In your head, you can visualize asking them something and you can imagine their response based off of what you already know about them. This does not mean they are actually talking to you. Then there was the emotional aspect of God. When I would ask God something that was morally neutral, I would go with the option that appealed most to my emotions.

All of these things—the gender inequality, the problems with a literal Bible, and my personal experience—came together over this last year of high school. Over the summer, I was able to talk to some of my siblings about it, and I realized I was not alone. My older brother and sister were both struggling with the literal interpretation of the Bible. One day, my brother posted a Facebook status explaining to everyone that he was now an atheist. I watched as replies poured in from family and friends, telling him that he really needed to think it through and talk to a pastor. They treated him as though he was just rebelling against God and had just decided to become an atheist overnight, instead of the years of thought I know he had given it. I admit, even after all that we had talked over the summer, I was still a little bit shocked that he was an atheist. I had always thought that atheists were angry people who believed that there was absolutely no god. I thought that this was a rather strong position to take. But seeing my brother become an atheist helped me to separate actual atheist beliefs from the stigma against atheism. I knew he had thought this through, and I knew he had reasons for why he felt this way, despite what others thought. That past year had left me mentally exhausted, and I really did not want to keep thinking about God. One day I asked myself if I still believed that Jesus was the son of God, and the answer was simply no.

I don't know how I managed this, but for the next few months, I gave myself a mental vacation. I'm always constantly thinking about things, but I realized for the moment that I didn't know what to believe, and I left it at that. I stayed open to new beliefs and read up on evolution, feminism, and gay rights with a new perspective. Eventually I started thinking about religion again. I found a few different blogs by atheists and saw that these were still good, thoughtful people. Most of them had been very religious in the past, too. I realized that I really was an atheist. The label surprised me at first because of all I thought I knew about atheists, but there was no denying that that's what I was.

I've been an atheist for almost two years now, and so much has changed. As a Christian, I hated the moments that I would try to let God control my life because it has never been natural for me to base a decision off of my feelings alone. Now I can be rational and make my own decisions without feeling guilty that I'm not letting some imaginary deity take over. Atheism is incredibly freeing in that I am much more open-minded. Before, any new idea had to be filtered through a biblical perspective. I was against gay marriage, sex before marriage, drinking, smoking, swearing, and many more immoral things, and I would judge other people for their decisions. I am much kinder to people now and understand that they have a right to make their own choices for themselves. If I was still a Christian, I might still be in an unhealthy relationship because I was so convinced that God wanted me to marry my ex-boyfriend. Now I am with someone who is perfect for me in every way, but I never would have dated him before because I wouldn't have dated a non-Christian. I feel so much happier now because I feel more in control of my life, and I'm making the decisions that I know are best for me. I feel so free from the guilt I used to feel every time I swore or doubted God or thought about sex. I feel much happier and calmer than I used to.

At the moment, I am only halfway out of the closet. I have told my close friends and siblings that I know would be okay with my beliefs. It is also up on my Facebook page, so anyone who has looked at my information will know, but I'm afraid to officially announce it. I'm so afraid of what people will say to me. All of my extended family is deeply religious, and I know it would disappoint them very much. I'm also afraid of what my friends from church would say, and especially my old youth group leader, who can be very assertive of his opinions. I know most of these people would just think I'm rebelling and living my life in sin, especially since I have moved in with my boyfriend. All I want is for people to understand that this has not been an easy process. It has nothing to do with ignorance, rebellion, or anger at God. I simply don't believe anymore. Faith is belief without evidence, and I can't force myself to believe something without any proof.

3

CLAP OUR HANDS LIKE TREES

———————

Chris Matallana

Chris, twenty-seven, hails from Texas, where he lives with his partner, Marisa, and their dog-child, Fonzie. He is currently pursuing a writing career while working at a bookstore to make ends meet.

I want to tell you a story about narratives; more specifically I want to tell you a story about how I left the narrative of religion, specifically the Christian faith in the Evangelical tradition, and how I came to embrace the narrative of humanism, of "good without God." To be human is to align one's life with a narrative. Whether we realize it or not, we circle our lives around a particular narrative. It is no coincidence that once human language rose, so did our myths of how we got here, why we are here, and where we are going. The power of story links us together. For example, how else do we get to know someone other than through the stories they tell us about themselves? How do we learn about hope, about joy, about facing adversity? Through stories. This is mine.

I grew up in the suburbs of Dallas, in cookie-cutter houses that my family made into homes. We were nominal Catholics, and throughout my early teens I experienced deep, existential crises. The blackness and the vastness of the universe terrified me. I felt that it was the gaping mouth of a giant creature waiting to devour us. The summer between my junior and senior year of high school, however, my crises met their resolution in the most likely of places in suburban Dallas: the Christian narrative.

Some Evangelical Baptist friends of mine invited me to attend their youth group service with them—in retrospect, they all probably thought that their Catholic friend was bound for the flames of hell and wanted to save me from it. There's no purgatory in Evangelicalism: you either turn or burn. Even though I had no idea what was going to happen, I decided to go because I had always heard that youth groups were a great place to pick up girls and that this one was swarming with Baptist babes. My hormones conquered over the fear of the unknown, and I found myself on the third floor of a Baptist church in a darkened room with a few spotlights on the stage that illuminated the band playing music that my friends were clapping to. Some of them had their eyes closed, while others had their arms raised. The bravest ones did both. (As an aside, even though Baptists scoff alongside everyone else at the ridiculousness of their past that taught you could not be a Christian and dance, it is quite uncommon to see much movement going on in Baptist churches during their services. Movement still equals sin.) It was in this room that I discovered the Christian narrative, explicated by the Evangelical tradition, and it was here that I began my long journey into this narrative.

This was the Christian narrative first explained to me: Adam and Eve disobeyed God, and this disobedience introduced sin into the world. Sin was responsible for all kinds of things, including murder, pain, suffering, and the menstrual cycle. God has enacted a plan to bring back humanity to Himself. The plan consisted first of using the Israelites to save the world, and when they failed, He came down fleshed in the first-century Mediterranean peasant by the name of Jesus. This Jesus lived a sinless life, died on the cross, taking my punishment, then resurrected. He then ascended to heaven and afterward sent the Holy Spirit to dwell in his believers who preached His message.

This narrative sounds like complete and utter foolishness to me now, but there was a time when it was not ridiculous; it marked and defined my life. It was not merely a story to me but fact, the true explanation of our life on earth, the ultimate story, the metanarrative. It eventually led me to decide to become a pastor. I wanted to help people, to save the world, and this occurred when one turned his or her life to Jesus and attempted to live life as He did.

I wanted to help people do this. I graduated with a degree in biblical studies from an Evangelical school and was pursuing life to this end. But while this was all going on, a steady undercurrent of doubt existed beneath my beliefs. A singular question would often rise up: "Do you really believe this?" I would push the question down, or answer myself, "Of course I do! How could I not?" But this question would continue to rise in my mind, vine-like, moving into the cracks and eventually overtaking it.

After graduation, I began an internship at Providence Community Church. Providence was unlike any church experience I ever had, and if you've ever had a church experience, it was unlike that, too. And this is meant as a compliment, because the people of Providence strove (and still do, I am supposing) to replicate the first-century church as much as possible in a highly churched culture like Dallas. As an example: instead of wasting money on owning a church building, Providence rented a space in an art center. We would meet on Sunday mornings there, first in the art center proper, and eventually in the little theater located across the courtyard. These people were like family to me, the pastors were my mentors, and my time here expanded my view of the Christian narrative to its bursting point.

The main thrust of the internship was reading all sorts of Christian theology and New Testament studies very different than the theologies I'd learned in college. It widened my view, evolving my views on God and Jesus. During this time of study, I began to realize that the Christian narrative had an underlying theme of Jesus' universal salvation for the world, meaning that when He died and resurrected, it wasn't just for people who believed in Him; this was also for people who didn't. A severe tension rose within me, because I had been taught otherwise and held (very begrudgingly) to the idea that those with faith in Jesus were rewarded with eternal bliss and those without condemned to eternal suffering. Instead, I was now learning that different traditions in Christianity held to a view of Jesus saving everyone. After numerous months of painful growth in this area, I came to the conclusion I no longer believed hell existed. It seemed ludicrous to me that a God who was supposedly a God of love would ever banish anyone to hell. I knew the arguments for hell: God is a god of love but also of justice and therefore had to punish evildoers or He couldn't be God; or He gave us free will to choose Him or not; or

He didn't REALLY send anyone to hell, their own choices did. I studied views on hell that had people going there for a while, but eventually they would get to leave and join the redeemed in glory. It was kind of like a "time out" version of hell. And others believed that people would merely stop existing, that they would disappear into the ether and be as forgotten as a gust of wind. The arguments for hell are weak, flawed, and exposed the power that religion could have if you scare someone enough, or if someone really wants to justify their frustration at not getting to do anything fun. Getting to this point was huge, because my view of God had truly changed. He resembled less the traditional Christian god and more an amorphous being who benevolently watched over us. This evolution continued until I finally admitted to myself that I didn't know if I even believed in God anymore and eventually to where I am now: we have created God in our image, a fiction that does not exist. This degradation to the foundation of my belief in God was monumental, and alongside two additional degradations, led me to my unbelief.

The first was this: as my theology began to drastically change, I was also faced with the fact that if this version of the narrative was true, I had to basically change a lot of who I was in order to fit this mold of a Jesus disciple. I was no longer to truly be able to be myself, who, incidentally, God created me to be. In order to be a pastor, I had to be what is called a "godly man," meaning I had to watch how and what I joked around about (sex jokes were considered a snub on the beauty of sex within marriage), or about the types of shows I watched (*The Office*'s "that's what she said" jokes were considered too immature and ungodly), or the things I exposed myself to (pretty much any movies with bare breasts in them). Also, I wasn't supposed to masturbate since this meant lust dwelled in my heart (and honestly, the biggest jerk-off move religion has done is make millions of people feel bad about masturbating, and I feel a lot better these days knowing that Jesus isn't watching me). The realization that I could not be who I was became a growing source of frustration for me. The narrative of Christianity was forcing me to stop being myself and to become someone I was not. Like the arguments for hell, I understood the arguments for striving to be holy quite well: God created us perfect, but sin ruined that perfection, and in order to be what God called us to be (holy), we had to fight for it. But it rubbed the nerve of my doubt raw, because as the falsity of this story was growing by leaps and bounds, it became more and more difficult to think that was any type of sound argument. I began seriously considering the idea of leaving the faith, of living my life as who I was, not the way some invisible, Bronze Age deity demanded. I would imagine life without God, and the initial fear of leaving everything I'd poured so much of myself into slowly metamorphosed into an enticement.

The second came when the exclusivity of Christianity became repulsive to me. I had become attracted to a coworker who was an atheist. She was cute and funny and smart, and I enjoyed being around her, but the boundaries of the Christian narrative kept us separated. Good Christians, especially those wanting to become pastors, only dated and married equally good Christians. The combination of my changing theology of who was "in" and "out"—and my growing frustration of not being able to be who I was—culminated in the realization that to continue down the Christian path meant that I was not free to love whom I wanted. Because of the difference of our religious views, I could not hope to be anything but a friend to this coworker, despite the fact that we both wanted there to be more (P.S.: At the time of writing, this coworker and I have become "more." We currently share an apartment and the cutest dog-child that evolution ever produced). And what if things didn't work out with her, but someday down the line I met a Buddhist or a Muslim or another atheist, and we were not free to express our love because of the boundaries of these narratives? What kind of God, supposedly of love and acceptance, would demand such a narrow and confining view to His people? And on a larger scale, why was I not able to do what I wanted? Why was I bound by these rules and regulations from an ancient time that would hinder me from watching *The Office*, or making sex jokes, or any other thing that I would want to do?

These undercurrents of doubt grew and grew until they were a tsunami-sized wave heading straight for the coast that was my faith. The narrative I had invested so much time, energy, and money into was unraveling at the seams, and for the first time, the allure of leaving the faith overpowered the fear of leaving it. I awoke one morning with all of these things on my mind, arguing with myself about the state of my belief. As I was getting into the shower, I took the first step on my pilgrimage to unbelief and admitted I no longer believed in the Christian God. I let out a deep sigh of relief. Admitting this fact to myself was monumental. In the Gospels, those cornerstones of the Christian narrative, Jesus tells people to come to Him if they are weary and they'll find true rest. The true rest came for me when I finally left this narrative that offered me "meaning" at the expense of being shackled as a human.

After admitting I no longer believed in the Christian narrative, I wrote an e-mail to Mark, the pastor of Providence, and told him of my unbelief. I stopped going to services, to classes, and to our weekly missional community, where we ate meals together. Mark responded to my e-mail of how hurt and shocked he was but also promised me that if I ever returned to Christianity, I would always have a home at Providence. Other church members would send me Facebook messages or e-mails, letting me know they still loved me and were available to talk if I so desired. It felt like I had broken up with a hundred people all at once, but this was a cost of seeking truth in my life.

I was living at home with my parents, post-college, when all this happened. They began to notice my being at home much more and eventually asked why. Unlike most Evangelicals, our family did not gain the tradition from our fathers. A short time after I embraced the Christian narrative, my parents and brothers followed suit. The story of Christianity had bonded my family with a sense of tight-knit connection, and I now had to come out to my parents that I no longer believed. My parents reacted with shock, with anger, with heartbrokenness. They would corner me in my room, with gentle voices that would rise and eyes filled with tears, and ask what I believed, if I thought that anything happened after death, or if I thought that Jesus was real. My first step away from Christianity was agnosticism, and so my response to these questions was, "I don't know." It took time for me to come out and admit fully that I not only disbelieved in the Christian God but no longer believed in any type of God. After a while, my parents and I stopped discussing my religious beliefs and met on more neutral ground. Since moving out, my relationship with them has bettered, they and I both comfortable in our views to openly and freely discuss what we believe, knowing full well what the other does not.

I had to come out to Christian friends. We were bound by our shared belief of the Christian narrative, and I owed it to our friendship to let them know what I now believed. The most important conversation of this ilk was with my best friend of many years, Adam. He is a pastor at a church. When I told him of my loss of faith, he responded with shock and heartbreak but swore allegiance to our friendship despite our new difference of opinions. Adam and I had dreamed of starting a church together and reaching the inner city of Dallas with Jesus. I sat across from him in a Starbucks and told him that this narrative no longer meant anything to me. He has stuck to his promise, and we regularly meet and discuss our ever-evolving thoughts on theology and philosophy. He is on the same path theologically that eventually drew me out of Christianity, and while he hopes I will someday return to embrace this narrative again, I hope that he will leave it, to experience the joy of living life free from the burden of a fictional god.

When I left, it was important to me that the universe had answers for meaning, morality, and mystery without God. Could life still retain these things if there was not a divine being handing them down to us from on high? I quickly learned the answer to these questions was a resounding "Yes!" In the existentialist philosophy of Sartre and Camus I have found freedom in a life lacking any inherent meaning and joy that the task falls on us to decide the meaning of our lives. As I read books on evolutionary biology and evolutionary psychology, I have learned and embraced that morality does not come to us from on high but from here on earth, with us, as humans. Our moral standards are the outgrowth of our evolution as a species, and any so-called moral absolutes are merely brain waves so ingrained in us from our ancestors that we cannot imagine living life without them. Morality without God affirms our humanity, as we are the originators and followers of it, these things growing out from our experiences here, in this world.

The possibility of mystery without God was the most important element to me, and I have found two particular mysteries of our universe to be even more satisfying to ponder and stand in awe of than God: the realm of physics and the human mind. As I continue to learn more about curved space-time, or string theory, I am humbled at the fact that we are slowly learning how to define our universe. The mystery of using words to define these mysteries also resonates with me. And that our brains, these constructions of mindless neurons, give rise to thought, to consciousness, to our ability of discovering the universe: this is more majestic and incredible than some God who is so beyond our comprehension that all we can say about Him is that He is different from us.

Trading the narrative of religion for the narrative of humanism has been the most life-affirming experience yet. I am thankful to be alive, not to any divine being, but just thankful. This transition was difficult at first, because the onus was now on me to give meaning to my life. Whenever freedom of any kind is given, there is always joy and terror. The joy of new possibilities is tempered with the terror of living life in a completely new way. Living in a godless universe was terrifying for me because I had learned that God gave us meaning and without a god there was no meaning. But now I am overwhelmed with the joy of freedom that came upon the realization that we make our meaning and we do not have to carry the baggage of religious rules and regulations in order to live a life filled with love, happiness, and joy.

I want to end this story of my exodus from the narrative of religion by using a piece of religious poetry to describe life now, post-God. In the fifty-fifth chapter of his eponymous book, the prophet Isaiah writes down the words of God, who is promising Israel that although He has let them be conquered by yet another heathen empire, He will someday return them to their former glory. To celebrate this return to glory, Isaiah uses some gorgeous anthropomorphized language, stating that when this happens, the mountains and hills will break out in singing and that all the trees of the field will clap their hands. Glory became mine the moment I stopped aligning my life with the narrative of religion and instead with the narrative that I am creating. I can wake up each morning, take a deep breath, and realize that today is all I have, that it is sacred, and it is enough. And I am not the only one who can do this, all of us who have participated in this exodus, we have glory. We all clap our hands like trees, and no God is necessary.

4

EX-MORMON

Cora Judd

Cora, forty-nine, is a paralegal and lives in southern California with her husband and three grown children. She volunteers at Legal Aid and for a Nicaraguan charity for young girls.

I had my first bona fide life-altering spiritual experience at twenty-six. It came quietly during a fast and testimony meeting and changed me in a single moment. I believe my epiphany was the result of all that came before it.

I was raised as a strict Mormon with all of the usual requirements to prepare me for a temple marriage: Utah pioneer stock through my mother; no Coke, coffee, tea, liquor, or tobacco; family prayers in the mornings and evenings; family home evening; endless meetings; service activities and church jobs; and full-coverage, modest attire.

As any active or ex-Mormon knows, there is unrelenting pressure in Mormonism to study more, pray more, repent more, forgive more, feel the Holy Ghost more, pay more, and work more. When I got to wherever "more" was in my mind, it never felt like enough. There aren't enough hours in the day to do everything I was supposed to have done, and alongside this pressure was a real fear that my many daily failures were surpassing any meaningful accomplishments.

Even Mormon children know this pressure. There was supposedly the "still small voice" of the Holy Ghost whispering to me since my baptism at age eight, trying to guide my path. I was wide open to the Spirit, but I could never hear him or sense his presence for certain. I truly needed the guidance, and thanks to the doctrinal lessons that began in earnest when I was three years old, I had absolute faith that if I was worthy enough I could walk on water as Jesus did (many hours were spent falling in Maryvale Public Pool testing this particular faith). I had faith I could have a vision as Joseph Smith did or, at the very least, would receive the protection and the comfort I needed. I knew the trick was getting enough faith and making myself worthy.

We may have appeared to be the classic Mormon family to nonmembers: clean, wholesome, and obedient; but our secret (which I'll readily admit has no relevance to the truthfulness of LDS doctrine) was that our mother was a sadistic and manic woman. The ward members said nothing, although we knew they were aware. My childhood was marked by interactions with Child Protective Services and my brother's institutionalization when he snapped from our mother's abuse.

Our childhood misery was complicated by the fact that, like a lot of Mormons, my mother claimed to have heard spiritual promptings from the Holy Ghost, to have been given signs from God and received answers to her prayers. Us kids, on the other hand, couldn't get Heavenly Father to hear our desperate pleas to be protected from her cruelty. Why would God favor her prayers and turn a deaf ear to ours? Her prayers to get to church on time were miraculously answered with a succession of green traffic lights. Our prayers for protection from her were answered with silence. This raised a lot of questions as I grew up.

In my many, many church lessons I struggled to make the required leaps of logic in Book of Mormon, church history, and other doctrinal lessons. The answers to my questions about these points were typically obscure, or they raised yet more questions. With hindsight, I now understand the church's resistance to probing questions. The teachers who know the answers also know such answers aren't "faith promoting," and they pussyfoot around the questions. The teachers who don't know the other side of Mormonism rely on rote "lesson manual answers," which are deeply unsatisfying. There's a lot of in-between here, full of partial knowledge, freewheeling speculation, and a vast, beloved Mormon mythology.

Latter-Day Saints have the correct intuition that there's a category of doctrinal questions whose answers will open a spiritual Pandora's box. Once certain truths of the church are set free in their world, nothing will be the same again. Such questions get persistently "shelved." A typical example of this willingness to turn a blind eye to the gritty details of doctrine and history happened during seminary class one day when I was a sophomore.

I loved my seminary teacher, and I showed up in class each day due to his dynamic teaching. Nevertheless, some of his church history lessons aggravated my struggle for a testimony.[1] This particular lesson's topic was the Mountain Meadows massacre[2] (but since I've learned the rest of the history, I am having a hard time thinking this was actually part of the approved curriculum). I pestered my teacher to clear up some confusion about his lesson. I could sense that Brother C knew more about the topic than he was revealing, so I asked increasingly more specific questions. Brother C wouldn't give a whole answer. A classmate suddenly turned on me and indignantly demanded, "Cora! Just what are you trying to *say*?" I was bewildered. I wasn't trying to *say* anything. I just wanted a straight answer, and I said so. I looked around at my seminary classmates for a defender. But it was clear from the looks on their faces that this girl spoke their thoughts too.

Didn't we all want to understand? The Church was true, of course, but how can this bit of doctrine or that event in history also be Divine? It was becoming apparent to me that maybe my confusion wasn't due to my failure to grasp elusive concepts. Maybe Mormons just don't want to know. I understand now that questioning the words of the prophets and other doctrine is the same as challenging the validity of the Church. In doing this, you reveal yourself as someone whose testimony is weak, someone who has allowed Satan into his or her life, someone whose eternal salvation is in peril.

Frustrated, I went back to the school library and looked up the word "Mormon" in the encyclopedia at school. I read my first simple, nonreligious account of Mormonism. I was shocked reading those plain words about Joseph Smith and his visions and gold plates. It was the first time I'd read them without the soft-focus of LDS lesson manuals and the Church's romantic spin on its own history.

As I recall, there was nothing about that entry that was biased or negative. Nonetheless, my temper flared; how dare these so-called historians not include all the other details that could have prevented this naked accounting of facts from appearing so bizarre. Every word I read was surely "anti-Mormon literature," and I was sinning by reading the encyclopedia!

I could never forget what I'd read, but I continued to strive for a testimony. I obeyed every single Gospel principle . . . except chastity.

Interestingly, if I had stolen or lied, tasted coffee or tried a cigarette, I'd have been in an agony of conscience. The chastity lessons never "took" for obvious reasons: these were object lessons where, for example, the advisors would take a small wedding cake, "accidentally" drop it on the floor, scrape it back onto little plates and serve the dirty food to the youth. Of course no one would touch it.

It was explained that the spoiled cake represented how desirable a Daughter of Zion would be as a wife if she had sexual experience before marriage. I've heard of this same object lesson done with roses, chewing gum, and stained wedding dresses.

Did this give Mormon boys an aversion to sexual activity? Did it create a desire in the girls to be chaste? More interestingly to me, what effect did such lessons have on youth who'd already had sexual experience? Any of us could see that nothing would make our portion of wedding cake palatable again. All the forgiveness in the world couldn't unscramble such eggs. Sure, maybe God could grant his forgiveness, and the sinner could forgive himself or herself for breaking the law of chastity. Your ward and your stake, on the other hand, don't have anything to forgive, and they rarely forget.

I was one of the students who'd had a little sexual experience. Fortunately, I rejected the message of those chastity lessons. I already had a mother who spit-screamed in my face how worthless and repulsive I was, and I refused to accept that same message from my church leaders as well.

By the time I was eighteen I was more than ready for marriage (or so I thought), and I wanted to go through the temple soon. I'd gone through the repentance process for impure thoughts and deeds but ended up feeling less worthy because I wasn't sufficiently remorseful for my supposed "uncleanness." The little guilt I felt was nothing like the devastating descriptions I'd read in *The Miracle of Forgiveness*. I became, in my heart, a spiritual fraud for eventually accepting my temple recommend. On the other hand, I couldn't refuse it without walking off the only path to eternal salvation. A genuine dilemma.

Even though, as young LDS girls and teens, we'd sat though countless hours of lessons that prepared us for marriage and motherhood by focusing on the relevant temple ordinances, the particulars of the endowment rites and marriage ceremony were never discussed, only alluded to. All questions were answered with some variation of, "We can't discuss it. It's too sacred."

So when I fell in love with the man who was to become my husband and went to the temple to marry him, I was completely in the dark about the rituals. Throughout my endowment I was anxious about my inability to feel the Spirit. I felt mostly embarrassed during the anointing. And I remember the stress that bordered on panic while trying to make sense of the ritual while also memorizing it. Further, I was seriously frightened at the blood oaths.[3] I briefly wondered, who are the "Saints" that do the throat slitting and disemboweling? Or will I be required to do this to myself if I reveal the secrets? Is this even legal? Why haven't we read about this in the papers? But I was getting married! I stifled my skepticism and focused on the wedding ceremony.

My fiancé and I were shown into a small sealing room, and our marriage ceremony was over and done with in about twenty minutes. Although I have to say here, I was so happy to be getting married, I was grinning from ear to ear as I knelt across the altar from my new husband. My only regret that day was that I was so old, two weeks from my twentieth birthday.

Married life was good. After wrestling with all the sexual "no's" throughout our courtship, it was great to finally flip the master switch to "Yes!"

We soon found out I was with twins. Sadly, at about the fourth month, I miscarried them. I'd been in labor for over twenty-four hours when I finally lost the second baby. Much later, when I asked the nurse about them, she said their tiny bodies had been "disposed of."

A few days later when I was out of the hospital, an in-law scolded me about this, implying that failing to bury them properly could have dire repercussions for our babies (and thus myself) in the resurrection. Somehow, by not arranging a church burial—between contractions perhaps?—

I'd not kept some little-known protocol in this miscarriage. How was I going to repent of that?

Before the end of our first year I was pregnant again, and a beautiful daughter was born to us. A year later a second precious daughter was welcomed into our arms. Those were the days! We were madly in love with our beautiful baby girls. We were living in Provo during this time, and my husband was attending BYU's J. R. Clark Law School.

As a married woman I tried to live a worthy life, but I couldn't "Honor thy Father and thy Mother," which led to the sin of failing to forgive, which led to the sin of "judge not," which led to the sin of "pride." Otherwise, I obeyed the principles of the Gospel and kept the commandments. My faithless doubts weren't enough to stop me from saying "yes" to every single ward calling and every mindless assignment I'd ever been given, regardless of my ability to succeed.

I taught Gospel doctrine in my BYU ward for young married people (I was a disaster). My husband and I conducted weekly church services in a Provo retirement home, and I worked in the nursery in two wards. My husband was graduated, and we returned to Phoenix, where I worked in Cub Scouts (two tiny daughters and a husband accruing over seventy billable hours a week, and God decided via the brethren that I should be a den mother to eight rowdy Scouts). I also tried (and mostly failed) to be a good missionary.

This brings up an issue that nagged my consciousness as a member but that I couldn't articulate until after I'd been out of the church for many years. Why are women, while denied the authority and powers of the priesthood, nonetheless expected to shoulder the lion's share of the work in a ward? The auxiliaries of Relief Society, Young Women, Primary, Nursery, Scouts, Under 12, and many of the extraneous efforts, food storage, genealogy, special programs, choir, Service and Activities, feeding the missionaries, and virtually all other charitable endeavors that don't require heavy lifting are typically done by the sisters.

Both sexes teach classes, but even there I've seen a distinctive difference in the lessons. Women typically put hours of thought and toil into their lessons, preparing handouts and visual aids and trying creative approaches to the same old information. Men are far more likely to rely on their own knowledge base, with maybe some visuals from the ward library. The men take over the camping and hiking years of Scouting after the women have successfully managed the demanding work of the early years. Men handle the jobs that have the real church authority and do a lot of delegating of the actual work. They glorify the powers of the male-only priesthood and then tell the women that it's just a God-granted compensation for not being able to birth babies.

Of all my church efforts, none gave me any assurances of the truthfulness of the Gospel. I would search my soul and assess my prayers to identify any spiritual communication, but it always required an unnatural effort. Any feelings of spiritual "rightness" I felt were the same ones I enjoyed in a wide variety of positive experiences, and not necessarily religious ones.

By this time, I was overeager for some sign of the Holy Ghost's guidance in my life. Like my mother, I was starting to see it where it wasn't. When our girls were almost two and three years old, I wanted another baby. My husband thought this was a bad idea and couldn't agree to it. I had a recurring dream about this time. In the dream, I took condoms one by one from the ginger jar where we kept them and I punched a perfect little hole in the center of each packet with a paper hole punch. I almost convinced myself this dream was a sign that Heavenly Father wanted us to have another baby. My husband didn't buy it!

Six years into our marriage, I was twenty-six years old, and my one and only "witness" of the Gospel finally occurred. I had resolved a short time prior to this that, to combat the frustration and boredom of church meetings, I would show up at meetings willing and ready to learn some small nugget of truth.

One Sunday I was sitting in a Fast and Testimony Meeting with my husband and our two little girls. A man was bearing his testimony of the First Vision. As I sat in the pew listening and considering his words, an unmistakable feeling of clarity struck me. All my years of questioning and trying to puzzle together Mormon doctrine and history coalesced into that single moment and I knew: this brother's testimony was based on an elaborate fiction! Finally, suddenly, I could testify to something beyond a shadow of a doubt: the Church is not true. I believe this happened because I was spiritually and mentally ready to accept it.

I had rejected the Church's main premise, "truth," as faulty. In doing so, the veil parted, and I had the clear-eyed view of Mormonism I had always sought. This moment is one of the most defining experiences of my life. I couldn't keep this to myself and told my husband within the week.

I think I did a poor job of conveying to him the nature of the change in me because he asked me if I could go to church anyway. My Mormon identity, nearly my whole identity really, had vanished, and yet it was unthinkable to attempt to recover it and try "going to church anyway." Overall, he was far more understanding than I suppose most Mormon men would have been.

My bishop heard about my apostasy from my husband (I had made such a clean break from Mormondom in the week after that meeting that I didn't even bother telling the bishop that I was done with the Church—who was he to me now?). The bishop asked to speak to me in person about my decision, and I agreed. During our conversation he insisted I read *Mere Christianity* and then we'd meet again to discuss my decision to leave. I sensed I was being set up for a battle of dogmas and told him "no thanks." I was done with fruitless debates and unanswerable questions.

My husband continued attending church without me, and he took our girls with him.

The prophets and apostles have always looked like spiritual and kindly men to me. But since learning about how key events in the course the church's history have been handled by them, I regard them differently. It's difficult to ignore the overall absence of any powers of discernment in these "prophets, seers, and revelators" regarding everything from the Kinderhook plates to the "Book of Abraham" papyri to the Hoffman documents and many other important issues in between. Despite this lack of discernment, they seem quite shrewd in earthly matters. Unfortunately, all that I intuited to be false and disturbing about the Church was more than validated in my research.

My reaction at being so thoroughly duped, at surrendering so much of my identity and my life's decisions, was a righteous fury. It lived in a strange coexistence for many years with the sense of having been miraculously cut free from the chains of the church. Today I try not to give the anger any power, but after all these years, I still savor the freedom.

A Mormon will glibly say my apostasy is the influence of Satan. But even though I submitted to the authority of the Church and struggled to gain a testimony and followed the commandments and the Plan of Salvation, the darkest parts of my life were also my most religiously obedient.

In contrast, there were a lot of wonderful surprises in becoming an apostate. No cloud of darkness hovers over me. In fact, I'm far more optimistic about myself and my future. My joys aren't tainted by any attached feelings of guilt for not doing "more and better" in so many other parts of my life. I also enjoy a certain serenity with who I am and the problems I (still) have and how I'm living my life. And there's no longer the fear that I'm paying for (or will eventually pay for) a trail of inadvertent sins left in my wake. This is not a lifelong, arbitrary "test of faith." Over time, I also lost an arrogant view of the world that I hadn't been aware that I had.

As a Mormon, I'd disregarded almost all non-Mormons as misguided people. Even if they looked like loving people who were engaged in meaningful lives, I knew their happiness was counterfeit. Non-Mormons didn't know real happiness because they didn't have the One True Church. They didn't love their husbands and children as I did because they didn't understand Forever Families. My marriage was eternal; theirs was only a little better than shacking up. My feelings were real; their feelings were delusions. I regret how I needlessly limited my "outside" friendships and considered non-Mormons as Heavenly Father's less-favored people.

Very little else has changed about me. Coffee found me quickly! I have no real taste for alcohol. I have no desire to lie, cheat, smoke, gossip, fool around, evade taxes, etc. Moreover, my goal to live a principled life, do good, and insure that our earth doesn't suffer for my presence here still guides me. I no longer believe I'm currying favor with God for any good I might do.

About a year or two after I left, I heard a statistic about the Church's fantastic growth and membership. I realized they were including me in that number. It bothered me because it seemed to be a little white lie. "The LDS Church has grown to X million saints worldwide." Including me and how many other "inactives?" I wrote and asked that they not include me as a saint in their future tallies, and my name was eventually removed.

Our children are now grown and have stories of their own about growing up in a part-member family. It hasn't been easy for any of us. Because my spouse is LDS and I'm not, none of us could have quite what we wanted in a family.

To me, the church seems to have an over-over-emphasis on obedience. The list of things that a true-blue Mormon fears is long. The overriding ones are: "What if I'm not worthy enough to pass the final judgment?" "What if I'm not righteous enough to keep my family together eternally?" "What if the feeling I'm calling the Spirit of the Holy Ghost isn't?" "What, of many things, should I be doing better but just can't seem to?" "What if the eternal salvation of my friend/neighbor/child/mother/sibling/mailman rests in my ability to bring them the Gospel?" "Am I under the influence of Satan?" and all the endless "Why . . . ?" and "How . . . ?" and "What if . . . ?" questions that they train themselves to stop asking and put on their "shelf." There's no real comfort from the Church leadership when it comes to these fears because they serve such a practical purpose.

The members internalize them and the accompanying guilt. Thus fearful, they blindly obey the very "principles" that keep the authority and influence of the Brethren intact. I think the saddest result of striving for such perfect compliance, as the faithful Mormons do, is that it prevents more authentic and healthy ways of experiencing one's own thoughts, feelings, and life. Because nearly all aspects of their lives are managed by the Church until their last moments on earth, the concept of free agency that LDS doctrine touts is an illusion.

Some ex-Mormons find solace in new religions, and I'm certain that because of their journey through Mormonism, they're unique and valuable assets there. As for me, I can't imagine committing to any other religion. I'll never again surrender any part of my ability to think and study freely about a thing and draw my own conclusions. I love to learn, and I love not needing to first ask, "What's the Church's position on this?" to know what my own thinking will be.

PART 2

CULTURAL CONTEXTS IN COMING OUT AS ATHEIST

F I WERE to ask you to draw a portrait of any key leader within the atheist movement, I'm guessing that you may be able to draft an accurate sketch. First of all, you would put away any crayons or colored pencils that were not in the peach or beige spectrum, as the vast majority of leaders in the atheist movement are white. Second, you would only be drawing men, men who are mostly older and middle to upper class. You would probably imagine this person sitting in a coffee shop in Seattle or eating a bagel in Manhattan. However, this whitewashed portrait of atheists fails to capture the experiences of many people who occupy other diverse identities and share in nonbelief. People of color, those from rural areas in the middle of the country, and people from disadvantaged economic backgrounds also identify as atheists, though their voices go largely unheard.

When it comes to religiosity, geographic region does matter; national data from the 2010 General Social Survey (GSS) highlights that people from the Midwest and South of the United States are far and away more active in their religious communities than those in other areas of the country. For marginalized groups (especially people living in poverty and/or communities of color), churches often play a key role in the spiritual geography of one's neighborhood. Religious faith can captivate, inspire, provide "a balm for suffering, a source of atonement, and a nexus for kinship and community."[1] For major life adversities, such as financial concerns, faith in God is comforting: it can inspire strength, coping, the amelioration of fear and worry—in other words, the ability to "surrender problems" or turn them over to divine intervention.[2] For individuals existing in poverty, the sacred salvation promised by religions may be viewed as an antidote to the hardships of daily living. Beyond providing escapism, religion and spirituality can help some individuals confront reality. For example, in regards to dealing with adversity, one woman who participated in a recent qualitative study noted:

> I guess for me spirituality . . . is seeing things as they are, not as I would like them to be. No matter how much you love someone or a situation, you go, "God, I wish." Yeah, you wish, but this is how it really is! And, it's the thing of when one door closes another one does open. But, keep your eyes open, and see that open door and go through it, instead of staring at that closed door.[3]

Unsurprisingly, in more rural and impoverished regions of the United States, churches often offer the only social functions, events, or community.[4] In this way, religiosity serves as a culturally specific survival strategy; to turn away from religiosity may mean shedding support systems and may lead to isolation. Specific to African American communities struggling with poverty, churches play a direct role in black family life, with some research suggesting that over 50 percent of churches provide outreach programs (e.g., financial assistance, food, shelter, clothing, medical or child care); in this way, churches take on roles and replicate key aspects of family structures.[5]

Recent GSS data further illustrates that, more than other people of color or white-identified people, black Americans attend religious services at a greater frequency. Specifically, 58 percent of black individuals reported attending church at least one to three times a month, whereas 40 percent of white people and 45 percent of all "other" racial/ethnic groups (the GSS lacks sophistication in assessing racial identity!) attended with this frequency. Data from a 2009 Barna survey found that among religious black Americans, 92 percent identified as Christian and were more likely than white people to identify as born again; they concluded that the faith of African Americans is moving to be aligned with more conservative biblical teaching.[6] Religious belief, therefore, is extremely prevalent in communities of color as it may serve as a tool to help cope with racism and transcend social boundaries. As described by one black participant in a recent study:

> I said, "Well, God, here is where I am. I have done all I can do! I don't know where else to go, or what else to do, the rest is up to you!" And—I'm talking to that spiritual—that self—that higher power within me. Then it starts working. "Okay, you can't do anymore, girl, so I'm gonna take over now." And, sometimes this power works through someone else. Someone comes to my aid, but it's after I have connected to the spiritual being, the spiritual higher power, then help comes to me through someone. It might be in the form of an individual or a thing, but that's how it happens.[7]

Reactions to the widespread religiosity within the black community are not uniformly positive. Sikivu Hutchinson laments that, despite a longstanding history of secular humanism within the African American intellectual discourse, in most black communities "atheism is akin to donning a white sheet and a Confederate Flag. In others it's ostensibly tolerated yet whispered about, branded as culturally incorrect and bad form if not outright sacrilege."[8] Donald Barbera further reflects on the "Negro Thought Police"—the belief that there are gatekeepers of socially correct black thoughts and behaviors and to go against the grain in the African American neighborhoods has serious consequences and penalties—and how this construct symbolically spread compulsory religiosity in black communities.[9] Anthony Pinn, a thought leader on black nontheistic humanism, writes that historical oppression, power, and responsibility must be accounted for in ethical atheism, with these five guiding principles:

1. There is recognition that humanity is fully and solely accountable and responsible for the human condition and the correction of humanity's plight.
2. There is a general suspicion toward or rejection of supernatural explanations and claims, combined with an understanding of humanity as an

evolving part of the natural environment as opposed to being a created being. This can involve disbelief in God(s).

3. There is an appreciation for African American cultural production and a perception of traditional forms of black religiosity as having cultural importance as opposed to any type of "cosmic" authority.

4. There is a commitment to individual and societal transformation.

5. There is a controlled optimism that recognizes both human potential and human destructive activities.[10]

This spirit is beautifully captured by the African American novelist Zora Neale Hurston's words: "So I do not pray. I accept the means at my disposal for working out my destiny. It seems to me that I have been given a mind and will-power for that very purpose."[11]

The stories of Naima, James, Shawn, and David explore the influences that racial or cultural group, community of origin, and social class have on atheist identity development. Interestingly, both Naima and Shawn describe sudden deconversions. For Naima, leaving her born-again Christian faith as an African American woman occurred in the midst of a sudden life transformation: she one day woke up questioning everything she had previously held true. Shawn's sudden deconversion from Islamic faith was triggered by an unwelcome visit from a faith-based healer, whom he believed duped his family and provided false hope. The deconversion not only removed his religious faith but also shook his connection to his South Asian heritage. Even though South Asian American communities are diverse and have distinct immigration histories, they share common cultural values such as collectivism, familial piety, and emotional self-control. In his narrative, Shawn expressed that he grew uncomfortable with the pressure his culture placed on individuals to have traditional marriages, and he resented that he could not be more open about a romantic relationship he had with a woman who was not Muslim. According to their most recent census, roughly 13 percent of the Indian population practices Islam; India is home to the world's third-largest Muslim population. Like Shawn, one prominent atheist woman of color, Ayaan Hirsi Ali, argues that "the Koran is inherently misogynistic, fascistic, and anti-human rights, and that 'moderate' or liberal Islam is oxymoronic."[12]

James and David, both white men from rural and impoverished regions of the Midwest, experienced much more traditional deconversion experiences, in that exposure to novel intellectual material—literature, philosophy, art, and punk music—shifted their perspectives away from religion. Interestingly, though, Naima, James, and David all cite social justice as one of their primary pulls away from religion and the force responsible for maintaining their atheism. Pointedly, Naima acknowledged the potential for religion to serve as a healing balm but explained that once she became aware of larger social issues, blind comfort was no longer an option: "Those churches could have been very soothing places for me to join, but I no longer wanted to be soothed. I wanted to know the truth—painful or otherwise." Such a statement sounds similar to the words of Zora Neale Hurston quoted earlier. Similarly, when James became more aware of the role that some religions played in social issues and prejudice he noted, "if God was mixed up in the mess his religions create, I really wanted nothing to do with him." For David, the link between social justice and religion is even more explicit. Growing up in poverty, he used spiritual beliefs as a way to cope with his class position; now, he draws from Marxist thought and believes "we need to demand to *give up the conditions* that require illusions such as religiosity" (i.e., conditions of socioeconomic inequalities). Taken together, the narratives point to significant shifts in worldview and life direction after becoming atheist.

5

AN UNEXAMINED LIFE

Naima Cabelle

Naima lives in Washington, D.C., with Phlo, a Jack/Jane Russell Terrier.

By the time I was conceived in Harlem, New York, my future as a black woman was already compromised. My mother married before I was born, but she didn't know that Dad was already married with children (making their marriage invalid) or that he used an alias (which is still on my birth certificate). He went to prison for bigamy, and she became estranged from her parents. Her family was Catholic, and she and her siblings attended Catholic schools. She also had a friend who was a housewife with young children, and I began living with this woman and her husband right after I was born. They were also Catholics, they became my godparents, and I lived with them until I was around five years old. My mother worked, came to see me, but there was no parent-child bond. She was just a visitor.

To deviate briefly, it's important for critics puzzled by the religiosity of black people to remember that the majority of Americans of all ethnicities are theists who also have a hard time challenging religious dogma. After the Civil War, the doors leading to social integration and economic stability remained closed to black people, along with the denial of the protections and opportunities that come with citizenship. From the cradle to the grave, slaves existed only to produce wealth, turning the United States into an economic empire. Yet as free people, black people were labeled as the "white man's burden," and their humanity, morality, and patriotism continues to be called into question. There was no choice but to seek refuge in religious institutions not because they were necessarily more religious than other groups but as a matter of survival.

Religious institutions often present the weakest challenges to the status quo. This is the primary reason why religion remains accessible to us. In 1865, however, refuge for four million American citizens of African descent was not to be found in America's "whites only" religious establishment. This perpetuated the creation of "the black church." Today, black atheists face hostility and marginalization within the secular community and must deal with challenges presented by white nonbelievers as well. In the United States, one cannot legitimately claim patriotism, humanity, or morality without also claiming a religious belief. If the claim of religious belief is used as a stepping stone for whites pursuing upward mobility—well-paying jobs, corporate ownership, election to political office, and more—it has been absolutely critical for the mere survival of black people. Black parents often see no alternative beyond making sure that their children, irrespective of all other values taught to them, embrace religious belief. Most theists prefer mainstream beliefs and reject "extreme" religious dogma (as well as atheism). Extreme beliefs held by African Americans may further limit access to jobs, housing, educational opportunities, etc. The most widely accepted beliefs are also wedded to American mainstream values and are more difficult to question because those beliefs come with social benefits while the more extreme religious beliefs and practices (as well as atheism) may trigger bigotry along with the denial of social benefits.

I experienced many losses: At five, our entire neighborhood was to be demolished to make way for massive public housing projects. Dozens of blocks containing tenement apartment buildings would be razed. Every friend I had, every girl in my ballet class, every adult I knew had to move. The family I loved and thought to be my own moved fifty miles away from Harlem. I spent every summer with them. At the end of each summer I had to leave them again, and after each separation I spent many months in pain. My parents legally married when I was five, so, at five, I was living with strangers, having never lived with either parent. They didn't see themselves as strangers! Violence was part of the home landscape, and when they weren't distracted with their own fights, I could end up on the receiving end of violence. During a time when parents could "discipline" their children without fear of legal intervention, even then I knew that if anyone had seen how I had been beaten, my parents would have been jailed. It was barbaric. Life at home generally meant being ignored, but if I did something wrong I would be whipped with ironing cords, belt buckles, or ropes. We lived in a somewhat suburban, mostly white, working-class neighborhood. Former neighbors from Harlem had purchased a two-family home, and we rented the top floor of the home. I had few playmates—black or white—and was never encouraged under any circumstances to invite them into the house. My mother absolutely didn't like it. I knew very few people in the neighborhood and knew more about the black people I saw on TV than the ones in my community. My parents separated after nearly one violent year together.

At six I started Catholic school, at seven my parents divorced, and at eight my mother remarried. I was nine when that marriage ended. I thought my second-grade nun would kill me after my mother signed my report card with her maiden name. I didn't know that parents who hated each other weren't supposed to divorce. When my mother signed my report card with her new married name, I avoided another humiliating lecture on sin, excommunication, broken homes, adultery, etc., by claiming my father had died. For the Catholic Church, death is obviously less sinful than divorce.

The school was regimented and sadistic. We endured name calling, insults, screams, and constant threats of expulsion from school. There were slaps, punches, assaults with rulers and yardsticks, and hair and ears were pulled. There were seven or eight black children, out of three hundred students, in a school run by Irish Catholic nuns who didn't care for blacks, Italians, Germans, Hispanics, Jews, and others. Students who were nine, ten, and older would sometimes urinate in their seats out of fear or because they didn't want to be humiliated by asking to go to the bathroom, so they tried to hold out until recess. There was vomiting, shaking, and nail biting by students who were clearly traumatized. We were perfect candidates for a collective nervous breakdown. Race and discrimination were never discussed in that world known as Catholic school. One discussion I will never forget occurred in a classroom at Christmas during a lesson about the Three Wise Men when I asked if one of them was from Africa and was told no, "He's not black; his skin is dark from the sun." Perhaps today, black students in Catholic school can receive a more balanced, inclusive, and honest education.

Ironically, I did not grow up in a Catholic household! The nuns provided physical and emotional trauma along with academic and religious indoctrination; home was much worse and included sexual abuse. My stepfather was a sick sexual exhibitionist and child molester. For six years I went to a school/church one block from home, but my mother, father, and stepfather never went to church. My mother's church-going days ended after high school. She probably resented the church's intrusions, accusations, and judgments. Many adults only went to church for weddings, christenings, and funerals. They thought that religion was for children and the elderly, but their faces lit up when they learned a child was attending Catholic school because "the nuns were so strict." In some communities it was prestigious for Protestant African American parents to send their children to Catholic school; as we were being brutalized our parents were somehow socially elevated. Adults were hypocrites who lied rather than help children understand life's complexities. We were kept ignorant about sex, but sexually deviant adults secretly talked to children about sex, and some did more than talk about sex. At eighteen, you were suddenly expected to know everything about managing your life, knowing how to have sex (and avoid getting caught) and prevent pregnancy. Any unmarried young woman who became pregnant was continually berated.

From the ages of fourteen to eighteen, I had an almost normal or at least happier existence. Due to my juvenile delinquency, I was sent to live with my godparents. They both worked on Sundays and no longer attended Mass, but their son-in-law was a born-again Christian, and I went to church with him and his wife. Belief now was expressed through biblical interpretations and in some ways appeared more "liberal" than Catholicism because the rules were now subject to interpretation. There was all of this poring over the scriptures in an attempt to determine exactly what God wants us to do.

How did I go from Catholicism and born-again Christianity to secularism and atheism? If there is the freedom to make choices, you can follow your own path, but it wasn't easy for me because I didn't know that there were choices other than a belief in heaven and hell, god or the devil. Gradually resisting parental control after I left high school wasn't easy, but it proved to be one small step toward free agency, yet I would eventually take several steps backward. I suffered from many forms of ignorance. I failed to interrogate my religious beliefs, avoided any critical examination of other aspects of my life, and would repeat destructive patterns out of habit, ignorance, and fear. I resisted making changes and never considered that I could both think and act differently. At the age of twenty-one, I was still locked in the prison of religious and parental indoctrination. I didn't understand that I could question things about my life until one day when I literally and figuratively woke up questioning my choice—and at that point I was finally able to see being religious as a choice. I left an upscale lifestyle for a neighborhood and an apartment that had both seen better days. For months I slept on the floor, lived out of cardboard boxes and suitcases, and ate miniature TV dinners. It would be a year before I could afford to have a phone. I didn't stop living hand to mouth until I found a second job; I would leave home at 8:00 a.m. and return at 11:00 p.m. No one knew that I traveled a rough road, and some may have pitied me if they knew. But I had no regrets. I didn't feel sorry for myself, feel cheated, or feel as though I was suffering. I was free and so happy to live my life, however imperfect, on my own terms. That year, I stopped buying Christmas cards and gifts. I was still a believer but suddenly viewed the Christmas season as a crass and disrespectful observance.

I soon became very interested in both historical and contemporary social and political issues. I didn't have money for many books, but I would purchase them when I could. When I became politically active, I'd collect the leaflets handed out by various organizations at demonstrations addressing social, economic, and political issues and read and reread them. There was no mention of the gods. Not every activist I met was an atheist, but almost every atheist I met was involved with social justice movements. I didn't suddenly become an atheist but gradually evolved out of the narrowness of religious dogma even as I met progressives who belonged to churches that were committed to social justice. Those churches could have been very soothing places for me to join, but I no longer wanted to be soothed. I wanted to know the truth—painful or otherwise. I was moving away from ideas about gods, devils, prayers, etc. but had no direct contact with any group of nonbelievers until I joined the

American Atheists Association many years later. I was only a dues-paying member and knew no other members.

However, blacks are invisible in the secular community. I'm often told by white atheists that they don't know any black atheists (which I assume includes me) and how awful it is that so many blacks are addicted to religion. If I say that there are black atheists, I'm told that they must all be in the closet. Trying to point out the contradictions found in many of their statements is like trying to unravel a knotted ball of yarn. However, I've challenged and questioned many white atheists who eventually admit to knowing at least one black atheist (not including me). We are marginalized to the point where it is easy as well as customary to claim that we don't exist; however, if we do exist, we must all be in hiding.

After joining a secular group I was asked for ideas to help attract more black people to the monthly forum, and I suggested that we come up with topics of interest to African Americans as well as posting announcements in areas where black people would access the information. This never happened. I think the idea of attracting more people of color to the secular community is only expressed to people of color because there are seldom any concrete plans, resources, or serious efforts taking place in order to make this happen. Yet the overall low attendance of whites to these meetings never leads any of these groups to abandon their efforts to continue to reach out to white nonbelievers even when those who do respond barely represent the numbers of nonbelievers in that community.

When it comes down to "race" some people just need to get things off of their chest. In our segregated society, it is possible that there are many whites who do not live, work, or socialize with black people. Talk radio and now the Internet continue to serve such people very well, and it allows them to vent about race without consequence. However, when there is an opportunity to do some face-to-face venting, that will happen as well. I don't initiate discussions about race because they seldom lead anywhere. However, I will discuss it when it is raised. In a discussion with two white atheists, I said that I'd been to many meetings in the secular community where no one white ever spoke to me first; some avoided speaking to me. When the woman who initiated the conversation said that whites don't know if black people want to be approached, I said that if we didn't want to be approached, we'd stay home. She also indicated that black atheists don't seem to go to many meetings, but she was trying to have it both ways by claiming that we don't come to meetings but then excusing whites for ignoring us when we do show up. Historically and even today, black people have been the group that had to know if, how, and when to approach white people, and not the other way around. It's a matter of survival.

While developing as a socialist and a feminist I began to see that religion was unimportant in my life. I also knew that atheism could not be a license to do as I pleased and that social guidelines and laws which apply to everyone are supposed to be for the good of humanity. Unlike religious directives, social guidelines and laws can be challenged, reevaluated, discussed, and changed. I was challenging the status quo, white supremacy, sexual oppression, militarism, and economic exploitation long before I came to think of myself as an atheist. While my activism coincidentally challenged religion, it was a direct and intentional challenge to all antihuman institutions. I'm sure my family members, at least those who may have taken me seriously, hoped that I could manage to stay out of jail since a young, outspoken, black woman was deemed to be more challenging to secular authorities than to religious authority. I'd been an atheist for about seven years when I came across approximately fifteen volumes of the writings of Robert Ingersoll (a Civil War Veteran, abolitionist, and vocal agnostic) and read all of them. That was the first time I'd been exposed to a comprehensive and detailed critique of theism. His writings also helped me develop ethical standards as well as understand the ongoing process for becoming a better human being. With every book I read, I am always searching for any lesson that might help strengthen my ethical standards.

As for the rest of my life, I'd like to be able to enjoy good health and remain active. As a former Catholic and born-again Christian, I spent over two decades bombarded with messages about death and dying and was often emotionally paralyzed by thoughts of death. As an atheist, I'm sometimes still plagued by these earlier thoughts although I've spent much more time thinking about having a good life as well as living a good life. So far, I've enjoyed the ride. I intend to die as an atheist, and I promise that once I'm dead, I won't return to exact revenge on my foes, visit my loved ones, or attempt to collect on any outstanding loans!

6

USER ERROR: COMING OUT AS ATHEIST IN UTAH

James Mouritsen

James, thirty, is currently living in Minneapolis until his wanderlust or artist partner of twelve years takes him elsewhere. He is a blogger at AnAtheistsMorality.com.

Being a Utahn and being a Mormon are, for all intents and purposes, synonymous. That's why the first thing I'm asked when I say I grew up in Utah is whether or not I'm Mormon. God I hate being asked that question because I have to say that I was Mormon, that I grew up Mormon but am not anymore. It's kind of embarrassing. I don't want to be associated with Mormons; I shed that part of me long ago, and I'd like it to go away. Sometimes I really envy my atheist friends that grew up in nonreligious households. But I also recognize the strengths I gained through my unique experiences. It's easy to be an atheist if you grew up in a liberal community—in Utah, not so goddamned easy. I always got the impression that even for those who weren't passionately religious it just made life easier and provided a much-needed sense of community to belong to "the church." It's such an ingrained part of the culture, not just a belief or a religion, not just something you leave at church on Sunday and return to a week later. It's more than an activity. It's an identity. It's a way of life.

When I was young, I knew about the few "nonmember" families in my small coal-mining town. I thought about them with a form of benevolent concern tinged with (more than a little) contempt. But I understood, even at a young age, the difference between those who simply haven't had the opportunity to learn "the truth" (like a blissfully ignorant child) and those who "lost faith." It's one thing to be alone in the midst of a tight-knit community but quite another thing to suddenly lose the community you used to have. I thought of it in one of two ways: a poor troubled, confused person has let life (and Satan) get the better of things, much in the same vein as an alcoholic falling off the wagon; or a person so filled with negativity, hatred, or even evil has decided that they hate God and, even though they "know" the "church is true," has deliberately denounced their beliefs.

The Mormon Church has a catch-22 that is mostly designed for potential converts but also covers questioning members. It's so simple: if you want to find out if the LDS faith is true, just ask God, and he'll tell you. Here's a Quick Start Guide to this process of divine inspiration:

1. Have a true desire to find out the "truth," and open your heart to all answers, no matter the potential implications (societal, familial, personal, etc.). This is called having a "Sincere Heart."
2. Pray, asking God to reveal the truth to you.
3. God will tell you "yes" through the Holy Spirit.

Note: The Holy Spirit is an unmistakable feeling inside of you.

Caution: User Error is possible. If you receive an error message via a conflicted or confused feeling, or no message at all, ensure all procedural requirements, especially "Sincere Heart," are in place, quit all conflicting applications, restart, and follow instructions again. If problem persists, it is likely that "Sincere Heart" is corrupt.

In summary, if God doesn't tell you the LDS faith is the only true faith, you fucked up. God, supposedly, doesn't mess around; you really have to want it before he'll bother giving you a sign. (He's busy.) His delivery method is also a bit ambiguous. Basically, whatever emotions you're feeling inside, that's the "holy spirit." It's all about interpreting whatever you're feeling, and that is the "clear sign." This is especially true of those who really want nothing more than to have it be true, to finally have some perfect purpose in life and a clear attainable goal, something they can feel certain about being on the right path for. It is also possible to misinterpret God's sign as anxiety, fear, etc. (He really doesn't feel like he needs to whisper louder); again, user error.

So there's the catch-22. Since the only conclusion you can come to is that the Mormon Church is true, if you don't come to that conclusion, the problem is you. That is a lot of pressure for a teenage boy in Utah wondering whether he really should be assuming he'll go on a Mormon mission, knocking on doors, and trying to convert people for two entire years of his life.

I was a rebellious teen, but not in a fucking-up-my-life kind of way. I was excited about pushing limits, but I was still responsible. It probably seems like a regular adolescent phase to most but herb and alcohol experimentation, ditching class to smoke cigarettes, being in a punk band, and spending all of my time skating with friends was kind of a big deal since even Mormon adults are not allowed to drink alcohol, smoke tobacco (or pot), listen to offensive music, or even drink caffeine. But I was less of a rebel than a lot of my friends because I still somehow balanced it with getting nearly straight A's and helping my single mother with all five of my younger siblings, including being a good example by going to an agonizing three-hour block of church service every single week and attending church youth activities besides. In the beginning I assumed it was a phase I was going through, stretching my wings and testing my limits, like Amish Rumspringa, because it scared me to think of the consequences of not pulling myself together to go on a mission when I turned nineteen.

It was certainly an inner conflict dealing with the guilt of some of the things I was doing. I didn't feel like a bad person, and I couldn't logically argue that the things I was doing weren't understandable or even natural. But I knew the black and white of it all, and I felt horribly weak at times, trying to resolve what I wanted and what felt right with what I had always been told should feel right.

At the time I became rather obsessed with politics and philosophy, not in a small part due to the music I was listening to. The punk bands I admired the most advocated an idealistic justice, fairness, and equality. An equality of gender, sexuality, race, spiritual beliefs, economic class, you name it. They were scathingly critical of all institutions that stood in the way of such equality, particularly governments, economic politics (capitalism), and of course religion. I became quickly impassioned about my newly realized moral compass. I certainly couldn't understand the overwhelmingly conservative outlook of those in my community. Utah is, after all, consistently labeled as the most Republican state in the union. It's a strange unspoken bond, Mormonism and the Republican Party, one that's understood but not "official." My impression has always been that members feel it something of a moral duty to support the Republican Party. It always seemed so backward to me since the equality and tolerance I was passionate about that was pushing me toward liberal politics seemed to be a logical extension of Christ's teachings.

I began looking critically at my own religion, and the clear violations of my ideals that I found were troubling. A woman's role is very subservient, she must obey her husband, she cannot obtain the priesthood, she is not the head of a household, she cannot pass "Go," her salvation is directly reliant on her husband. Black people were not allowed to obtain the priesthood until 1978; dark skin is a curse from God. I became aware of the LDS church's active involvement in the campaign against gay rights, diametrically opposed to the equality I felt was so important. I started feeling that if anyone should be right about these kinds of things from the beginning, it would be God. I thought that the policy against blacks, for example, should never been in place, let alone the fact that God supposedly waited a good couple decades after the civil rights movement began (come on, he's not that busy) to change his mind that blacks were inherently unworthy of the blessings and rights of the priesthood because of their skin color.

I was quickly becoming disenfranchised not only with my religion but also with organized religion in general. It was an incredibly liberating feeling: I no longer felt overwhelming guilt for the most trivial of things, a cigarette I smoked, masturbation. I had never felt more like a good person; I still knew what was right and wrong. This was mind-blowingly contradictory to what I'd been taught: that people who were not fortunate enough to be a part of the "true" faith were miserable. I did ask God, like I was always told to do, if I was on the right track. I suppose it was user error. I felt incredible about the direction I was going, and I was filled with dread at the possibility that the LDS faith could be true. I got no divine inspiration other than self-realized epiphany. I reasoned that any god would know I was a good person and judge me accordingly, not based on the number of hoops I was willing to jump through. And I further reasoned that if God was mixed up in the mess his religions create, I really wanted nothing to do with him. I just couldn't ignore these issues because I was scared of hell; I had more self-respect than that.

But I still had to play it cool because I lived with my mother, and I respected her rules, and I also didn't want to be the sole reason my younger siblings gave her problems (though they all made similar decisions when they grew up, decisions they came to themselves). But the least noble reason I waited to come out as atheist, and probably the biggest reason, was that I was afraid of the confrontation and how much it would let my mother down.

Sundays were the "Lord's Day," and anything not related to religion was out of the question. Spending money, watching TV or playing video games, reading nonreligious books, seeing friends: all off limits. Reading Dickens or Dumas or Dostoevsky on a Sunday was an act of rebellion. I napped a lot. I also went to choir practice, ironically, as something enjoyable to escape the repressive feeling of Sunday (my love of music was an escape). In addition to three hours of church and an hour of choir practice, there were often additional church meetings for youth or just for the men (priesthood meetings). I guess the idea was to be completely occupied by the gospel on Sunday.

On just such a depressing Sunday afternoon when I was about sixteen or seventeen, not wanting to leave the solace of Middle Earth, I refused to go to a big-deal, twice-a-year, church leadership priesthood meeting that was broadcast worldwide from Salt Lake City. My mother was understandably upset; she'd dealt with this type of thing before from all of her six children several times. But it was when she started talking about how important the meeting was and I interrupted her with, "it's not important to me," that she really lost her shit.

It was likely a confirmation of her fears. The writing had been on the wall: all of the subversive music, CDs she'd confiscated and broken; having to refuse my requests to dye my hair green or red or black (the body is a temple and whatnot); seeing the kind of friends I was hanging out with. I had seen her angry plenty of times, but I'd never seen her display such a strange mixture of anger, disappointment, confusion, fear, and overwhelming frustration, at least not with me. We yelled at each other for a while, and it only got worse. I'm not sure why I bothered making a big deal out of it when I had been telling myself that I could and should continue to be a good example until I turned eighteen and moved out. I certainly didn't decide I just couldn't keep that part of myself quelled any longer and needed to "come out"; I wasn't even certain what I did believe, only what I had problems with. But I suddenly felt like I needed to stand my ground, and I couldn't relent.

I can't remember what exactly was said, but I do remember that it was definitely the first time I conveyed my doubt about the LDS faith to her, hinting even at the beginnings of agnosticism, and also the fact that I didn't want to go on a Mormon mission. After a while she gave up, angry and devastated.

That was the first time I came out. And it wasn't like working up the courage to just come out once and be done with it, like that first big hump of a scary roller coaster. There were smatterings of mini-coming-out instances later on, peppered throughout the course of my late adolescence and early adulthood, most of them involving coming out to my mother one step at a time, or maybe more like subtle, stinging incremental reminders of what I believed (or rather did not believe).

The guilt machine especially among Utah Mormons is as well oiled and on message as a national political party. So, although one's decision to believe in the faith seems like a personal thing, between that person and God, it's really not. You'd think that even family members, even the ones who were sad about the possibility of you going to hell, could at least say, "well, it's their decision, at least I'm saved." But one of the main hooks of the faith is that families are together forever in something called the Eternal Family. So if you decide to not jump through all the hoops (mission, temple marriage, etc.), you are also fucking up heaven for your family, not just for yourself.

But the guilt works both ways. Mormons are utterly terrified when a family member is questioning or has left the faith. I can only imagine how often my mother wondered where she went wrong raising me. I know that she believes I'm a very good person, and she is usually tactful about respectfully disagreeing with my lifestyle and beliefs, but she still finds occasion to tell me that I "know" what is "right," and I think she holds out that I'll return to the faith someday; I'm sure she prays about it.

Not being Mormon is not like being picked for the other kickball team to Mormons. They find absolutely no solace in even other Christian religions. There is only one true church with one true way. When someone chooses not to be a part of the church, it's not just a choice that creates difficulties for them; it's understood as a choice that personally attacks their friends and family, like they've done something deliberately destructive to the community.

Moving out of the rural community helped me. I went to college and found out that because the Mormon community is so strong, so is the community of Utahns who are nonmembers. I realized that there is support in a community of like-minded individuals, and it seemed more real and organic than the one I grew up in. Coffee shops and bars are very literally refuges from a culture that can feel too eerily like a 1950s propaganda film. Having piercings and tattoos is tantamount to a secret sign that you flash to a stranger as you walk by each other on the street and smile with a knowing look in your eyes. I grew up feeling like I was part of something superior, like a prince born into royalty, and I was surprised at how embarrassingly arrogant that felt after I found out how to value everyone and their beliefs, even if they are different. And maybe this is where my embarrassment comes from when I say I'm from Utah and I'm asked if I'm Mormon. Maybe I don't want this sudden inquisitor to know what I was a part of, the things I actually believed, the contempt I actually felt for nonmembers.

It's a strange thing: when you stop thinking in black and white, you become more empathetic to others, and it makes your sense of morality stronger even as you recognize the legitimacy of opposing views. Really, the irony is that understanding the legitimacy of opposing views, and respecting everyone, and pushing for fairness and equality are all values I learned from my mother.

7

THE NAMES WE CALL HOME

Shawn Mirza

Shawn, twenty-three, is an author, entrepreneur, and financial professional from New Jersey.

They named me Shawn. For years I thought it was inconsequential, but being born to South Asian parents, I was never bound to that culture, never created an identity in that context, never had anything holding me to it, save for religion, and Islam's grasp on me proved temporary. Looking back, Islam really stood no chance. Even though it was an Americanized spelling of a similar Urdu name, Shaan, I was simply Shawn, just like any other non–South Asian. And I love it. I was the only South Asian in my schools when I was a kid, and I think for this reason I never really considered myself any different. Me and my siblings were almost fully Americanized. Religion was really the only thing tying me to that cultural identity, and now it's gone, and I am now fully free to continue to create my own identity.

Though my parents always bent over backward to spoil their kids, it is the emotional and social aspect by which they drop the ball, though not for lack of trying. It is religion, the teaching of falsehoods as truths, that so severely undermines all of their strengths. Seemingly so educated, their possession of advanced degrees did nothing to allow them to think for themselves, to question everything. We see this often, in all parts of the world.

This is merely training, rather than education. And thinking is a new trick for an old dog.

Islam is the specter that ruined my family. The same mother who would give her life for her kids, like any good South Asian mother, is the same who genuinely believes she will be punished in hell for not raising a good Muslim child. The sister who is a physician is the same who believes in black magic. The college-educated big brother is the same who set up the very religious event where I witnessed my old, familiar, secular family die.

It is often the case that when one is involved in the process of self-creation, the death of one's former self—when ushered in through grit and rigor and perseverance—is a triumphant affair. You can almost hear the trumpets as they announce the arrival of that "new you" toward which you have been struggling. It is a victory.

But this is not always the case. Sometimes the world destroys you. Some three years ago, my family—my parents in response to their ill health, my brother and sister in response to not achieving their goals—invited a Muslim cleric into our home in order to seek advice. This man (who I perceived as backward, uneducated, and grotesque and who barely spoke English) was sought to give advice to my family. His advice, of course, invariably led back to being more religious and praying more often being the solution.

The imams, like all "religious leaders," share the vocation of lying to children for a living, and they are praised for it. In a sense, all adults who claim godliness are children too—fearing their "heavenly father," as they are wont to call their imaginary friend. The religious figure, like all professions, provides a service: the ability for adults to suspend their disbelief and escape reality when dealing with life's most important questions. Faith—belief coupled with the wanton disregard for evidence—is the drug they push.

My sister, the physician, was seeking advice from a purveyor of untruths; this was insanity. I was nineteen or twenty—I no longer remember even though it was only a few years ago—not long after I had become an atheist. My thoughts were racing: This is a pity party. This is pathetic. I can't believe this. We sat on the floor in a circle, each one explaining our "problems" to this stranger. This was when I witnessed my family—previously rational—die before my eyes. Perhaps I never knew them that way, perhaps they were never rational, and perhaps I was just like them, so I just never noticed. Now it was inescapable. And with them, that day, an old version of me finally died as well. I couldn't look at them the same way. I suppose it still could have been a good thing. But it wasn't my doing.

I played along, so my family would not be embarrassed. In South Asian culture, the cleric is respected in the utmost, no matter how uneducated. When such things happen, when it is not you who has ushered in the new you—when it is murder—in that moment, there is nothing that could be less triumphant. You are defeated. You are naked. You are ashamed that you backed down. You do not rage; you do not wail in despair. Not then, not ever. How can you? You just let it writhe in you. There it stays. You do what you do. More masks, more pretentions, more nervous smiles and stupid grins at what I knew to be non-sense. And oftentimes, you will even appear intelligent and sound eloquent, and the sound of your own eloquence will be sweet—but it remains: the most gruesome sound on earth you will ever hear is the sound of your old self dying.

There you are, angry, bitter, scrambling to collect and reorder that stack of papers that was once you, now blown off the table because someone opened a window they should not have. Now a few years later, that anger begins to be replaced by sadness. You are sad that they did not know any better; you are sad that they do not know the world as you do, with all its beauty and complexity and history, and probably never will.

I brought it up a few months later, in an angry discussion where I finally declared I was no longer Muslim, that I did not blame my problems on black magic and fairy tales, nor did I seek out fraudulent clerics to alleviate them. Since then, it seems my brother has become a bit less religious, and my mother has learned, at the very least, to never invite this cleric back into our home, despite him being a friend of a particularly religiously zealous friend of hers. But I am writing this still from under their roof, having finished college less than a year ago. This shows not that the issues around my lack of faith are resolved but that they have been covered by denial. I barely talk to them. They try to, but I am done—because it is not over, and in a few years, they will attempt to pressure me into marrying a Muslim girl, and if not, insist she convert. The next fiasco is coming, in a few years, partly due to my older siblings' complicity in following the "traditional" marriage process, which, though only completed with the children's consent, is largely conducted by the parents themselves. It is approached like a business agreement, with parents seeking out other parents with children of marrying age, even going so far as placing ads in Islamic magazines and engaging in phone and e-mail correspondence—sending their child's picture along with essentially a resume—often without the consent of their children. Old hags charge by the phone number for "matchmaking" services. The fiasco moves forward when the entire family is invited over. This is how it was always done, so this is how they do it, despite the fact that most marriages from my parents' generation are unhappy and remain that way, since divorce is also frowned upon. This, for me, is out of the question. I need the permission of no one. I accept conditions from no one. And, like those years ago when I finally decided: I need no one's permission to become the person I wish to be.

My life exists largely without them knowing the details, and it has been like that for some time. When I was twenty, I wrote and self-published my first book—without them knowing. A book on personal philosophy, written by a young man railing against the world around him, a world where the things he took for granted, possibly the most important things—health and family—were falling apart.

I know the damage that is done to children when they are scared into believing fairy tales, when these fairy tales form the basis of their opinions of the world, and then the shame that comes when that child, now freed, remembers those times when they once asserted and defended those opinions to others. For these reasons, marrying a theist is out of the question. From my perspective, arranged marriages are unhappy and dysfunctional. And with divorce being taboo in South Asian culture, especially in my parents' generation, mothers smother their children (usually having no career or their own to give them pride and no discernible marriage to keep them happy). In doing so, those in my parents' generation do not view children as individuals but extensions of themselves. This shall not be the case with my children. To paraphrase Nietzsche, in having children, I shall be creating living monuments to victory and emancipation, and it will be the result of two self-created individuals trying to create something better than the sum of its parts—rather than two trying to free themselves through slavery.

In truth, the chances of me even marrying a South Asian woman, even an atheist, are slim. None of the women whom I have dated have been of my own ethnicity, except for one, a half-Pakistani, half-Italian woman who was raised Christian but was thoroughly agnostic. I met her in September 2010. Over the next few months, we spent some time together, but it never became serious. It was both odd and significant for me, but we were both also seeing other people. In March 2011, she passed away. I had not known before that she was suffering from schizophrenia and would at times go off her medication, and due to this, she hanged herself on a night she and I were to go out.

I never told my family. How could I? Dating is not approved, much less understood—and even if they tried to be consoling, I would likely receive condolences of a heavily religious variety. I would receive enough of that at her funeral. And lest we forget, those who take their own life, according to Islam, end up in Hell. Perhaps my siblings would have been more help, having been born and raised here like myself, but what would have been the point? We are not close; I was not going to begin with this. Would I have wanted the emotional support of a family? Sure, but not my own. I never gave them a chance. But for people like me, our friends are our family, the family you can choose. Blood alone does not a family make. Last month was the one-year anniversary of her death. A week after that, I was let go from my job, and now here I am, at home, dependent again on them financially, writing this.

At her funeral, there the pastor stood, pretending to know something about her and, for most of his service, speaking about her last living moments. Was this supposed to be consoling? Forget about me—I had only known her for a mere five months. What of her family? Was this supposed to be consoling? That we should put our trust in god for only "He" knows what she went through, in those moments? Did this man not know how she died? That poor girl hanged herself. Her last moments were agony. And the pastor, the purveyor of untruths, stood up there and reminded me of it: she was supposed to be with me that night. I hope I was the only one, because I hope everyone there, who knew her better, was actually comforted. He could have chosen any other topic. I guess I wanted to believe, just this once, seeing her family there, that it was alright for people to feel good because of something that wasn't real. A religious person can still do good, and they often do, even if it is for the wrong reasons. And I guess for myself, I expected some level of comfort, some level of tact and grace that could be appreciated despite one's beliefs, not because of them. But as the saying goes: for good people to do bad things, you need religion, and there I was, sitting there, just listening to this man doing something so bad while believing it was so good—I couldn't take it. I had seen it before.

For me, it is still the beginning. I am only twenty-three. We are in the exposition, the rough place where all the good movies start. One of the most compelling arguments against theism is to illustrate the sheer variety of religious belief, the vast contrast between victims of Taliban cruelty and the majority of peaceful, loving Muslims—like my family—and in doing so, illustrate that both have scriptural justification for their beliefs. But the latter are who they are for secular reasons derived from things like ethics, reasoning, and humanism, which transcend and predate the major religions. Since my deconversion from Islam, I feel we must show that religious teachings are too diverse and contradictory to hold merit in a modern world.

Our past is simultaneously a burden and a source of strength.

The day I wrote this I turned onto my street from a busy intersection and saw a peculiar sight. Not far from this busy intersection, a family built a new house some years ago, and outside the family had set up a basketball hoop for their young son (both a well-intentioned and ill-thought-out gesture). I guess my life has been a little like that. In some ways, the boy is much better off than most kids—the kids who do not have a basketball hoop, whose parents do not care enough or cannot afford one. But no matter how good he gets or how many shots he makes—and he might very well get very good—he will always have to pause for cars. And wait. And watch other people go down through the intersection and down the street, until he can continue his game. He is stuck, for now. Those of us who were not raised as atheists must learn to play in traffic, until we eventually go play somewhere else. When your home is in the wrong place, you do what you have to do.

8

A LIFE OF
CLASS CONSCIOUSNESS

David Hoelscher

David, fifty-one, lives in Collinsville, Illinois, with his wife and two cats. He is an adjunct instructor of philosophy at Southwestern Illinois College.

I grew up Christian. My earliest memories of the religious life are from the time my stepfather arrived on the scene when I was a six-year-old living in Leavenworth, Kansas. For the next nine years, he forced me and my siblings to attend regular Sunday (Wisconsin Synod) Lutheran church services. I usually found church to be excruciatingly boring, but because my stepfather was strict and stern I was in no position to object to his commands. Lutheranism was important enough to him that several times he spent the only extra money he had to send us to religious schools (St. Mark's, Watertown, Wisconsin, second grade; Good Shepherd, Omaha, Nebraska, part of fourth grade and all of fifth; Jerusalem, Milwaukee, Wisconsin, sixth grade). At those schools recitation of the pledge of allegiance to "one nation, under God" was a daily ritual, and the principal book of instruction was Luther's *Small Catechism*. At home, our family always intoned a prayer before meals; naturally, I supposed that we had to be talking to somebody. Four or five times we watched Cecil B. DeMille's *The Ten Commandments*, which I was told was an accurate portrayal of ancient history. I loved the Christmas season, in part because of the beautiful religious music that was such an auditory fixture during that part of the year. My dislike of churchgoing notwithstanding, all these things and more inculcated in me the unquestionable a priori conviction that God, although transmundane and mysterious, was a core part of reality.

I also grew up economically disadvantaged. My family alternated between being downright poor and existing at the borderline separating the working class from the lower middle class. I was born to a seventeen-year-old high school dropout, a refugee from a violent and abusive family. Because my twenty-one-year-old father was already an alcoholic who worked only sporadically, when I was a baby my mother was forced to ask for milk from our neighbors. My parents' material possessions were hauled away by creditors. We lived in poverty until my mother remarried when I was seven. During her nine-year marriage to my stepfather, during most of which he was an enlisted man in the army (there was a short interval between enlistments when he tried his hand at factory work), material conditions were a good deal better, although his pay never rose above the level of working class.

When that marriage ended I had just turned sixteen. My mother, now receiving child support for just one of her four kids, worked a low-wage job at a retail box store. More or less overnight we descended back into poverty, before long we became undernourished, and within a year the family fell apart altogether. We were a kind of shrunken mirror image of the socioeconomics of religiosity: poor but full of religious faith, turning to prayer to lift us from our economic constraints. Believing that God would make things better but not realizing that giving control of our circumstances to an unreachable, unknowable force actually made things worse. Looking back it is clear to me that religiosity and social class are inextricable.

Through most of my twenties, I was on my own and in many ways completely floundering. Unlike during my childhood, I needed God's help in coping with life. I was no longer a passive recipient of religious training but an active seeker of a proper and beneficial relationship with the Almighty. Recovery from drug and alcohol addiction, loneliness, poverty, lack of opportunity—these challenges and problems, literally dozens of people told me, had the biggest part of their solution in reliance on a "higher power," code for one's own preferred conception of the God of Christianity. During those years I prayed often. Although I feel somewhat embarrassed to say so, I actually thought God was listening and that he cared about my earthly problems. And to my credulous, culturally programmed mind things sometimes worked out in such a way that it seemed reasonable to infer that God did answer my prayers. Psychologists call this kind of thinking, for which the human brain is hardwired, hyperactive agency detection. And from the perspective of hindsight, although at the time I lacked the philosophical vocabulary to express it in such terms, God had become instrumentally valuable.

Reflecting on my experience, I pondered the inevitable question: was my thinking irrational? In many particulars as well as in the wide, general sense, of course the answer is "yes." But such a judgment ignores the fact that our subjective experience of life is not nebulous but, rather, intimate, concrete, and existential. So, given my upbringing, my appalling ignorance, the very limited range of my worldview—which could only expand and improve organically over time rather than by fiat—the fact that praying actually made me feel better and gave me hope at times when there was no other source of it, the proper answer is a definite "no," my thinking was not irrational. Sadly but verily, in a general sense I was behaving in the most rational manner available to me as a situated agent, subjectively and often desperately trying both to survive and to discover some path by which I might come to flourish in this world.

Once started, the process of losing my religion played out fairly quickly. The groundwork had been forming for several years during my late twenties when, reflecting that the suffering I endured seemed a good ways beyond reasonable, I began to have nagging doubts as to whether God was really out there at all. My belief in the efficacy of faith was beginning to lose what the psychologist and philosopher of religion William James famously called its "cash value." The big transformation happened when I was in my early thirties and finally finishing my bachelor's degree. A few years earlier I had completed an associate degree at a community college, an accomplishment made possible only by my spending two miserable years in the Army. It was the first degree anybody had ever earned on either side of my family. Now I was taking out student loans and going deeply into debt. But between the courses I took and the wide reading I was now doing on my own, I discovered the beauty and value of the liberal arts. It was neither planned nor expected, but an epiphenomenal effect of my reading was the complete loss of my faith. The religious fog that had partially clouded my vision for as long as I could remember was hit by an intellectual wind—composed of psychology, art, literature, philosophy, history, and science—and it disappeared within two or three years.

During the two decades since my apostasy, I have seldom been shy about letting people know I do not believe in God. Although, during everyday social encounters, I am not in the habit of trying to convert people and do not go out of my way to advertise my nonbelief, most of the time I do not hide it either. When the subject of religion comes up in social situations or with family members, I am forthcoming about my beliefs so long as it seems I can be so without being unduly provocative or in any way rude (although this pattern took a few years to develop, and at times early on, I wielded my newfound atheism with a somewhat immature cockiness). To be sure, it is a sometimes tricky business, maintaining openness and restraint in the proper measures, but I have found it fairly easy, most of the time, to finesse my way through such encounters so as to avoid being party to unpleasant pothers.

I am fortunate in that openness has brought with it few problems, most of them fairly minor. During the early years I had to learn that going out of my way to start arguments with Christians was both rude and counterproductive. Through practice and trial and error I taught myself how to handle religious topics diplomatically when talking with believers. Because antiatheist bigotry is a fact of life, in some situations—such as when applying for work—I have chosen to exercise prudence by pulling the shade down in front of my unbelief. After joining an online social network site, initially I struggled a bit in deciding how to fill out the "religious views" profile box. For some days or weeks I had "none" there, because I was thinking about things like avoiding conflict with my mother, of not hurting certain people's feelings, and so on. But one day, feeling somewhat ashamed of my timidity, I said to myself: if somebody like me, who is (becoming) well versed in the arguments for and against God, who cares a great deal about the bad effects of religion, who is a sensitive and serious humanitarian, does not "out" himself, who besides a tiny brave minority ever will?

I have had one difficult and somewhat major problem. It involves my mother. She and her husband are Protestant fundamentalists who are as unhappy about my godlessness as they are baffled that a son of God-fearing Bible Belt Christians could actually be an atheist. Their religious beliefs are of a seamless piece with their right-wing politics, opinions about which they are in the habit of freely and frequently and spontaneously sharing. Getting along with them is often very difficult for me. When she and her husband act on their compulsion to express certainties like, say, God gave us the U.S. Constitution, or gay marriage should never become legal because homosexuality is deemed to be immoral by Scripture, or Barack Obama is an Islamic socialist, it is very difficult for me to remain silent. My almost unfailingly polite arguments against such claims are seldom if ever accepted, but I make them, even at the inevitable cost of incurring resentment that sometimes lasts for months, because I want to feel the satisfaction of knowing that I have made a well-intentioned effort to promote better understanding in my own little corner of the world.

There are many truths that, given my secular humanistic values, render the option of hiding in the closet pretty much unthinkable. At the personal level, religion usurped something like a couple thousand hours of my life, precious time during which I could have done something worthwhile and for which I will never get any temporal compensation. Despite a court order to pay child support, my Christian biological father never paid a single penny for the three children he had with my mother. My mother and stepfather, with the support of the wider society, raised me in such a way that as a young adult I found it necessary to resort to the undignified and ridiculous expedient of talking to and pleading with the metaphysical equivalent of Jupiter or Zeus. I lived a quarter of a century with a theoretically avoidable cognitive disability that substantially delayed my achieving intellectual autonomy. Poverty and a thoroughly anti-intellectual childhood environment prevented my blossoming as a student and thinker until I was in my thirties.

At this point, my primary passion is a concern for social justice. I feel profound sadness about class and other kinds of oppression and have long been involved in various types of activism. In a world with two to three billion poor people (economists' numbers range widely) this passion seems to me an individual moral imperative. Unfortunately, the atheist movement has been slow to direct any significant attention to social justice concerns, and that is especially true regarding economic injustice. This needs to change so that we can more easily undo the inextricable and mutually reinforcing links between religion and systems of class oppression.

In 2002, during a talk calling for "militant atheism," Richard Dawkins, speaking about his inevitable funeral, stated that, were he able on that occasion to feel anything, he would "feel triumphal at having lived at all, and at having lived on this splendid planet." Of course, in countless ways ours is indeed a "splendid planet." However, for most of the world's poor, this splendidness is hidden from view by the strains and stresses and limitations that accompany material poverty, or it is perhaps distorted or dissolved as it passes through the filters of religious dogma and superstition. Probably most atheists agree that it would be a very good thing if we could enlist many of these people into the ranks of the godless. Interestingly, extrapolating from recent research, the most effective way to do that would be to markedly improve their economic, health, and safety conditions and their educational opportunities. Drawing from Marxist thought, we need to demand to give up the condition that requires illusions such as religiosity. We atheists can best promote progress on this front by being out in the open and crusading for social justice.

PART 3

TWO CLOSETS?
IDENTIFYING AS BOTH
LGBTQ AND ATHEIST

A S PREVIOUSLY DISCUSSED, religious affiliations can provide social, community, and familial support systems for marginalized groups. Still, "religions in general, and Christianity in particular, are often perceived as anathema" to LGBTQ identity.[1] Countless studies have documented the persistence of heterosexist attitudes and policies within numerous religious groups including the Catholic Church (Buchanan et al. 2001), fundamentalist Christian sects (Barton 2010), conservative Jewish sects (Kahn 1989), the Mormon Church (Cooper and Pease 2009), and Islamic sects (Boellstorff 2005).[2] Highlighting this heterosexism, in a recent study, one woman reflected upon growing up as a lesbian youth in the Pentecostal church, stating that "the preacher would preach on homosexuality. He would always group us in with the so-called perverts, you know, like child molesters and just awful people."[3] Such a traumatizing early experience is depicted frequently in research with religious LGBTQ people.[4]

Specific to gender nonconforming or transgender individuals, the strict patriarchal gender roles outlined by many religions may feel particularly oppressive and incompatible with their identities. Indeed, for people who have transgressed the societally proscribed dichotomy of what it means to be a man or a woman, upholding rigid gender expectations for religious practice may feel like a step backward. For lesbian or bisexual women, patriarchal

beliefs may pose similar concerns. Some scholars claim that women's participation in religion is a paradox; as women continue to make strides toward
equality across work and social contexts, the gendered stereotypes of women
offered by most religions seem increasingly disparate with queer and feminist goals.[5]

Links between atheism and identification as LGBTQ have been widely
discussed within sexuality and religious literature.[6] Scholars even discuss
the religious deconversion process as ritualized, in that, "a flight from religious intolerance is a central aspect of personal 'coming out' stories" for many
LGBTQ people.[7] As reviewed previously, within many religious groups,
LGBTQ-identified persons are taught that their identities are unaccept-
able and immoral and that the expression of these identities is incompatible with being a moral and good devotee.[8] Considering the open hostility
from many religious organizations, it is no surprise that many LGBTQ individuals make the decision to abandon their faith in favor of atheism. Until
recently, it was unclear how rates of unbelief differed between heterosexual
and LGBTQ populations; however, through their analyses of General Social
Survey data, Thomas Linneman and Margaret Clendenen found that lesbian,
gay, and bisexual individuals are three times more likely to be agnostic or
atheist than heterosexual people.[9] It is important to note, however, that the
direction of this relationship is not clear. It may be that LGBTQ individuals feel cast out of religious organizations because of their orientations and
subsequently become atheist, or it could be that people who identify as atheist
are free from religious oppression and more able to explore and acknowledge
their LGBTQ identity. Thus, the following narratives explore the experience
of three people who navigated coming out twice—once as LGBTQ and again
as atheist, though not necessarily in that order!

Stephen, Sherilyn, and David each struggled with their faiths and simultaneously with coming into their own sexual orientations and gender identities. For both Stephen and David, coming out as gay was a laborious process,
made painful by their membership to Christian religions. Stephen, who was
a member of Disciples of Christ Church, felt that the members of the church
were more liberal than evangelical Christians but largely silent on gay issues.
As a boy struggling to come to terms with an attraction to men, he learned

to internalize this silence as shame. Stephen's same-gender attraction became harder to suppress, and in college he eventually came out as gay to his peers and family. David's coming out trajectory was similar to Stephen's in that both men handled "one closet at a time" (gay first, atheist later), and both write that their families took the news of their coming out as atheist much harder than the news they were gay. David noted that he suspected that he was gay for almost a decade and, like many others before him, had attempted to *pray away the gay*. He was raised in a very evangelical faith and reported feeling like an outsider in his church's congregation. There were stages of anger, disappointment, bargaining, and eventually intellectual acrobatics and acceptance; he explains: "I wrote out a letter to God saying that I couldn't believe that he would make me gay only to require that I stifle the desire he supposedly gave me."

Sherilyn, who transitioned from biologically male to a transgender woman in early adulthood, explained that she had always felt something was amiss with her gender. Much like the research suggests, she was raised Catholic, and any information that she managed to garner about transgender issues had a tone of pity and conveyed a message that to have feelings of gender incongruency was abnormal and inappropriate; thus, there was really no room for self-exploration. Sherilyn begrudgingly attended church and CCD, though she was not moved by belief, and, eventually, her protests led to a victory: her mother stopped waking her up for Sunday services. So, in contrast to Stephen and David, Sherilyn first left religion and several years later began her gender transition to become the "godless woman" she was always meant to be!

All of the authors noted feeling free, lighter, and finally "becoming themselves" after coming out as both LGBTQ and atheist. Similarly, they each expressed that there was no way of "unknowning" their atheism once they had critically thought through their beliefs.

9

A TALE OF TWO CLOSETS

Stephen S. Mills

Stephen, thirty, lives in Florida with his partner of nine years and their miniature schnauzer, Sebastian.

When I sat my parents down to tell them I was gay, my mother thought I'd called the family meeting to tell them I was an atheist. Perhaps this false expectation caused my coming out as a gay man to go a bit smoother.

I spent twenty years living in denial. When you grow up in a small Indiana city, gay isn't an option. I'm a child of the early 1980s and a teenager of the 1990s, and even though TV was beginning to fill with Ellens, Wills, and Jacks, Indiana was still a gayless place. I didn't know any gay people growing up. There was a random rumor here and there. I think my rich uncle's business partner was gay, but I never met him and rarely saw my uncle. Gay people weren't talked about. Neither were atheists.

I attended church every Sunday from the time I can remember all the way through my freshman year of college. It was expected of me. Church was a centerpiece of my family. My parents were deacons. I participated in church plays, attended Sunday school, and went to youth group. I woke up early for sunrise services on Easter and stayed up late for Christmas Eve services in the dead of winter.

One summer, my parents even insisted that I go away to Bible camp for a week. I got there, saw the tiny cabins that slept twelve, saw the counselors with their big smiles and cross necklaces, and I felt sick to my stomach. I complained long enough the first day that I got to sleep my only night at church camp in the air-conditioned clinic. Mom picked me up the next morning.

My first eleven years were spent attending a Quaker Meeting House, which was as liberal as you could get in Indiana. Quakers believe in an individual and private relationship with God. None of the hoopla or pageantry of the Catholics nor the strictness of the Baptists. To Quakers, there is no one right way to love God. They also cut out all of the symbols: no blood of Christ, no crosses, and no baptisms. They believe in peace and aren't big on recruiting others. All in all, they aren't too bad when it comes to organized religion.

But as time went on, the Quakers in my hometown got older, and the congregation began to shrink. My mom thought my sisters and I needed a younger church, so we switched and began attending a Disciples of Christ Church, which had a married couple as co-pastors. This was also fairly liberal leaning, but completely different. As a person who has always overanalyzed everything, this switch was confusing. Suddenly, we were taking communion, which I'd never done before, and we were getting baptized. This switch made me question my own parents' devotion to religion. How could one so suddenly switch all the rules and be okay with it? It didn't quite make sense.

The Disciples of Christ Church provided me with more insight into the religions of the world. My pastors led the middle school youth group, and we spent a few months learning about other world religions. I'm not exactly sure what their point was, but I realized rather quickly how similar these religions were, and most had the same basic stories but with different names. Of course, this was pre-9/11, when it was okay to see the parallels between Islam and Christianity. I appreciated their open approach to other religions and for not taking everything so literally.

See, my childhood was not filled with fire and brimstone sermons. I never remember a pastor preaching on the evils of homosexuals or abortions or ever mentioning politics. In Indiana, people are polite. You don't really talk about those things. My parents never said anything negative or positive about gay people in front of me. Yet this silence spoke loudly.

I internalized that silence and turned it into shame. I lived in a state of fear. Fear that I was gay. Fear of what that would mean for my life. I had no real understanding of what being an openly gay person would be like or look like. I pretended to be the perfect son. The only son in my family. Much like I pretended to be the perfect Christian. I didn't stay out late or rebel or drink or smoke. I did everything to make myself "normal" in the eyes of my parents.

Atheists were rare in my hometown. Not as rare as gays, but rare. My best friend in sixth grade was an open atheist, the first I can remember meeting. This fascinated me. I couldn't imagine what his Sundays were like not waking up early to attend church. He was a nice guy. A smart guy. I admired him and maybe even had a bit of crush on him. He was so different from everyone else, but that difference scared me. I had my doubts early on about God, but I always figured it was better to believe just in case all those people were right. It seemed a bit too risky to state: "I don't believe in God."

Toward the end of middle school, one of our family friends died in a plane crash in the Everglades. She had been my troop leader in Cub Scouts, and I was friends with her son. I knew they didn't attend church, but that never seemed to matter until that plane crash. She was a travel agent and was heading to Florida to scope some places out. She'd brought along her parents. I remember the phone call. The shock of it all. The thought of losing my mom and my grandparents all at once seemed unfathomable. If there was a time for God, this seemed like a good one.

Her funeral was held in a civic center. Not a funeral home. Not a church. There wasn't a minister or prayers. She was only the second person that I really knew who had died. When my grandmother passed away, God was very much a part of her service, a part of understanding her death. My parents didn't let me go to that civic center funeral. I'm not entirely sure why. But suddenly the fact that I knew that family didn't believe in God or attend church felt like a warning. I didn't need fire and brimstone from the pulpit; I could create my own. I've always been an anxious person and could easily create enough fear to keep me in both closets for years to come.

In May of my senior year of high school, I was asked to give a sermon for Graduation Sunday. This was a service that all the high school seniors led. My sermon had to be about gifts from God, so I spoke about how my dream of becoming a writer was attached to my spirituality. I'm sure I have a copy of this somewhere, but it would pain me to read it now. I knew what people wanted to hear and what was expected of me, and it worked. I was greeted with open arms by all of the elderly church ladies, who wished me well and kissed me on the cheek. I'm sure they all imagined I'd write some great American novel that would reflect the wonderful values I learned there in church. They'd be surprised to find out my first book is actually a collection of poems about sexuality and violence.

But the boy who stood before the congregation on that day wasn't me. He was a version of me living in an alternative reality where I was the good, straight Christian boy. I wonder where his life would have gone had I kept giving him breath.

I went to a small liberal arts college in southern Indiana that was two and a half hours from my hometown, which was enough distance to create a new life. One might expect that I would shed my false self right away, but instead I found a church to go to and a girl to date all within the first week of school. I so wanted to be "normal." The girl only lasted a month, but I attended church almost every Sunday my entire first year of college.

One weekend, I brought my parents to the church. The minister was a lively woman in her early forties. She was passionate and a good storyteller. She'd often have tears running down her face at some point during the service. I was never that moved, but she kept my attention, as did the shaggy-haired high school boys who played in the church band. I always sensed in her a troubled past and that perhaps she'd found Jesus later in life. You don't typically have that much passion if you're simply born into it.

As I was leaving church that Sunday with my parents, the minister stopped us. I'd spoken with her before, as she often greeted everyone after the service. She introduced herself to my parents and said to them, "the greatest thing in the world is knowing your son loves Jesus Christ." Her eyes were welling with tears and her poof of blonde hair bobbed with each squeeze of my mother's hand. She meant it.

I knew right then and there that I was a fraud.

By the winter of my sophomore year, I'd fallen into a depression. I was no longer attending church, and my sexuality was coming to the surface like a life preserver that had been there all along. One day, I woke up and simply said, "I'm gay." I found the last piece to the jigsaw puzzle hiding under the chair leg. The pieces fit together. This was who I had always been. I still didn't know what being gay would mean, but I no longer cared.

I spent a few months in counseling sessions with the school therapist, where I could talk out my feelings and plan how to tell everyone in my life. I figured the quicker, the better. I was eager to start over. I told my close friends first, like my best girlfriend from high school (a Jew), who, of course, had known all along. I then told my older sister and brother-in-law, and we planned a family meeting to tell my parents and younger sister.

It was April. Spring was just beginning. I had blond highlights in my red hair, a new shirt on, and I was preparing to leave for Europe for two months as an out gay man. What better time to tell my parents? We were a close family—but never a family who had meetings—so calling one seemed unnatural and sent up some red flags.

When I uttered the words, a weight came off of me. My parents took it fairly well. There were tears, of course, and then my mother admitted she thought I was going to say I was an atheist. At this point, I wasn't ready to say those words. My struggle with my sexuality and my sudden departure from attending church were linked in my head, but I wasn't quite ready to give up on the whole God thing. One closet at a time.

I had other things on my mind. I had a whole world to explore, boys to meet, sex to have, and love to find. It wasn't until a few years later that I realized I'd made it without God or religion. I'd always known that it didn't quite work for me or add up, and after spending seven years in higher education and getting my master's, I knew too much to believe in God. I knew what religion had been created for and how it has always been used to control people, to comfort people, to keep people in check. I didn't need God anymore, because I finally believed in myself.

I've never spoken the word "atheist" to my parents, but as the years wore on, they stopped asking if I'd found a church to attend and stopped calling me on Easter. This past Christmas when I was visiting them, I was asked for the first time by my mother if I minded attending Christmas Eve service. It felt funny that my mother would ask me something that had always been expected of me. Perhaps this was her way of accepting me as an atheist nine years after she accepted me as a gay man.

Now on Sundays, I often find myself in a gay club in Florida, where I live with my partner. We sit there with friends and drinks, and we watch a black drag queen in a church dress and a big hat lip-synch to a gospel number. This has become my church. My sanctuary. It has nothing to do with God, but there are rituals here. Patterns. A Captain and coke from my favorite bartender, who will share with me a funny story or the latest piece of club gossip. A handful of dollar bills to tuck into a drag queen's sweaty palm. A hug to the old man who works the door and thinks I'm the cutest guy there. A dance to my favorite song of the moment with the man I love. His hand on my back. His fingers just slipping below my waistband. Men all around. Different men. Different ages. Different skin tones and sizes. There together, dancing, drinking, and imagining all the possibilities this world holds. This is my religion.

10

THE PERMANENT
PRODIGAL DAUGHTER

Sherilyn Connelly

Sherilyn, thirty-nine, lives in San Francisco, where she is pursuing a master's degree in library and information science.

I have a distinct memory of the moment: I was on the San Francisco Muni 18 line one day in 1997, traveling north along the lower edge of Lake Merced. I was finishing up Carl Sagan and Ann Druyan's 1992 book *Shadows of Forgotten Ancestors*. When I reached the final sentence of the final page, I finally came to peace with something I'd known for a long time: I had to start transitioning to female. I was twenty-four years old.

I'd known by the time I was five that there was something amiss with me gender-wise, that the whole "boy" thing didn't suit me at all, but I couldn't put it into words until I was older. As a teenager in the late 1980s, I spent many a Saturday in the Fresno State University library, reading everything I could find on transsexuality. Most of it was outdated and academic, with a "be glad you aren't one of those people!" tone that was hard to miss when you knew you were indeed one of those people. While it did make me quite knowledgeable on an unmentionable subject—I was probably the only boy in Fresno who knew who Roberta Cowell was, let alone who wanted to be her when he grew up—none of it gave me the courage to come out of the closet. (Roberta

Cowell, by the way, was a British trans woman whose 1954 memoir endlessly fascinated me.)

I'd been a fan of Carl Sagan ever since my family watched *Cosmos* when I was seven years old, and in more recent years I'd been reading all his books. I never quite grokked most of the harder-core science stuff, but that was one of the great things about his writing: it was accessible to those of us who were lousy at math. Though the need for rationality over superstition had always been a recurring theme in his work, it had been coming to the forefront of his work in more recent years.

Shadows of Forgotten Ancestors was less about god and religion per se than some of his other work, like the more recent and explicitly atheistic *The Demon-Haunted World*, but it did have a fascinating chapter about the power of testosterone—the substance that I felt was poisoning my body and that I desperately wanted to replace with estrogen—and the second half of the book was an examination of chimp society and how it related to humans.

It made me realize that my life was my own to lead, nobody else's, so I had to live it by following my own heart. I was not beholden to any higher power, theological or parental.

I've never known anyone else to have quite that reaction to the book, let alone it helping another transgender person find the courage to come out. But it wasn't the only impetus, either. There was also the fledgling World Wide Web of the late 1990s, which had two profound effects on me.

The first was reading about and communicating with trans women, which gave a courage that I had been sorely lacking when I was younger, when the only representation available to me had been the unrelentingly negative images in movies and television. Growing up in the 1970s and 1980s, the mass media was very clear on one thing: boys who wanted to be girls—or who even simply wanted to dress like girls—were sick and wrong, pathetic creatures to be pitied and scorned. So I had learned to keep those desires to myself.

But the communication I had with other, already out transgender people, talking to them online and even meeting them in the flesh, proved that it was a real thing, that not only was I not alone in feeling this way, but that a path was being made. It could be done.

One trans woman, who herself was long since out and transitioning, asked me this question: "Can you see yourself as an old man someday?" Oh, wow. That just floored me. And, no. I really could not.

The other subject I researched online was atheism. Much like the knowledge that I was transgender was always inside me, just waiting for me to have the courage to do something about it, I'd always known that I would someday reject religion altogether, and it was getting to be about that time.

Sundays were the worst when I was growing up.

Okay, Tuesday nights were bad, too. Tuesdays were CCD, which stood for "Confraternity of Christian Doctrine." Not that I ever remembered, and I asked my mom every few years, but the information never stuck in my head, probably because I resented it too much. I'm pretty sure it was what other churches called catechism. All it meant to me was that my Tuesday evenings were ruined because my mother was putting me through the Catholic rigors.

That still wasn't as bad as Sunday mornings. After all, Tuesdays were doomed from the start because I had to go to school. But at least Sundays had potential, since I didn't have to go to school and thus could theoretically sleep in. Instead, whichever parent I was with that weekend would wake me up early, force me to put on the "nice" clothes with the collars I hated so much—I was nowhere near being able to admit to myself or anyone else that I didn't like boy clothes at all, but I was especially irked by those thickly striped shirts with the button-down collars—and drag me to nine o'clock mass.

The service was over by ten, and my current parental unit's postritual socializing was typically over around eleven. Sometimes we'd go to brunch afterward, which was cool, but more often we'd just go home. Even though I'd have the afternoon and evening to myself, it didn't matter. The day was shot. There was no way I could relax or enjoy myself. All I could do was count the minutes until it was the time that I normally got home from school, at which point it ceased feeling like the weekend, and my depression increased. Even now, late Sunday afternoon light depresses me a little.

It was from going to church that I developed the habit of always having a book on my person. I learned it from my oldest brother, who would read in church until the last possible moment, usually our mother telling him to put it away because the service was starting.

Aside from being able to get in some reading time, the other respite from the deadly banality of Catholic mass was the Children's Liturgy. Shortly before the sermon began—but after what felt like an eternity of sitting and kneeling and sitting and standing and kneeling and standing and sitting and then doing the whole thing over again—anyone under the age of consent was sent out of the main chapel into a smaller room where we were given a dumbed-down version of the Bible readings. At least there I could get a bit more headway into my book. It also provided me with the means to avoid the rest of mass.

Painfully shy, I hated the ritual of exiting the chapel and heading for the Children's Liturgy, since there was no way to do it without being seen by the entire congregation. I was convinced they were all looking at me, this tall misfit boy, uncomfortable in his own skin, already towering over the other kids and quite a few of the adults.

Even worse was returning to our seats after the Children's Liturgy. I eventually realized that I could get away with not returning to my seat in the chapel, and I could instead lurk around the back entrance, paying nominal attention. I really wanted to just go into the lounge or cafeteria and read until the service was over, but I was just afraid someone would narc me out. At least if I was standing in the back, or drifting just outside the doors, I had plausible deniability. Suuuure, I was listening to the priest! You betcha! Just listening from out here while I pace in the hallway!

I did everything I could to resist church indoctrination. Getting baptized sure as hell wasn't my idea, nor was First Communion. There was talk of me becoming an altar boy, just like my closest brother had been. I found the idea heinous and wanted nothing to do with it. Wearing that robe, everybody watching, having to remember all the steps? More pressure than I could handle. In a display of self-determination that was downright uncharacteristic for me at that age, I made it clear that I did not wanna, and the bullet was successfully dodged.

First Confession was also my Last. I went into the booth and soft-pedaled like mad, confessing to having negative, non-Christian thoughts about the kids who bullied me at school. What, did anyone think I was going to tell the priest, someone I knew and considered a nice guy, about the really bad things I'd done? About my genuine misdeeds, the ones I'd managed to cover up? Or what they would surely consider to be my worst sins: that I was fascinated by the concepts of cross-dressing and changing sex, that I was already spending hours researching the subjects, that deep down I knew I wasn't really a boy? Uh-uh. No way.

I like to make jokes now about being a lapsed Catholic and having residual guilt issues and stuff, but the truth of the matter is, most of what I know about Catholicism comes from Martin Scorsese movies. Or, more accurately, from reading about Scorsese movies, like the countless interviews where he points out all the recurring instances of Catholic guilt in his work. But I didn't pick up any of it while I was there.

As it often will, salvation came from a secular force. When I was sixteen, I got a job at a video store, and I worked until midnight on Saturdays, often not getting to bed until one or two in the morning. My mother either took pity on me or admitted defeat, possibly both, and stopped getting me out of bed on Sunday morning. (It also helped that I often went to my brother Jonco's house on Saturday nights, and Jonco was no more a churchgoer than I was.) She expressed some hope that when I no longer worked late on Saturdays that I might return to church. I can't fault her for trying.

The last couple years of CCD was supposed to lead to Confirmation, but it never happened, largely due to my will finally growing stronger than my mother's—which also accounts for why my hair started to grow long around that time. She began to grudgingly accept that in spite of her best (and certainly well-intentioned) efforts, I would never be the short-haired Confirmed Catholic boy she so wanted me to be.

Eventually, I would even stop being the boy.

Intellectually, religion based on nationality had never made any sense to me. Around the time that I began to realize that I wasn't really a boy, when I was no more than five or six, I began to suspect that if I'd been born somewhere else, I wouldn't necessarily have been born into a Christian family. And weren't people born in other countries into other religions (like, say, Muslim people in India) just as certain that their religion was the correct one? Didn't that make the entire concept kind of arbitrary and pointless?

Coming out as both transgender and atheist was a matter of rejecting certain things that had always been presented to me as absolute: I was a boy, and that I was made that way by a god who knew what it was doing. And the fact that it took me so long to decide to transition—although, in those days, coming out in your mid-twenties was somewhat ahead of the curve—had nothing to do with any fear of what god might think of me. Admitting to the world that you're going to change from male to female is just a big scary leap no matter what, and the real danger is presented by people whose belief in their god would allow them to act in judgment on the rest of us.

I knew some transgender people who were determined to hang onto their faith as they transitioned, and I respected them for that, but I didn't envy them the number of hoops they had to jump through to justify it: "Hey, god doesn't make mistakes! If this is who I am, then this is how god intended me to be!" Some were able to use that logic to make peace with themselves, but for others, it resulted in a feedback loop of self-hatred that was even stronger and more destructive than the gender dysphoria itself. They had no choice but to be transgender, but they also had to live with the certain knowledge that they were going against the will of their god.

It seemed a lot easier, at least from my perspective, to not believe in a judgmental man in the sky to begin with. Solved a lot of problems.

This is not to suggest that my atheism is a kind of intellectual rationalization. Like becoming female, I believe it was always hardwired into me. Nor did the lack of god result in a world with no rules, one where I could do whatever I wanted with no thoughts of the consequences. I suppose it might have if I'd lacked a conscience, but instead, I'd always lived in mortal fear of hurting or disappointing other people.

It's one of the reasons why I refused to marry my high school girlfriend, even though she very much wanted us to wed in our early twenties. I knew it would not last, that it was absolutely guaranteed to end in a painful, icky divorce when I eventually came out as trans—and it did end in an icky, painful breakup, but she only lost a boyfriend, not a husband. If I believed in anything, it was harm reduction, doing what I needed to do with as little damage to other peoples' lives as possible. I didn't see any need for a bible to tell me what to do and what not to do, let alone a bible that has been used to justify great atrocities throughout history and was allegedly written by a being who was, by definition, unknowable to the human mind.

Perhaps most important of all was the knowledge that when I was dead, I would be dead, period, dot, end of line. When I embraced atheism, it took away any lingering fears of a punishment that might be waiting for me when I died, nor any hope for a heavenly reward to make up for the trials of a nasty, brutish, and short life.

It meant my life was to be lived now, and I would live it as a woman, the godless woman I was always meant to be.

11

FAR FROM HOME

David Philip Norris

David Philip Norris, thirty, is a writer and composer from St. Paul, Minnesota.

For many of us there was no one to explain the truth about the monsters we were taught to fear as children—and as adults—and the journey toward self-discovery, freedom, and accepting reality is often a lonely one that is dearly fought and paid for. There's no going back from what you learn.

Growing up, my home life was shaped by the reformed fundamentalist theology of my parents, who had both grown up in largely secular environments and become Christians early in their twenties. They wanted my younger sisters and me to avoid the mistakes they and their families had made and tried to bring us up in the "fear of the Lord." It was rare for us to miss church on Sunday, and the rest of the week was filled with church activities—Bible studies, potlucks, Awana clubs,[1] drama team, choir, orchestra, and band rehearsals. Since we were homeschooled until high school, our schedule of activities was ambitious.

According to my parents, they were likely the first couple in their respective families in decades to be honest-to-goodness virgins on their wedding night, and for Christians challenged to "wait until marriage," this is a big deal. For example, my grandparents were married after my grandmother became pregnant with my father's older brother, and my mother's parents divorced after my grandfather left my grandmother for a Mormon woman. The lesson imparted to my sisters and me through these stories was that no marriage—or human effort—can truly succeed without Jesus.

True to form, sex, drugs, alcohol and "unclean speech" were moral minefields for our family, and we were given plenty of motivation to steer clear of them. Sermons, television, and radio programs were littered with cautionary tales about those who'd fallen prey to the devil's wiles, the moral inevitably going something like, "If only I'd listened to my mother," or "Don't make the same mistakes I did, kid." The Bible was given to us by God as a guidebook for life, and we were expected to accept its teaching obediently; the promise being that Jesus would guide our steps if we followed it to the letter. The true believer would be empowered by faith to resist those temptations and persevere to the very end.

To young minds raised to believe that demons and potential antichrists lurked in even the most innocuous of amusements, every experience became a test of devotion. Christian life demanded total commitment, and anything could be used to lure us away from that calling. To live outside of the church (and especially in the company of nonbelievers) was to court hell and damnation, because Satan was prowling about the world seeking the ruin of souls.

I once asked my mother: "If God created everything, that means God created Satan too. So did God create evil?" These existential questions inspired a variety of responses that mostly ended with a shrug to the ineffability of the Divine, and ultimately the answer was to trust God, pray for faith, and spend more time reading the Bible.

The real question, though, was about eternity. The first time I said the salvation prayer was after watching a Billy Graham crusade and being scared to death after his graphic description of eternal damnation. I prayed again to be saved soon after, this time with my father, though I'm not sure if it was entirely genuine since my parents had made a huge deal over my younger sister getting saved earlier, and I didn't want to be left out. Still, for a few days after, I was sure I felt the power of the Holy Spirit making me into a new creation. It would be the first of many prayers, a brief spiritual euphoria followed by backsliding into what my parents called carnal behavior. I read the Bible and prayed every day, but connecting to God felt like trying to connect with someone on the other side of the world.

In the years since graduating from the small conservative Christian college where I'd spent four years, I've talked to classmates who struggled privately there with serious doubts and questions about what we were taught as Christians. We rarely shared these struggles; there was fear of being looked down on or condemned for not persevering. If there was a conversation about temptation, it was on how to resist it in order to be better godly men and women. While these talks were probably intended to inspire and encourage, often they only deepened the feelings of guilt and shame over our impure thoughts and motives and for our failure to truly believe.

Even more, as hard as I prayed and begged God for help, the heavy secret I carried for ten years never went away. For a Christian, it felt like the worst thing one could possibly be—gay.

Around the onset of puberty, I started noticing odd physical reactions that seemed to happen when certain guys were around—a panicky, heart-racing, stomach-in-your-throat feeling that would make me break into a cold sweat. Since I was painfully introverted, shyness seemed the logical cause, so I worked at developing friendships with guys and being more outgoing. But despite my efforts, these friends still made me strangely uncomfortable in a way that I instinctively knew was different from what they were experiencing. There was one particular guy at church who I couldn't even look at without feeling like I was going to throw up. At the time it was bewildering and confusing, but it became clear later what this reaction was—my first crush.

My first television crush was Chad Allen, who played Jane Seymour's handsome, hunky adopted son Matthew on *Dr. Quinn: Medicine Woman*. It was one of the few shows my family watched together, and it was a paranoid hour for me trying not to blush and raise questions that might lead to an awkward conversation I didn't want to have.

On a family vacation one summer, we were swimming outside at a hotel when a young couple got into the pool, obviously very physically attracted to each other. My parents balked at the lewd display, but for the rest of that trip I couldn't resist replaying the image of the man in my teenage mind—his bare hairy chest, muscular shoulders, the wet cut-off denim shorts that barely covered his crotch.

I don't have an exact recollection of when—sometime around age fifteen or sixteen—but one autumn afternoon while raking leaves outside it suddenly hit me, like sunlight suddenly cutting through grey clouds. I'm gay. This was before I knew about Oscar Wilde, William Burroughs, or W. H. Auden—that day, I only knew three things about homosexuality:

1. It ranked with murder and blasphemy as a grievous sin
2. Parents kept their children away from homosexual people
3. Homosexual people went to hell

Naturally, as the eldest child of Evangelicals I didn't know much about sex and had absolutely no clue what gay sex entailed. But I knew that heterosexual men were attracted to women.

And I was not.

Men in the Christian community are raised with the expectation that they will find a nice Christian girl who was raised to be a nice Christian wife. The implication is that they will have nice Christian children, who will themselves grow up to be nice Christian spouses and parents of their own Christian children.

As I considered this possible future, I knew that it was not the life for me. After all, I'd need to be physically attracted to the woman I'd marry one day and presumably have sex with—which was the whole point, right? In hopes that the female form was an appreciation I could eventually acquire, like a taste for food or music, I tried to force myself to have sexual thoughts about women. These were sad, half-formed, half-hearted fantasies that inevitably became male focused, ending in the routine of despair, self-loathing, and falling asleep pleading for God to deliver me from the demon of homosexuality.

Of course, a powerful sense of relief came with figuring out my sexuality. Everything finally made sense, and as much as I didn't want to admit it, I was curious about this new aspect of myself. It felt really good to look at attractive guys. They seemed to be everywhere. My eyes wanted to look even though I knew what I was feeling was supposed to feel wrong—and it didn't. It never once crossed my mind to act on that attraction, at least at first, since that wasn't even an option—nor was telling anyone about it. After all, there were places they sent boys like me. (As an adult, this fear was confirmed when my parents told me that they would have done anything to correct what they saw as a failure on their part to raise a heterosexual son.)

So at sixteen I began my double life, trying to be a good Christian while keeping what I saw as the monster within me at bay.

In January 2001, my high school ennui had reached its peak, so I decided to start a semester early at a local Christian college that had a decent music composition program. There were required biblical and theological courses, and this seemed the perfect way to rekindle my wavering faith and curb my homosexual thoughts. After all, if my days were spent thinking about nothing but music and God, how could my life not be transformed?

The fall semester began abruptly with the shockwave of September 11. The entire student body gathered, horrorstruck, to watch as the first and then the second plane flew into the towers in New York City. The speaker in chapel that morning shelved his prepared talk and spoke from Habakkuk, a book that expresses outrage over God's seeming ambivalence to evil. It was hard to believe, but this was the time for faith, he said. No matter how awful or senseless the act, God was still good and still in control. I wanted to believe that, but his words rang hollow and empty in my ears.

That evening I watched replayed images of tiny falling dots against the burning towers, people jumping to avoid burning alive. One image was of a man and woman holding hands as they fell to their deaths, and as I stood in front of the television, the images of fire, smoke, pulverized airplanes, collapsing buildings, and doomed human beings coalesced in my mind to form a single coherent thought, "There is no God."

In June 2005, the summer after graduating college, I sat in my car listening to the radio. A version of Julia Sweeney's *Letting Go of God*, her story of becoming an atheist, was on *This American Life*. In the dénouement, after trying every path she can think of to find God, she realizes that there has been a tiny voice in the back of her mind whispering, "There is no God." And it gets louder. "There is no God."

As I sat in my car, I too realized that there had been a tiny voice whispering in my mind for some time, but either I hadn't wanted or I had not been able to hear it until the moment that God seemed to have abandoned humanity. After a day or two I backpedaled and gave God another chance, but the effort felt labored, artificial, and more hypocritical than ever.

The next three years were a blur of staying as busy as possible to keep ahead of the growing doubts about the nature of the faith I had been raised with and of the sexual desire that was growing harder to control. Music provided that distraction, and after graduating I started working in theater, which took up most of my free nights, and to fill the social void left after graduating college I became more involved with music and young-adult ministries at my church. Staying busy worked, but the momentum was exhausting to sustain.

In the summer of 2008, I was working overnights at a store not far from my apartment. It paid well, but aside from the schedule, the downside was that I was often left alone with increasingly unsettling thoughts. I was running out of reasons to keep resisting the sexual desires that felt as normal to me as wanting a glass of water. The previous year I'd even told one of my friends I was gay, but that was only to explain why I couldn't reciprocate her feelings for me.

Earlier that summer I had sought out a prayer healing ministry recommendation; they had helped a friend of mine experience deliverance from what she believed was demonic oppression. I met with a married couple there, and when they asked how they could help, I barely got the word homosexual out as the despair that had been stored up for years poured out of me in sobs. They showed incredible kindness and compassion and none of the hatred or condemnation I was expecting, and for a few days it seemed to have worked. I was a new creation. However, it took one glance at a sexy, shirtless man running by to realize it was hopeless.

So on the night of August 24, 2008, I wrote out a letter to God saying that I couldn't believe that he would make me gay only to require that I stifle the desire he supposedly gave me. I decided to find out what the Bible really said about homosexuality, and for the next two years I poured through exegetical texts, alternative interpretations of the verses used to condemn homosexuality, and even books reexamining traditional notions of Christianity. It felt like I was encountering the Bible for the first time.

Instead of finding certainty, though, the further I dug the murkier every-thing became. Making the Bible harmonize with homosexuality required as much a leap of faith as it took to condemn it, reading between the lines of often vague and questionable texts. There are only eight verses that even men-tion homosexuality, and these are usually taken out of context. We don't know why Paul wrote what he did to the church in Rome or why lesbianism isn't mentioned in Leviticus. Those instances seemed to be describing sexual abuse, prostitution, or pagan worship—things I had no intention of doing.

But I discovered something even more disturbing—how did I even know this book was true? For example, we were taught that Genesis contained an exact account of creation—that God spoke everything into existence. Around this time I'd also begun reading more books on science, and what I was find-ing there seemed to present a better explanation for the world and for the universe at large than what the Bible taught. Even by treating Genesis as met-aphor, that metaphor seemed far removed from the observable facts.

I was introduced here to the idea for the first time that the first eleven chapters of Genesis were drawn from Mesopotamian creation myths. We cer-tainly hadn't heard about that in theology class or church. Of course, that didn't mean that God couldn't speak to us through a flawed book. Did it have to be literally true? After raising this question during a Bible study, the room went silent a moment, then one man said quietly, "That's a dangerous road."

I started considering the implications of the idea that the origin story was nothing more than myth. If there was no historical Adam and Eve, that meant there was no original sin, which meant there was no sin to forgive—and no reason for Christ to have died. I was suddenly struck by how ridiculous and barbaric the concept of atonement was and how petty the God of the Bible must be to have set up an experiment intended to fail—yet blame us for its preordained outcome. The institution of Christianity I'd been raised in, which had been home for so many years and which as a child had offered such surety and comfort, began to look like a two-thousand-year-old house of cards that was now falling apart.

My parents took the news late in 2009 that I was gay with surprising poise. They'd had suspicions throughout the years, so it wasn't a shock, but they made it clear that they couldn't accept me as a gay man, insisting I was a broken heterosexual who needed both Jesus and a good woman to fix me. While they said that they loved and accepted me, they maintained they could never accept any future partners or celebrate a relationship of mine as they had my younger sister's marriage a year earlier.

While they were never overtly hostile, over the next two years our relationship became increasingly distant as family gatherings became exercises in tiptoeing around this issue. At the same time I was beginning to feel less connected to my friends and to the church that had been my social group since graduating college. One Sunday, my doubts grew several decibels louder while listening to the pastor's sermon, and I became less sure that we had much in common with each other anymore. It felt disingenuous to sing the songs, and each sermon left me feeling cold and more like an outsider. So I stopped going to church.

Everything came to a head on the night of my twenty-eighth birthday with the agonizing end of a year-long on-again, off-again physical relationship with a young man who was studying to be pastor. It was the first time I'd been deeply in love, and when he said that he'd met someone else and wanted us to just be friends, the rejection hit me with an emotional intensity I hadn't been prepared for. As if a blindfold had been ripped off, I saw that he was the only reason I'd even called myself a Christian that year. I'd stayed for the sake of my friends and family, but the fear of losing those relationships wasn't as keen, and I didn't care that much anymore about God or my faith. There was no reason to pretend any longer.

During the following months, a growing sense of rage and feeling of utter betrayal welled up in me, over the decades I'd wasted chasing after a god who was turning out to be nothing more than human invention. I thought of the years spent suppressing the red flags and questions about Christianity and faith that my intellect had raised and denying myself the opportunity to seek out a partner with whom to grow and build a loving and committed relationship. I had subjected myself to years of intellectual and psychological torment because I was gay and because of my doubts, all because I'd believed an outmoded holy book and a crowd of people who said that I was an abomination.

Because of the distances involved, there's a gap between when a cosmic event like a supernova occurs and when we actually observe it. Were our own star to die, it would take eight minutes before we even noticed. It took nine years, four months, and twenty-two days—roughly 9.4 light-years, the distance to the seventh-nearest star—from my first time saying "There is no God" to finally accepting the fact and for the light of twenty-eight years of indoctrination, inculcation, and fear to fade enough to ultimately let go.

My quest to reconcile homosexuality with Christianity was a last-ditch effort to find reasons to continue believing. I'd hoped that in discovering what the Bible really said that I would find God, that the questions and doubts about my faith and about why I was born into a family that could never accept me would be appeased. In the process, I found instead that there was no compelling reason to think that God even exists. As nice as it would be to return to the familiarity of ritual, to the belief in a benevolent God and a blessed afterlife, there's no way I could even pretend again. I would know that I don't believe any of it.

Ultimately, my family took the news of my atheism harder than they took my being gay. As a result I've lost that and other relationships but have gained a lot too. I'm finally free to ponder, love, be amazed, and make my own choices without the fear of divine retribution. The earth and the universe seem more miraculous to me now for having spontaneously generated than they did being created, and every moment is that much richer and precious for being the only moment that will ever be.

In shutting the door on one life, I discovered in return who I truly am. And that's not a bad trade.

PART 4

AIN'T NO MOUNTAIN HIGH ENOUGH

Navigating Romantic Relationships
as an Atheist

OVE AS AN atheist? To remix the beloved Tina Turner song, "what's God got to do with it?" Specifically, how do atheists navigate dating, long-term relationships, and marriages in a predominately Judeo-Christian country? Despite prevalent folk hokum that opposites attract, decades of research on relationship satisfaction among couples shows that similarities are the true key to domestic tranquility. Homogamy in terms of interests, education level, lifestyle, and religiosity are all-important determinants of the well-being of a couple. Unsurprisingly, religious and spiritual beliefs have been examined extensively in couples research.[1] Some studies suggest that religious couples have greater marital satisfaction than nonreligious couples, and copious research has found that mismatches among religious belief (e.g., different belief systems; a wife is religious and a husband is not) are linked with relationship dissatisfaction.[2] And if we're going to get physical with research findings, one large-scale correlational study found that atheists have better sex than followers of religion; further, satisfaction with sex increased when religious people deconverted to atheism.[3]

Looking back to the introduction, we know that the rates of atheist identification in the United States are low. Considering this, are atheists placed at more of a disadvantage in finding compatible romantic partners than religious people? Simply, yes: stigma against atheists tarnishes romantic possibilities.

According to national data from the Pew Research Center, roughly 48 percent of Americans said that they would disapprove if their child married an atheist, even though atheists get fewer divorces than Jewish people or *any* Christian group per capita. Thus, if individuals are sensitive to their parents' or family's endorsement of their romantic partners, atheists are placed at a loss.

In recent years, a few atheist-only Internet dating sites have sprung up, suggesting that there is a market for nonbelievers attempting to find love. One site, atheistpassions.com, proudly boasts the tagline: *"You have a better chance of finding Waldo on this site than you do of finding God!"* and another, atheistdatingservice.com states: *"Meet someone for a deity-free romance today!"* However, memberships to these sites are relatively limited compared to more mainstream online dating venues such as match.com, eharmony.com, and others that boast memberships in the millions.[4] Recent controversy has even sprung up regarding eharmony.com and the apparently biased "unmatchability" of atheist users within their system.[5] However, one mainstream site, okcupid.com, seems to be a mecca for atheist users. With over ten million members worldwide, OkCupid analyzed messages from more than five hundred thousand users and found that including the word "atheist" in a first message to another member was more likely to garner a reply than inclusion of any other religious descriptors, except Christian.[6] Thus, mentioning atheism was one way to spark dialogue for many members. OkCupid has received praise from nonbelieving communities for being one of the only dating sites open to and affirming of people of all backgrounds and belief systems; its founder, Maxwell Krohn, won the Harvard Humanist of the Year award in 2012. The market for online atheist dating may be improving, though challenges still persist.

The following narratives explore how three atheist men and women have found (and lost) love, in the context of their nonreligious worldview and belief systems. Ethan was raised by atheist parents who, drawing from their own experiences, have acknowledged the difficulty that he may have in finding a romantic partner in the religious climate of the United States. Originally adamant about dating only women who are nonbelievers, Ethan found that his perceived "ideal" situation (finding an atheist girlfriend) shifted when faced with real emotions and dating experiences. He describes two past relationships, with a Muslim woman and with a woman deeply involved in her own uncertain spiritual quest, and his current partner, a Buddhist. Despite the marked differences in belief, Ethan has deeply cared for and connected with each of these women. Through these experiences, Ethan came to terms with the fact that, though finding an atheist partner was important to him, finding someone with shared worldview was *more* important.

Similar in some ways, Matt became involved with a woman who was devoutly Christian. While he was adamantly atheist himself, he found himself drawn to her energy and kindness. Despite months of trying to come to terms with and overlook her evangelical beliefs, Matt finally realized that he was unable to commit further to their relationship, specifically explaining: "I pictured our kids not believing dinosaurs existed and instead talking about how beautiful Jesus' horse is in heaven." Indeed, casually dating someone with different belief systems may be sustainable for many atheist people, but when it comes to imagining a long-term future or building a family, similar values and belief systems become more critical. Matt laments that if his ex-girlfriend had not been so religious, they would certainly married.

When Sen (short for Kristen) met her future husband, Kira, she was spiritedly tomboyish and nonreligious. Kira was from a conservative Russian Christian community, and Sen felt obligated to take on traditional gender roles and his faith in order to be a perfect wife. While this guise lasted for many years, Sen eventually realized that Christianity and its marriage norms did not fit for her; gradually, she expressed these views to Kira, and they eventually both came out as atheist. The couple has struggled together against the exclusion, fear, and stigma they have faced from the Russian Christian community in northern California, but the strength of their love for each other has endured against leaving faith and losing community support.

Borrowing from Ethan's narrative: love is complicated. And it is even more so as a nonbeliever in the United States.

12

AN ATHEIST'S SIMPLE REVELATION ABOUT LOVE: IT'S COMPLICATED

Ethan Sahker

Ethan, thirty-one, was raised by atheist parents in the foothills west of Denver, Colorado. He has a master's degree in psychology, is seeking a Ph.D. program, and is currently an adjunct psychology instructor at a small university in Pittsburgh.

"I'm sorry that we've made it so hard for you to find a partner." These words and many similar variations have been uttered by my mother on several occasions. My father, on the other hand, is brazenly unapologetic. My parents are atheists, and I am an atheist, an agnostic-atheist to be more specific. My mother was right. It has been difficult for me to navigate my romantic relationships. I also believe that my father was right; I should not apologize for who I am and what I believe. My beliefs have made it difficult for me to develop relationships, and even more difficult when the relationships are romantic in nature. When you look at the numbers, my chances of meeting a lifelong partner seem a bit grim if being an atheist is requisite for a meaningful connection. Suppose 15 percent of the United States is irreligious, and, of those, 6 percent identify as atheist, then haphazardly estimating that 2 or 3 percent are women means my chances of finding love are bleak (at least in terms of percentages). I get it: love is complicated. Being an atheist only presents a different set of complications. I would wager that looking for meaningful relationships as an atheist is an experience shared by a relatively small portion of the population. Discussing these narratives normalizes our experiences, and it helps to develop a sense that we are not alone.

You cannot say that I was raised as an atheist; this would be offensive to my family. Instead, you have to say that I was raised without religion. This might seem like a small distinction, but my parents always stressed that they wanted me to come to my own conclusions about religion and spirituality. However, from my perspective, I sat at the same dinner table as they did, and I took part in the same conversations. For me to picture religion differently than they do is like trying to picture myself with different parents. My conclusions about religion and spirituality were certainly informed by the model my parents provided, which, I suspect, is true for most people. However, being raised as an atheist is different from the norm, as I never had to unplug from religion. It is hard for me to even conceptualize why someone believes in god. It is even difficult for me to put a capital G in god, because I cannot possibly see it as a proper noun, and I never have.

This rigidity is imbued in many aspects of my development and in my social interactions, but none more resolute than in my romantic relationships. When it came to identifying a romantic partner, not being an atheist was the deal breaker. I know in my heart that my parents would accept anyone I chose as a partner, but in my head, I can imagine that they would not understand if I chose to become involved with a religious woman.

When I first began to have real dating experiences, I treated the situations as interviews. It was routine for me to begin discussing the meaning of life, children, and religion on the first date. These are weighty topics for sure, but I wanted to meet an intelligent woman, a woman who wanted to talk of such substance. More importantly, I wanted to meet an atheist woman. When I was younger, even if a woman told me that she was spiritual but not religious, that was over the line, and I could not see myself becoming serious about the relationship. That is how rigid I was.

Both my younger self and my current self have a "list" of six issues that I believe must be agreed upon or at least considered in order for a long-term relationship to work: children, education, money, politics, sex, and of course, religion. This is not small talk and might not be the first-date fodder that usually accompanies a cup of coffee. I feel like these are things that couples must agree upon (at least to some extent) in order to last through marriage, and I often wanted to know these things right up front. I thought of this paradigm as a guide to love, and as a result I never met anyone I could take seriously because I was using these issues as a nonnegotiable imperative. I was especially rigid when it came to religion. I was uncompromising in my atheism, and I thought a suitable partner must be undifferentiated in their irreligious resolve. This all began to change around the age of twenty-three when I met Maysa—and the "list" became more malleable.

Maysa was a Muslim woman I met in school. She was intelligent, a bit awkward, brave, a writer, and she was completely breathtaking. I completely fell for Maysa and didn't think about my "list" of relationship needs once. We barely even talked about religion. I did immediately tell her that I was an atheist; she really didn't seem to care, and I didn't care that she was a Muslim. We connected in a much more important way. We had similar worldviews, and we were both thoughtful of others in the same way. I was so in love that I did not see that she was hesitant to tell her parents about me and that religion might be an issue with her family. Our relationship only lasted about three months, but I learned a great deal about myself in that brief time. I learned that I was capable of loving someone who did not share the same beliefs as I did and that our shared worldviews were more important.

I grew a bit older and a bit wiser because of this brief tryst, and as a result, I began to look for different things in prospective partners. I still disclosed that I was an atheist right up front when I dated, but I started to become more flexible in my own needs. I could now be more accepting of a woman who did not share the same religious beliefs as I. However, I soon learned that family, religion, and community acceptance have a far greater reach when I became involved with a woman named Shauna.

Shauna was younger than I and was still searching for meaning. She was unsure about god and was incredibly engaged in her quest to find her own meaning. She knew I was an atheist, and I think that that was intriguing to her, as she had not really spent time with someone who thinks about life in quite the way that I did. She was an agnostic of sorts but came from a religious family. Shauna's mother worked for her church. Her mother was deeply religious, and she wanted Shauna to attend church on Sundays. Shauna would go to church even though she did not want to go. I could not understand this behavior, and I saw it as a weakness. She would tell me that this is not the battle she wanted to have with her mother and that she was only going to preserve their relationship. I did not understand. Her family knew that I was an atheist, and they were not happy about it.

After dating for about seven months, we decided to move in together. Again, her family was not happy about this. After we lived together, I became more involved with Shauna's family, and they began to see who I was. Though we never talked about it, I feel like her family saw that I was a good person, and my lack of religion, as well as Shauna's changing beliefs, soon became less and less of an issue. As a result, I began to look at her family differently. I had preconceived notions about how they must disapprove of me based solely on my lack of faith. Though they may have felt this way initially, they became completely accepting of me over time, and I too accepted them for who they were. We were together for about four years, and in that time, Shauna's parents never once asked me about my atheism or my beliefs at all. Her father invited me to church on one occasion, I respectfully declined, and the issue was never brought up again. When our relationship ended, her parents sent me a letter saying that they saw me as part of the family and that they would miss me. This is when I truly grew as a person in regard to my views on relationships. I learned that though religion might be an issue up front, the real issue was family and community acceptance. I was now walking through life feeling as though I had become exponentially more mature from my relationship experience.

Regardless of my evolving flexibility, religion and spirituality continue to be the most important issues I consider when meeting women. I still bring up my philosophical and existential beliefs on the first date. These are topics that I enjoy discussing, and if it seems too deep for my date, it can be a red flag. I am currently in a relationship with a woman named May, who describes herself as "basically an atheist." She was raised with Shinto and Buddhist traditions, and, on occasion, she visits shrines from her culture. This would have bothered me in the past, but I have learned that culture is strong. May still holds on to some aspects of animism. This does not bother me because she does not view these beliefs with a literal interpretation. In fact, I am learning a deeper sense of her cultural and traditional Shinto practices in a way that helps us connect on a level with which I was previously unfamiliar. This also means that I am (slowly) learning that all of these facets of a relationship are not just about me, and a difference like this can be enriching to our connection. We do share a common distaste for the gross permeation of religion in American culture and government, and perhaps an accord on dissenting views is more powerful than an agreement of faith.

My resolution to all of this is simple: love is complicated. As an atheist, I feel that my thinking only got in the way of making connections, and this had affected platonic connections as well. I now feel that love is inside, and I try to see beyond the words to find the more powerful connections of worldview, community, and family. Because I am irreligious, I am missing the sense of community and connection that comes with religion, and I need to identify as something in order to fit into a community of some kind. Maybe I like the idea of being an outsider. Regardless, I sometimes wear my atheism like armor in response to living in a religious America. I am a hidden minority, but I don't want to remain that way, and so I will continue to work at being vulnerable, open-minded, flexible, and exposed.

13

SWEPT UNDER THE RUG

Kristen Rurouni

Sen, twenty-three, lives in California with her husband. She is currently pursuing degrees in history and deaf education.

The sound of the out-of-tune guitars strumming to folk music, the smell of the pirozhki (Russian fried buns stuffed with a variety of savory fillings) and vinaigrette, the sound of hard and mushy syllables slamming through the air, heels clicking on the tiled floor of the kitchen: these are examples of simple, seemingly insignificant little things that can define part of my culture. Little things like this can define anyone's culture whether they were born with it or adopted it along the way. In mine and my husband, Kira's, case, I am referring to the ever-growing Russian community in northern California. Kira spent the first thirteen years of his life in Russia with his parents and siblings. His father was a reputable and beloved pastor, and the people, as he loves reminding us, worshiped him. Their faith in Christ defined everything in their lives and was attributed to every success and failure (while other's failures were attributed to Satan). Jesus was always there to cleanse their mind of threatening thoughts. I, on the other hand, was raised in California with Jesus as nothing more than background noise. I became heavily involved in Wicca as a young teenager and suffered depression after realizing that none of it was true. Christianity entered my life when I was falling in love with Kira.

I was awestruck by the muscley seventeen-year-old with the thick accent, and I wanted to make sure that I won his affection. I tiptoed into his culture and peeked around every corner to make sure that I wouldn't walk into where I was forbidden. I had to look the part of the quiet, innocent, obedient little girl in order to win his parents' approval. I learned how to speak Russian, cook Russian food, and suppress enough of my tomboyish ways to act somewhat Russian. We fell in love with each other, and his family fell in love with my mask. I went to the family church whenever I could and, despite the hard questions I would sometimes ask Kira about the faith, I learned just how much Jesus could be used to justify every belief and behavior that they partook in. Our relationship was strong, and there was no doubt that we loved each other. Kira made a promise to me: he would stand by me no matter what for the rest of his life. This promise that he made to me would prove to be a bond stronger than any God could promise to me.

After four years of brainwashing myself into an aspiring housewife that served Christ and Kira, I started to question inconsistencies. I questioned why God would allow such misery in the world while allowing somebody like me to live a comfortable life with access to food. I questioned why there was no evidence for the miracles of Jesus or God. I questioned why God would send my nonbelieving brother to burn for all eternity and expect me to forget about him if I was in Heaven. I tried to question Kira on these matters, but he always had an excuse. There were too many times to count that I ended up in tears because of how afraid I was that our faith was not true. I also feared that if I was wrong about my doubts that I would be sent to Hell. I feared even more that I was trying to send my own husband to Hell by making him question everything. He never got angry with me for questioning, though he did show some worry and fear in response to the questions that I made him ask. His mind ran from what it was processing.

When I could not make him listen to my concerns more, I turned elsewhere for answers. I did something so simple that almost killed my faith: I read the Bible. I did not find a loving God. I kept pointing out passage after passage to Kira about the way women are portrayed in the Bible. He was realizing that making me a submissive being was immoral and that the excuses he had made before were ridiculous. Though, he still held on. What destroyed the rest of our faith was when I finally managed to convince him to watch Bill Maher's *Religulous*. Strangely enough, I was crushed after watching, while he felt a sense of anger that he had ever followed such beliefs. It took me almost a year to fully come to terms with reality and not fear the prospect of no Heaven. So, there we were. Atheists. We had wandered from the flock. We had a new desire to pursue knowledge and replace our previous fantasies with the wonders that could be found in reality. We were free and standing together. Well, we wanted to be free. There was still that issue of a culture that held on to us like glitter stuck to a hand. No matter how hard we shook or scrubbed ourselves, we couldn't escape from it.

This was one of my major problems with the general Norcal Russian culture that I adopted: everything that was not of Russian origin was evil or to be feared. I already had a strike against me as an American, so there was no way in hell that I was going to come out in the beginning and tell them that I was an atheist. The conversation where I had to educate my mother-in-law on the actual meaning of Halloween was enough to get me labeled a devil worshiper by several family members. Kira tried to make them listen, but he knew it was pointless. I wanted to make things right with his family because I didn't want Kira to become separated from them over what I viewed to be trivial matters. We butted heads at this point because he was perfectly happy with the idea of never seeing them again. In time, I would soon feel this way. Trying to make them understand anything would prove to be more impossible with each interaction: the video game character Mario is in cahoots with the devil, Spiderman is evil because he is drawn with a black outline, and kanji is the writing of the devil. Playing cards are considered evil by most of his family, but they are considered to be a gift from Atlantis by one of his relatives.

As I said before, I decided that we would not tell his family that we had stopped believing, but we did stop going to church. That, in itself, is a huge no-no in the Russian community. We couldn't bear to even pretend to be believers in that building full of people spreading hatred and lies about how gay people spread AIDS to everybody. This was the time that Prop 8 was being fought over. When we were asked why we were no longer going, we did another huge no-no: we stood up to the pastor of the church. We told them that every "fact" about AIDS that they stated was completely wrong and that we would not tolerate a pastor that blatantly lied to his congregation. They made excuse after excuse. They followed the next golden rule perfectly: never question another Russian Christian person because a Russian Christian never lies.

Even though we no longer went to church with them anymore, we did make an effort to spend time with them. However, we could not escape any mention of religion. We were respectful of this because it would have been unreasonable to ask them not to pray in front of us or mention it at all, but when they wouldn't stop trying to force us to go back to church and wouldn't stop spewing hatred about gay people, we couldn't pretend anymore. It was unfair to them and ourselves to pretend any longer, so we came out to them.

They were in denial. They just kept repeating that we needed to think about it more and that we were still believers. Then, they changed the subject and ran. I couldn't believe it. We were expecting a huge fight, along with crying and damning, but there was none of it. That's when I remembered the next rule about the Russian community: it is physically impossible for a Russian to be an infidel.

They kept pushing for us to go to church and accept their ideas, and we kept pushing back while telling them that we couldn't believe. Finally, they started to question why we didn't believe, and we told them honestly. We told them about biblical inconsistencies, the recycled hero myth, the immoral God of the Old Testament that they cherry picked from, the fact that nobody can help it if they are gay or not, and on and on and on. They were afraid of what we were telling them, and they fought back. I can't blame them for that. While their resistance was understandable, we tried to make them understand that we could have a relationship without religion because none of us would convert the other and that love was more important than religion, but they wouldn't listen to us. They said that we were betraying our culture and family by being nonbelievers. As atheists, we were accused of being immoral and lacking in love. How much more wrong could they be? The very fact that Kira and I had fallen from a faith that defined our lives and rebuilt our lives around atheism and a new pursuit of knowledge strengthened our love for each other more than it ever had been.

To make themselves feel better, the family kept saying that Jesus would clear our minds from the devil's influence and would pray for us every night, and my mother-in-law would continue to have periods of denying that we were atheists. I have since been informed by a trustworthy family member that we are no longer prayed for. They swept us under the rug.

One might think that it was only the parents' love for us that was making them force Christ on us because they feared for our salvation, but one would be wrong. It was their fear of the loss of their perfect reputation that made them desperately try to convert us. As Kira's father so delicately put it, "I would be stoned to death in church if they found out that my son was an atheist that supported gay people." I don't think that would have happened, but he was right in the fact that the people would look at him as if he was a huge failure. Because of this, Kira's parents went to great lengths to lie about our actual beliefs and whereabouts when not in church just so they could avoid ridicule for our actions, which they had no control over any longer.

After coming out to the family, Kira ran into an old fellow churchgoer outside of his parents' house. Naturally, the man asked if we had found another church home, but Kira was honest. The look of fear in the man's eyes said it all. He honestly couldn't comprehend that a Russian could possibly not believe, and he had no idea because Kira's parents had hidden the fact so well. Kira calmly explained and asked the man to not judge his father because of our nonbelief. The man couldn't believe that Kira would say something so nice like that. Kira questioned him on why he thought that, even though he really did know the reason. Of course, the man eventually admitted that it was because he was an "infidel," which is the word they use for atheists.

During this time, I was also turning back into my own person as I was accepting my atheist identity. My so-called Americanness was blooming right before my in-law's eyes, and they couldn't understand what had happened to the innocent little girl they once knew. Surprisingly, they attributed it to my husband corrupting me, but his other siblings knew that it was I who had corrupted him. The parents openly condemned him for warping my weak and feminine mind, but together we told them that I had a brain of my own and that I needed no man to give me my own thoughts. One sibling in particular accused me of destroying the family, when, in fact, we were the only ones that had been cast away. When confronted by former church members that discovered our atheism, we presented our strong and happy relationship to them and showed them that our lives had not fallen apart because of our atheism. I started to not care even more about what they thought about me. I was honest with who I was. I was open about the music I loved, and I started to dress androgynously again and got my beloved tattoos. This was completely against the sexy clothing trend that all nice Christian Russian girls (and those that married into it) were expected to adhere to. Even if I were to adhere to all of their cultural standards, the one thing that would still make any attempt that I made useless would be my lack of belief. We were shunned from most family activities after we started openly telling everyone that we were no longer Christian, since the subject was impossible to sidestep. At a birthday party we attended, a man tried to force Kira to pray and couldn't believe it when he wouldn't. Kira's father almost completely cut contact with us. We have only seen him twice in the past two years. At the one event we did attend, I wore a Victorian man's outfit to his sister's wedding and was immediately looked upon with disgust for my heathen atheistic ways: fashion is directly attributed to religious belief and nonbelief in all situations to them. At the same event, it was revealed to some that we had no plan of having children, and that too was immediately attributed to atheism and being against God. We were no longer invited to weddings. Russian friends dropped all contact with us. Even those rare few that never brought up the topic of religion in our conversation dropped contact. People that we once went to church with ignored us in public if we happened to cross paths. It feels like going to a Russian store is near impossible without having people scatter out of the way and shuffle their children away from us.

Since I have written this, I am happy to say that my mother-in-law has slightly discovered that religion was tearing apart our relationship and has learned how to leave it out of our lives. She is learning that we are never coming back to Christianity, and she is finally letting go of her periods of denial. A few siblings of Kira's are now atheists, and we are often in contact. The rest of the family still shuns us, and the rest of the community has exiled us since we have abandoned their religion and, with it, the foundation of their culture. Kira and I have never been better together. We stand firm together and work hand in hand through life and continue to build each other up.

14

ON LOVE AND CREDULITY

Matt Hart

Matt Hart, thirty-seven, is a professional ultrarunner and endurance coach who lives and trains in the Wasatch Mountains bordering Salt Lake City, Utah.

When I first laid eyes on Lynn, in a yellow spring dress, she was holding the attention and respect of coworkers, both men and women. It was 1998, and we were standing in the anomalous sun of the Pacific Northwest. The San Francisco–based startup I was working for had been purchased by Microsoft, and this was our "Welcome to Redmond" party.

Lynn and I seemed to have an instant connection, but it was hard to tell if I had any edge over the swarms of geeks and freaks that made pass after pass at her. Thankfully, she was a skilled swatter, which gave me the time required for a man of my mediocre panache to make a true impression.

After some time as "just friends," we fell into a passionate love affair. It turned out she was an extremely rare breed: a beautiful, smart woman who was twenty-six years old . . . and a virgin.

She lived at home with her parents. This would normally be a pretty big red flag; however, it became apparent that she was simply so adored by her supportive family that she had zero pressure to move out. Her parents genuinely liked having her around, so when she moved home after graduating cum laude from an Ivy League school, it was natural that she lived with them.

Her family members were wonderful, kind, and welcoming. They were also very wealthy and insulated. They weren't preachy about god, but expected Lynn to at least attempt to attend church regularly. I've always had a white-trash chip on my shoulder, so I'm keenly aware of when the pious silver spooners are talking with their mouths full. Weekly church service reminded this amazingly wealthy, hard-working, and lucky family to be grateful. I felt like they needed that.

We fell into a habit of having dinner or brunch with her parents each Saturday. One week we were invited over a bit earlier than normal, and on a Sunday. They had somehow neglected to tell me there was a requisite church visit before breaking bread. The service was long, drawn out, confusing, and mind-numbingly boring. Lynn's father apparently felt the same way, since he slept through the entire event. I joked with Lynn afterward that it had been a dirty trick, and I let it be known I'd have rather been mountain biking.

A few weeks later I had somehow forgotten their tactics and fell prey to it again. This time I found myself listening to the preacher talk about pornography. Previous to the service that day, I had been working in a Starbucks attached to a Barnes and Noble bookstore for a few hours. On my way through I stopped to admire the *Sports Illustrated* swimsuit issue. I was twenty-seven years old, and my testosterone didn't allow me to pass up such wonderful opportunities to admire the female form. As a matter of fact, everything about my previous 2.5 million years of evolution would not allow me to pass that magazine rack without checking to see if there were any nipples showing through wet t-shirts. The audacity of the priest to try and make me feel guilty about this angered me. There is nothing inherently wrong with my attraction to women; it's innate.

After the service I struggled with a way to bring this up with Lynn. I found a private moment and told her that every guy she's ever met, including her dad, has looked at pictures of a naked woman. If they denied this, they were lying, and that it doesn't make any of them bad people.

Unfortunately, no amount of praying for health allows a family to escape the random acts of nature. We had been together for about three years when Lynn's sister-in-law had a miscarriage. The family was devastated. It just deepened my resolve that there could be no omniscient supernatural being in charge of things. To me this was inescapable proof. Here we have a Catholic family who plays by the rules, prays often, and shows continued reverence. There is no doubt that they prayed about the health and well-being of the fetus. How, or why, would an omnipotent being in charge of everything decide to bring such horrible grief to a family that really did do everything he asked of them?

That week, after dinner one night we retired to the family room, where Lynn decided to bring up my obvious disbelief. She said, "What if we had a miscarriage? How would we possibly deal with such a thing if you don't believe in God?"

"How would that help the fact that a child dies before it's born?"

"Well I know that God had a reason and has taken the little one to a better place. That he's up there with God. I couldn't imagine dealing with such loss without that base belief."

Having to look at a floating unborn fetus hanging out with Jesus and God didn't seem to comfort me at all. How exactly does a fetus exist in the celestial kingdom? He can't walk or talk. Does he just float there while we stare at him? How does he get fed? Who changes the diaper, or is he still attached to his mother? Is he floating in amniotic fluid? Shaking these thoughts from my head, I responded, "That doesn't make any logical sense to me. To throw it to God's divine plan is just another way to sidestep the reality of the situation. We can just blame God and move on? That doesn't explain anything."

The conversation devolved a bit; I can be condescending at times. Plus I had never read any of the theological or atheist arguments at that point in my life, so to be honest Lynn held her own to some degree with the "faith" argument. But the damage was done, and this was the beginning of the end for us.

The next day I really couldn't focus on my work. How could this very smart woman believe such obvious untruths? I felt embarrassed for what she believed. This, to me, was an intellectual flaw.

I left the Microsoft campus for my home in Seattle that day a bit earlier than normal and called my mother for some advice. I was struggling with the fact that I had to break up with Lynn. She was, without a doubt, the sweetest person I had ever met. The decision was not coming easy, but deep down I knew I had to do it.

I explained the situation to my mother, focusing on our differing religious beliefs. Her response was, "Just tell her you believe in God; that should be enough." Silence extended as my response welled up inside of me. My heart took a break from beating for a minute. I was breathless but somehow managed to spit out, "But Mom, I don't believe in God."

Silence.

I felt like I had to instantly defend my position, a chore I wasn't yet capable of doing. However, my mother didn't challenge me after I said, "I mean, come on. What reason do we have to believe in a God? I've seen zero proof of it my entire life, and the story makes absolutely no sense." While trying not to sound disappointed, my mother responded, "Well then, just tell her the truth. That's all you can do. I have to run; we'll talk later. Goodbye."

The breakup was probably the hardest I've had to do, so I chose to do it at work in her Microsoft office. As with any relationship, I had a list of other things that weren't perfect. Although it was central to my reasoning, I wasn't yet versed in the discourse of disbelief. So I simply mentioned it as a bullet point but didn't focus on it.

Looking back now I can say that had she not believed in the make-believe we would likely be married, and I still teeter on regretting my decision. However, I just couldn't see past it. I pictured our kids not believing dinosaurs existed and instead talking about how beautiful Jesus' horse is in heaven.

The woman I was in love with had a credulity that I simply could not live with, and it broke my heart.

Shortly after our breakup, I heard through a friend that Lynn's parents had wondered out loud if I was gay. That would certainly make me a whole lot easier to dislike.

PART 5

FAMILY LIFE AND
ATHEIST PARENTING

W HEN UTTERED TOGETHER, the words "atheism" and "family" carry a lot of ideological baggage.[1] In the United States, "the transmission of cultural values and beliefs through primary socialization within the family context greatly influences the values and beliefs that children will adopt and carry with them into adulthood."[2] Religion is a primary source for providing moral structure. Paradoxically, even as the United States grows more secular, ties between religion and family remain the same. One hypothesis for this link may be that secularism is largely viewed as an individual pursuit of youthful freedom.[3] So, as individuals "grow up" (i.e., settle down and begin to raise families) they must shed their youthful ways and embark on adult commitments.

As discussed in the introduction, religion is often perceived as uniformly good for physical and mental health—thus, families may feel disinclined to deprive their children (or elderly parents) of faith and a religious community. Captured by the adage "the family that prays together stays together"— individuals in the United States feel that shared religious beliefs are a glue that strengthen familial bonds and deepen love between relatives. Indeed, for many, religious practice provides a weekly (or more frequent) time for family members to get together and share an experience. Important events such as births, deaths, and marriages that further bind families may all be marked by religious ceremony.

The ramifications of being a nonbeliever can be perceived as quite dire to religious relatives. For example, in the Latter-Day Saint faith, family members must all be believers and undergo shared rituals in order to remain together in an "Eternal Family" during the afterlife.[4] Therefore, nonbelievers are not just abandoning their current family obligations but also sealing the fate that they will not be together in Heaven.

Beyond coming out to family members, coming out to children and rearing them in atheist households presents another layer of complication. It is no secret that raising children is exceedingly difficult. Parents work hard to try to give children the best of their values, experiences, and morals. Historically, families have also relied on religious institutions to help instill moral fiber into the diet of their progeny. In many ways, religion has a lot to offer parents. As noted by McGowan, religiosity ensures that parents will have access to "an established community, a predefined set of values, a common lexicon and symbology, rites of passage, a means of engendering wonder, comforting answers to big questions, and consoling explanations to ease hardship and loss."[5] However, for atheist parents, the perceived benefits of religion may not weigh up to the perceived detriments. As stated bluntly by Seth Andrews in his memoir, *Deconverted*:

> Along with talk of faith and bliss, religious parents are also cultivating guilt, shame and paranoia. As a result, many of these children spend the rest of their lives chained to the obscene notion that they're broken, tainted and unworthy, constantly apologizing for being born a sinner and scrambling to escape punishment by pledging allegiance to an invisible sky wizard and his book of spells. Even those [children] showered with saccharine assurances that they are precious children of God still often wrestle with the most basic human experiences relating to identity, worth, sexuality, etc.

As a result, atheist parents must learn to forge meaning and morals for their children without the traditional maps, guidebooks, or compasses provided by religiosity. In a nation that fully embraces religiosity in childrearing, a scarcity of resources exist for those who choose to raise children without faith.

To begin to tackle the perils of raising kids as an atheist parent, the first books on this subject, *Parenting Beyond Belief* and *Raising Freethinkers*, were published in 2007 and 2009, respectively. Reactions to *Parenting Beyond Belief* were overwhelmingly positive, and when it was released, it was the top-selling parenting reference book on Amazon.com for seventeen weeks.[6] Described by the author as "a book for loving and thoughtful parents who wish to raise their children without religion," the tone of the text is warm, humanistic, and welcoming. These seminal books posit that raising children without religious beliefs requires parents to be able to articulate the foundations of their own values and beliefs and engage in constant reflection on what they view to be good and true. Parallel to their own identity explorations, parents must facilitate the formation of their children's beliefs without controlling the process or being overly proselytizing in deconversion. Some suggested ways to begin this process are to promote curiosity, encourage religious literacy, normalize disbelief, invite the questioning of authority, and encourage active moral development.[7] Moreover, atheist parents must focus on counteracting negative societal views of nonbelievers by demonstrating that atheists, like religious people, can lead good, compassionate, and moral lives without supernaturalism, belief in higher powers, or a God/gods.[8] Summed up by McGowan in *Raising Freethinkers*:

> Secular parenting can be a wonderful experience, even for those living in intolerant communities. We have the opportunity and responsibility to help our children develop effective reasoning skills, a trait sorely needed on our troubled planet. It is rewarding to know that our children will be empowered to think for themselves as they navigate this credulous world.

So, what happens when a family member decides to shed their religious beliefs and "come out" as atheist? Ripples may be felt throughout the family as relatives adjust to the news (particularly older adults). The following narratives capture the unique experiences of culturally and racially diverse individuals as they navigate decisions to come out (or keep quiet) about their atheist beliefs to family members and to raise their children without religion.

Ronnelle, an African American gay man, describes his process as coming out as atheist to his elderly and Evangelical Christian grandmother. While he had largely been "out" in all other realms of his life, Ronnelle was nervous about revealing his atheism to his grandmother because he had a deep admiration for her fiery, funny, and kind spirit; severing a connection with her was a big risk. His mother and other family members reacted very poorly to the disclosure. While Ronnelle waited for a long time, when he eventually did tell his grandma he was atheist, she wasn't thrilled, but she also still accepted him. For Adrienne, however, the narrative progresses in a different manner. Raised in a deeply religious Pentecostal Puerto Rican family with "a lot of enthusiasm for God," Adrienne was active in religious practice until her late teens, when she finally acknowledged her lack of belief. Upon coming out and having a nonreligious wedding ceremony, she has been faced with the realization that her family fears for the safety of her soul. They prayed in tongues for her "godless marriage," and she laments that they do not take her seriously. Despite some awkward moments, Adrienne notes that they are largely respectful and nonconfrontational about her atheism; in general, it is known but not acknowledged or discussed.

Kevin and Amy both describe their journey parenting as atheists. Kevin grew up secular, converted to become a Latter-Day Saint, and gradually deconverted in his thirties. In his narrative, he describes the struggles of raising three children with a wife who is still very strong in her Mormon faith. In a household where one spouse is religious and one is atheist, parenting is particularly tricky; Kevin notes feeling that initially he believed that either his wife or he would have to be inauthentic with their children. However, they both have found ways to be open about their beliefs, best summed up by his idea of *influencing without indoctrination*: "to present my point of view, letting my kids know what I believe, and then saying as often as I can that there are other good people who believe differently, and encouraging them to seek out those people." As atheism parenting books recommend, Kevin teaches his kids about science and various religions and also still works hard to instill appreciation of diversity and skepticism. Amy, who was raised a Seventh-Day Adventist, describes that when she became pregnant and gave birth to her daughter, she and her husband began to do some hard thinking about their belief systems. Specifically, she noted feeling as though they needed to feel solid in the difficult questions that their daughter would inevitably pose about life, death, and belief. The more she read scripture, the more she began to feel that the Bible was inconsistent, sexist, and violent—she realized that she wanted her daughter to have the freedom to answer her own questions about the world, not rely on a religious filter. She and her husband feel that not having "a model for raising a child without religion is both a challenge and a joy."

15

DINNER WITH GRANDMA

Ronnelle Adams

Ronnelle, thirty-one, lives in Washington, D.C., and writes children's books.

I recently forgot my grandmother's birthday. It was on the sixteenth, so she called me on the seventeenth. After about five minutes of random conversation to confirm that I was oblivious, she added "It's cold outside . . . and I was born January 16, but it's *still* too cold for me." Nice delivery, Grandma. It took me a few seconds to figure out what had just happened but then I could almost see her smirking over the phone. A long overdue night out to dinner was in order.

The next night we were off to her destination of choice, Bugaboo Creek Steakhouse. We caught up, and I got to pick her brains on some family history. After attempting to match dates with historic events ("Just missed World War II . . . Little Rock . . . *Brown v. Board,*"), she let me in on what's been happening more recently. She's a very active member of her church and has taken to evangelizing door to door with her friend Barbara. As she went into detail about her activities spreading the gospel, I got self-conscious about my facial expression and made sure to keep smiling. My natural inclination to question religion was taken off guard, and my antitheistic views had to be suppressed. This wasn't some wide-eyed, apocalyptic street preacher; it was Grandma.

Most of my thoughts of her have only ever been attached to goodness in the world: eggnog, Loony Tunes, ice cream cake, the *Gremlins* movies, nature watching, Charlie Brown, and shih-tzu puppies. And now my favorite whacking mole sat comfortably protected in her lap. Of course, I always *knew* she was religious, and considering past arguments I've had with more belligerent Christians in the family, I suspected Grandma had *heard* that I'm not.

Coming out directly to my mother went over poorly, and after a decade of on-and-off relations, we're now permanently off. "I rebuke you, you abominable lil codependent faggot! I curse the day I had You. You are dead to me. Get thee behind me Satan." That was her final e-mail to me after an argument over my sexuality and atheism. It wasn't anything new at that point, and the cycle was more tiresome than hurtful. I now happily keep my distance. Other family members (a few aunts in particular) have been better about it, and we stay in touch mostly through Facebook. It's not at all clear whether they've changed their theological views on atheists or homosexuals, but I appreciate the kindness.

Still, I never officially came out to Grandma as gay or an atheist so much as left the closet doors ajar. This omission has had a chilling effect on my ability to be candid (myself) around her. It's a concession with roots going back to my childhood, and its existence has had implications on the strength of our relationship. I ordered the Bourbon shrimp, and she had a chicken salad.

A scene from when I was five years old may help illustrate my reluctance. While playing with my He-Man action figures in the backseat of her Buick on the way home from church, I noticed a similarity between my toys and the supernatural attributes of Jesus. "Grandma Feni, does God have the same kind of magic as He-Man?" I could see her wince through the rear-view mirror, and even though she didn't respond angrily, I immediately wished that I hadn't asked the question. After an awkward pause, she explained that He-Man did "make-believe" magic whereas God performed "real" acts of power. Her distinction between magic and power reminded me of He-Man's signature line, "By the power of Greyskull! I have the power!" That only left me with more questions, but by then I knew better than to pursue them. Having already upset her with my initial question, I didn't want to make things worse by appearing unsatisfied with her answer. My faith held until my late teens, when a renewed zeal to get closer with God had an unintended effect. I uncovered even more problematic questions. Reading history books about Christianity and seeing the manmade nature in which it developed, I was at once devastated and refreshed with information. Being a fan of Greco-Roman mythology also didn't help, given its similarities with scripture. I couldn't call Pandora a myth and take Eve seriously. All that combined with a growing contempt for biblical morality gradually ended my religious beliefs. By twenty, I wasn't afraid to talk about my newfound infidelity in most situations, but Grandma was a different story.

To her credit, she's a good representative of the faith. I'm willing to bet that her engaging smile and cheerful character would complement any religion in that way. As dinner went on, I told her that I'm usually nice to missionaries of different stripes when they come knocking. (I left out that my kindness toward handsome Mormon Elders in particular had a more prurient connotation, but that's a separate closet.) I had identical reasons to (1) suspect that she had heard and (2) not to bring it up. This, surprisingly, was when her inner sectarian briefly surfaced. "But Ronnie, they don't worship my God. They're going to Hell." I had never heard such a gentle rendition of that last sentence. I was intrigued and felt like the inquisitive kid in the Buick once again. But despite being grown up and more intellectually prepared, all I could manage in response was to wash down some nacho chips with my margarita.

I didn't get the feeling that she relished the thought of others being tortured in eternal fire; she seemed concerned for them. That may sound condescending, but it's better than the scornful mindset of others I've known in the beloved community. I also recognize that my grandmother is no feeble woman incapable of critical thought. Along with my now passed grandfather, she has always been one of my favorite nerds. Like many of my younger religious friends, she seems unwilling to use her powers of reason on that particular subject. Moreover, being raised on a terrifying idea is harder to shake off than one presented at maturity. The idea of Hell becomes an accepted reality that kids get used to through time and repetition—like "Feni" but *infinitely* less cute.

After we were done and I had kissed her goodbye for the night, I got home and pictured my young grandmother sitting attentively in a Danville church pew. Of all the things the preacher could have said and all the wonderful impressions he may have made on the young minds around him, he delivered his spiel on angels and demons. With the same certitude that the preachers just across town spewed their venom on the inferiority of blacks, her preacher must have rambled on about divine intervention against oppression and the dangers and rewards in the hereafter. There, she was groomed with the same overrated image of faith that she eventually helped instill in me. The pastor's opinions on other religious groups, homosexuals, nonbelievers, and a list of other undesirables helped to create unnecessary divisions not only between the saved and some unrelated other but also between family members. That's actually one of their stated goals.

> Do you suppose that I came to grant peace on earth? I tell you, no, but rather division; for from now on five members in one household will be divided, three against two and two against three. They will be divided, father against son and son against father, mother against daughter and daughter against mother, mother-in-law against daughter-in-law and daughter-in-law against mother-in-law.
>
> (Luke 12:51–53)

In spite of all this, the earthly goodness of people like my grandmother remains, even as they're taught to minimize the terrestrial in favor of the supernatural.

When I finally managed to come out to her—almost a year after publishing my first children's book criticizing religion—she confirmed that she *had* heard but didn't want to believe it unless it came from me. I didn't expect her to be happy about the news, but she was graceful as always and even complimented my book. Since then, things have stayed nearly the same, and I'm interpreting that as the best-case scenario. Where there was once vagary and silence on my beliefs and sexuality, there's now clarity and silence. I still have my grandmother despite the tradition that I'm contending with.

The tradition held from before Grandma's generation to mine and beyond, and I now find myself an uncle a few times over. In hindsight, I would have loved a second opinion when *I* was the impressionable child in the pew. I would have also benefited from the ability to voice honest questions about religion without coercion, scare tactics, and shame. The time and trouble it would have saved me had a single role model nudged my arm and said, "I don't buy it, and here's why: religions are just opinions and it's okay to disagree." That nudge, instead of the uniform and stagnant "truth" I was given, would have inspired greater curiosity in my developing mind, worked miracles for my self-esteem, and better prepared me for critical thinking. It would have given me intellectual breathing room and lessened the necessity of closets.

There weren't as many nonbelievers to go by when I was a child, but that situation is changing rapidly. Though many of us who have apostatized now find relief in our own expanded freedom of thought, we would do well not to neglect the youth who are currently being herded through the same process. Children remain the highest-valued targets of religious indoctrination, and unbelief (among other things) continues to be stigmatized. If you don't give full disclosure about your unbelief to a sibling, nephew, niece, or grandchild, clergy and other relatives get to repeat the cycle unchallenged. The various social and intellectual barriers that may result are as pernicious as they are preventable.

I'd like to grow old in a world more thoughtful than the one I grew up in. To make that possible, I suggest that like-minded nonbelievers give young people in faith-based predicaments a good nudge: a considerate, reasonable doubt.

16

PARENTING AUTHENTICALLY IN AN INTERFAITH MARRIAGE

Kevin J. Zimmerman

If he's not serving as chef, butler, chauffer, or housekeeper to his three boys or buying quilting supplies for his wife, Kevin, thirty-eight, is either preparing a lesson, teaching, or responding to student e-mails.

I grew up in a largely secular household, where books by Carl Sagan and Joseph Campbell punctuated our bookshelves. But I "picked up religion" from those around me, eventually joining the Mormon Church, to my father's great disappointment. Unsatisfied with the local public schools, my parents opted to send me to a private, Christian school from kindergarten through third grade—a time when children are most vulnerable to indoctrination. I loved the school, but there my child's brain was infected with the tedious supernatural beliefs of religion, beliefs such as mind reading (prayer), vicarious sacrifice (the atonement), and survival of one's own death (the afterlife). Once people's brains have been infected by religious dogma, they are often crippled in their ability to think critically. I had caught a bad case of religion that I didn't shake until my thirties.

Ever since I was a youth, I knew that I wanted to have children, and at the time, I thought the more the better. The day that I decided to join the Mormon Church was the day I watched the video *Together Forever* (1988), the LDS film that underscores the church's emphasis on families. I figured that my likelihood of finding a woman who also wanted to have a large family would be highest within the church; the specific doctrines that I had to accept were of only secondary concern. I served a two-year mission and then went to Brigham Young University. Even though I truly believed, both decisions were calculated to maximize my chances of marrying and having children. When I proposed to one of my classmates, Roseli, while sitting around a large table for lunch with some friends at a beach house in Mexico, I told her that my major purpose in life was to have a large, healthy, prosperous family and that I wanted God to be at the center of my family. "I want to raise my family with you," I told her. She said yes, and we married in the Mormon Temple.

Three boys and much graduate education later, I no longer believed that the Mormon Church was the only true church. In fact, I no longer believed in God at all. Becoming an atheist did not happen overnight but was a long process, just as one doesn't become an adult overnight but over time. I became an atheist when I decided to be honest and admit to myself that I couldn't reconcile the supernatural claims of religion with my experience of the world.

When I told Roseli that I no longer believed in God, she understandably felt devastated. After all, the information came as a complete surprise to her. She cried. She was angry. Her world had turned upside down. She insisted that we had agreed that we would raise our children in the church and that we needed to continue on this course. Yes, I countered, we began our family with the expectation of raising our children in the church, but there was no agreement that neither of us could ever change. I knew that I had to grant Roseli a good deal of time to adjust to my nonbelief and its implications for how we would raise our boys, who were five, three, and one. She wasn't comfortable with me being honest with the children about what I thought concerning religion, but I was just as uncomfortable pretending to be religious. Such an arrangement meant that Roseli could be authentic but that I could not. Fortunately, the inequality and deception by silence that Roseli expected of me has diminished over time as she has felt more secure that I am still committed to the family and that I support our children's continued activity in the church.

I had a form of "coming out" with my five-year-old as we walked together through his empty school playground one weekend. I told him that I thought

God was probably just pretend and that I didn't have any good reason to believe in him anymore. I explained to him that some of the stories of religion just didn't seem possible to me. He seemed a bit surprised but not upset. Like most five-year-olds, he was more interested in playing than in my theological opinions. My other boys were too young to comprehend that I had changed my mind about God, so I didn't have a coming out moment with them, but I feel committed nonetheless to being "out" as an atheist in order to inoculate them against what the researcher Robert Nash has called atheophobia, or "the fear and loathing of atheists that permeates American culture." My being out to my boys and to others as an atheist helps lighten the burden for the next generation. To children, "atheist" is just a word like any other, without all the stigma and baggage that American culture has burdened it with. It simply means that I don't believe in a god, just as I don't believe in ghosts. I figure that if I avoid the word, the avoidance implies a taboo, and taboo implies something too indecent or dirty to mention.

For a time after coming out, I felt a need to establish firmly my identity as an atheist by posting some of my thoughts concerning religion on Facebook. Many of my Facebook contacts were people from my mission, from BYU, or from church, and I didn't want to be in a situation in which someone incorrectly assumed that I was still Mormon. I was always respectful and thoughtful in my posts and comments, but the ideas still threatened many members of the church, who called me an antichrist, a Mormon basher, blind, ignorant, unrighteous, a waste of skin, and a waste of life, among other invectives. I imagine that those who made these comments replaced any semblance of what I'm actually like with a caricature of a scowling, hate-filled monster bent on abolishing the whole of Christianity. They assume that I'm immoral and don't see me as a real person anymore, playing with my kids, helping our neighbor's two-year-old get sand out his shoe, or momentarily diverting the spray of hose water from our newly planted grass to our neighbor's strawberry patch that also needed a drink. They don't see me visit pleasantly with the store clerk wearing a cross necklace or put on my sons' ties on Sunday mornings. These are not moral behaviors of which only theists are capable; these are simply little acts of human kindness that theists and atheists alike perform every day.

In the early days after my coming out, there were some notable collisions between the differing worldviews that my wife and I were attempting to communicate to our children. One Saturday morning, the local congregation, or "ward" as it's called, had a missionary-themed activity for the children. Our two older boys each received a letter with a mission call, one saying that he had been called to serve in the Bogota-Panama mission and the other saying that he was called to serve in Thailand. At the activity, church members told the kids about the languages they had learned, the food they had encountered, the adventures they had experienced, and other stories designed to focus on the magic of these exotic places. Members who had served in the United States were notably absent, presumably because stories of serving stateside would be less effective at motivating children to want to serve a mission.

Toward the end of the activity, one of the primary leaders asked, raising her hand to model the correct response, "Who here wants to serve a mission?" Every child's hand shot up, including our boys. Later, I asked my oldest son, Ethan, "Did you raise your hand because you want to serve a mission, or because you want to travel?" He said he actually just wants to travel and that he had confused that with serving a mission.

The activity ended with a sinister dollop of psychic bullying. A new missionary got up to bear his testimony about missionary work, saying that he knows Heavenly Father is very pleased when we serve a mission. The implication, of course, is that God is very *displeased* in those who choose *not* to serve a mission. Then, one of the children's leaders put on the LDS video, *Called to Serve*. Within the first ninety seconds, a boy in the film, underscored by sweeping orchestral music, says, "If you teach somebody the truth, I'm sure that they're going to feel good, and you're going to feel good, and Heavenly Father's going to feel good," again suggesting that the alternative also applies: if you *don't* teach others your "truth," then you're going to feel bad, and Heavenly Father is going to feel bad.

I perceived these statements as childhood indoctrination, plain and simple, and during the car ride home, I shared with Roseli what I was thinking. "Telling children that God will be pleased with you for serving a mission is a form of psychological manipulation," I said, "designed to make young people feel guilty for making decisions that might be different from what the church encourages. Let's say I want to instill in my children a desire to go to college. I would never say, even if I believed in God, 'Heavenly Father will be pleased with you if you go to college,' because the opposing meaning is implied, that God will be disappointed in them if they don't go to college. I'd rather take responsibility for my *own* hopes for them and tell them why going to college is a good idea, that they'll likely earn more or become who they want to become with an advanced education. And if our boys decide to serve a mission, that's fine, but I would want them to do so because they truly believe the church's doctrines and not because of guilt trips and social pressure." Having participated in the planning of the activity, Roseli grew defensive. Although she agreed in principle with some of my points, I could have chosen a better time and tone. After years of keeping silent about my slowly changing worldview, I was still on a learning curve of *how* to be open about my nonbelief.

With time, Roseli finally achieved a certain level of acceptance of my differing worldview and of my right as a parent not to self-censor on the topic of religion. There were still some uncomfortable moments, however. One morning during breakfast, Roseli began reading to the boys out loud from the Book of Mormon.

"Have ye walked, keeping yourselves blameless before God?"

"God isn't real," interrupted Joshua.

Roseli looked up from the book. "Who told you that?"

The answer was obvious. I never say it exactly *that* way. I don't believe God is any more real than the Easter Bunny, but I know that in our home I have to make it clear that this is my perspective and not an absolute truth.

"Dad," answered Joshua.

"That's my opinion," I clarified carefully, leaning against the kitchen counter. "Mom has a different opinion."

"What Papa meant to say was that he belieeeeves God isn't real," said Roseli. "And I belieeeeve that God is real." I was impressed by how calmly Roseli was reacting to Joshua's comment. It wasn't long before that such a comment would send Roseli spiraling into a day-long funk.

"I made up my mind that God isn't real," said Joshua.

But you're only four! I thought.

"Well, God is as real as you want Him to be," Roseli said, looking down to continue reading.

What a devastatingly revealing comment this was!

Roseli persisted, finishing her reading for the day with these last two appalling verses on the page:

And if ye will not hearken unto the voice of the good shepherd, to the name by which ye are called, behold, ye are not the sheep of the good shepherd. And now if ye are not the sheep of the good shepherd, of what fold are ye? Behold, I say unto you, that the devil is your shepherd, and ye are of his fold; and now, who can deny this? Behold, I say unto you, whosoever denieth this is a liar and a child of the devil.

I couldn't help it. I had to respond. "So every good Hindu, Jew, Buddhist, atheist—a majority of the world's population, in fact—are shepherded by the devil?" I asked. "Verses like these only serve to create an us-versus-them mentality. You either accept Jesus or you're of the devil! It's incredibly divisive!"

After a moment's thought, Roseli begrudgingly said, "That makes sense."

Well then why, I thought, would you want to read such verses to the kids? You know, selectively read the uplifting verses and ignore the distasteful. That's what most people do. I wasn't sure if Roseli agreed with me, but she seemed to understand how the verses could be understood the way I now understood them. Incidentally, I'm all for reading, including from sacred texts.

Perhaps my willingness to apply critical thinking to religion gave Roseli the permission to do the same. About six weeks after the scripture-reading episode, it was Mother's Day, and in Relief Society (the meeting just for women in the LDS church), the teacher read a quote about how LDS mothers are the best mothers in the world.

My wife spoke up. "I don't think that's true," she said. "There are plenty of wonderful mothers who are not LDS and many lousy LDS mothers."

The teacher backpedaled. "I'm just reading a quote from the prophet," she said.

"I don't care if you're quoting Jesus Christ," said Roseli, as women gasped. "I don't think it's true, and I think it's prideful and divisive to say LDS mothers are the best mothers in the world." When Roseli recounted the event to me later, I told her, "Good for you!"

As I pulled the garbage bin to the curb the following Sunday evening, the weather was ideal, the boys had just gone to bed, and so I asked Roseli, "Do you want to go for a walk?" Walking hand in hand, Roseli began to tell me the drama that had unfolded at church that morning. She had heard from someone earlier in the week that a family was moving, and when she ran into the woman who was moving in the hallway, Roseli attempted to ask her about the upcoming move. Now I wasn't there, but as Roseli tells it, the woman raised an open palm as if to say, "Talk to the hand," and said, "I don't even want to talk to you."

Roseli couldn't imagine what her issue was. Baffled, Roseli saw the woman again later during church and said, "Can we talk?"

The woman reluctantly agreed and they went into an empty room where she spewed forth about thirty minutes worth of angry, nasty, and vile comments about me on account of my disaffection from the church. According to Roseli, "Satan" was the least offensive name she had for me.

I felt bad that my sweet wife had to endure social consequences of my disbelief, and I found it genuinely puzzling that a mere difference of opinion about the nature of reality could generate such venom.

Roseli made a mental note of the list of women who had supposedly blacklisted us. A few weeks later, Roseli told me, "Well, I've talked to everyone on the list." She found that each woman denied keeping her distance from us, and most expressed some anger that their name would even come up in such a way. This means that either all these women somehow managed to enter into a long chat with Roseli, despite supposedly ostracizing her, and lied, or Liz got carried away and was just making up lies to justify her own anger. Or perhaps the truth is a little more nuanced. None of these women seems to have ostracized us, but one family has stopped bringing over their children, of whom their oldest and our oldest had been good friends.

Earlier, I alluded to religion as a virus. To carry the analogy further, I believe that I have a responsibility to inoculate my children against supernaturalism. I think that protecting my children from religion and its symptoms—such as dichotomous thinking, the externalization of blame, and perpetual guilt—

may be one of the greatest gifts that I can bestow. As my own upbringing illustrates, the mere absence of religion at home is not enough, just as keeping kids away from communicable diseases is not enough. I suspect that some secular parents are hesitant to share their thoughts about religion with their kids because they fear that doing so would constitute its own form of indoctrination, indoctrination into a naturalistic worldview. Indoctrination is the presentation of a single point of view to the exclusion of other opinions and the demand of unquestioning acceptance. Can atheists indoctrinate a child? Certainly, if they make it clear that they consider all religious people to be stupid, that religion is uniformly evil, and that any religious expression whatsoever is worthy of derision. In contrast, to *influence without indoctrination* is to present my point of view, letting my kids know what I believe, and then saying as often as I can that there are other good people who believe differently, and encouraging them to seek out those people.

I have described religious ideas as a virus, but I'm just not convinced that exposure to religion, at least the relatively benign strains of religion found in the United States, is as detrimental as some atheists claim. Most people grow up to figure out what works for them. I regard exposure to religion in small doses as a form of inoculation. In medicine, the way to inoculate against a virus is through exposure to a weakened strain of that virus. On a typical Sunday morning, therefore, you'll find me waking before everyone else and preparing breakfast for our boys, as I do nearly every morning, then dropping my family off at church. Roseli doesn't drive, but she wants to take our boys with her to church as often as she can, which is just about every week. The lessons that my boys are taught are all available online, which I have accessed on occasion, giving me the opportunity to share with them a secular response to the ideas that they have been exposed to.

For example, when they are told that Jesus is the Son of God, I tell them that Romulus, Alexander the Great, Augustus, Dionysus, and Scipio Africanus are also described as sons of God. When they are taught of Jesus' miracles, I share that people also believed that Vespatian's spit healed a blind man, that Apollonius of Tyana raised a girl from death, and that Dionysus turned water into wine. When they are told that Jesus was born of a virgin, I tell them that Horus of Egypt, Attis of Greece, Mithra of Persia, Krishna of India, and

Dionysus of Greece are also said to have been born of virgins. When they are told that they should be good because they are princes of a king, I tell them that they should be good because they understand that all people should be treated with respect and because they'll lead happier lives if they are nice to others. When they are taught that the commandments help them to choose the right, I contrast the ten commandments, which reveal the egotism of God through such commandments as "Do not worship other gods," "Do not make any idols," and "Do not misuse the name of God" with principles that are more human centered, like those presented in Dan Barker's *Maybe Right, Maybe Wrong*: "Respect the rights of others," "Try to treat everyone fairly," and "Try to be kind to other people."

In fact, I try to share some kind of thought related to religion or science with my boys daily. As an office elder on my mission and as a teacher at the church's Missionary Training Center, I had developed the habit of sharing an inspiring message every day. These experiences help me now as an atheist father to be intentional about opening my mouth, initiating conversations, and letting my boys know what I think. I have found a number of kid-friendly books, songs, and YouTube videos to be particularly helpful in fostering an appreciation of science, value in diversity, and skepticism of religion. My wife isn't thrilled about all of these resources in our home, but she has granted me the privilege of parenting in authenticity and in accordance with the dictates of my own conscience, and her own interest in science has been rekindled as a result. To paraphrase Carl Sagan, I wish to pursue the truth no matter where it leads, and I hope to influence my children to do the same. If they choose to accept a particular religious doctrine or philosophy of life that differs from mine, they are free to do so, and I'll love them all the same. I simply want to equip them to think critically and rationally, which in my case has led me to reject supernaturalism in all its forms.

17

HAVING A BABY MADE ME AN ATHEIST

Amy Watkins

Amy, thirty-three, is a poet, visual artist, and teacher who lives with her husband, their daughter, and a big, shaggy dog.

When I was pregnant, I was conflicted and insatiable, horny and self-conscious, restless and exhausted, empowered and totally helpless. And hungry. Hunger woke me in the middle of the night, made me nauseated and irritable during the day. I packed snacks for trips to the grocery store, stashed granola bars in my purse, dried apricots in my school bag, gummy bears and saltines in my desk at work. I craved root beer and taco salad with ranch dressing and hot salsa, peanut butter and jelly sandwiches, garlicky hummus, homemade chili, and thick strawberry milkshakes. My doctor, not one to baby the prenatal, scolded me for gaining too much weight—almost fifty pounds by my due date—but I couldn't get enough.

It wasn't just food I gorged on. I read with a voracity I hadn't felt since childhood summers when I read eight books every three weeks, the maximum our small-town library would allow me to check out. The apex of my compulsive reading was a love/hate relationship with *What to Expect When You're Expecting*. I read it obsessively, underlining passages and dog-earing pages, swallowing its wise aunt advice, but I loathed its placid-faced cover mom with her pastel sweater set, her smile as languid and enigmatic as the Mona Lisa's.

Clearly she did not feel how I felt: potent and sharp edged and inadequate, full of the kind of intensity I associated with high school, the adolescent belief that everything *mattered*.

What was happening in the wider world did matter. It was the fall of 2002. U.S. forces were fighting in Afghanistan, and war with Iraq was imminent. My husband and I attended peace rallies laden like picnickers with turkey sandwiches, bags of barbecue chips, and jugs of limeade. We didn't make posters or write protest songs, but if we had they might have said something about the terror of becoming parents in a world where both freedom and safety seemed lost.

In the wake of the Patriot Act, a coworker told me she was happy to give up some freedom in order to feel safe. When I said I felt the opposite—that I would rather face a little danger in order to feel free—she looked at me with a mixture of amusement and scorn and said, "You'll change your mind when that baby's born." No one else was so blunt, but the usual assumption was that becoming parents would make us more conservative. In fact, the opposite turned out to be true. Rather than turning inward, as so many new parents understandably do, Alex and I found our focus expanding to include more of the world. We both felt a new kind of empathy. Rather than imagining myself in the news stories I heard and read, I imagined my child. I felt new concern for gay rights, an issue that had always felt like someone else's fight, because it might affect my child, and Alex became a feminist the moment the sonogram showed us our daughter. "Everything changes when you have a baby," our relatives and acquaintances said, but they missed the point: everything had changed already. It was the baby, that fuzzy blur on the sonogram screen, pushing us further and further from our old worldview.

For Alex and me, much of that worldview was wrapped up in religion. We were both raised and baptized Seventh-Day Adventists (SDA). We attended church, prayed and read the Bible. We had both had doubts about religion in the past, but we had put them aside, believing that what our faith gave us was more important than the answers it couldn't provide. When our daughter was born, though, those elusive answers began to seem more important.

I looked for answers in books. I read the gospels while breastfeeding, feeling safer in the New Testament with Jesus' reassuring compassion than in the Old Testament with its endless wars and wrath of God, but I was not reassured. Had the Bible always been so inconsistent, so violent, so sexist? Had it always needed so much adjustment to fit with my own sense of right and wrong? I read Ellen White, the prophet of the SDAs. I read C. S. Lewis and found some comfort in Thomas Cahill's apologist histories on Judaism and Jesus Christ, but the more I read, the more I found myself saying, "Yes, but . . ."

I tried so hard to stretch my faith, twisting it like the rubber band I had looped through my buttonhole to give me a few more weeks in my premmaternity jeans, but it didn't fit. I tried to ignore my questions and doubts as I had in the past, but there was a new question I could not ignore: *What am I going to teach my daughter?* When our parents pressed for a dedication ceremony, sort of the SDA equivalent of infant baptism, Alex and I admitted that we could not raise our daughter in the church.

We named her after *Alice in Wonderland*, the story of a child who follows her curiosity and her courage to a place both dangerous and wonderful. It is only a coincidence that her name also means "truth." Truth, ultimately, is the reason that having a baby made me an atheist. The relationship I want with my daughter demands honesty from me in a way no other relationship has. If you're a parent, you know that we can't offer our children much in the long run. We can't make them good. We can't keep them safe. We don't have a just world to give them. We can give them ourselves, though. We can be honest with them. That's how Alex and I felt about Alice anyway. We would be trustworthy.

If we were to be honest with her, we had to be honest with ourselves, which meant admitting our doubts. They had been there all along, ignored because facing them was painful, confusing, and frightening. My journals from a young age are full of questions that I clearly felt guilty for expressing, even in private. I often prayed a version of the plea in Mark 9: "Lord, I believe; help thou mine unbelief."

When I was a child, my mother was very devout, but my father had "left the church"—a phrase that sounds silly enough to me now that I feel compelled to put it in quotation marks—but then was weighted with sadness and shame. Well-meaning church members would ask, "How's your dad?" as if they were checking up on the terminally ill. Others told me, in ways both subtle and explicit, that he was bad, that he would not be saved, that every wrong or rebellious action of mine set me closer to the dark path to damnation my father walked. Clearly, he would not go to heaven. He had no "relationship with Christ." He swore and smoked pot and shouted in anger. I couldn't deny those things, but I also knew that he was good, open-handed, and compassionate. He had a terrible temper, but he was infinitely patient with children and animals and confused old people. He never ignored a hitchhiker or a broken-down vehicle; I saw him change a hundred strangers' flat tires. Even as I internalized the fear of losing him for eternity, I knew that, no matter what the rules said, he did not deserve to burn.

When I was ten years old, my younger sister died in an accident. There was comfort in believing that we would be together again in heaven, but what about my daddy? The Bible says, "God shall wipe away every tear from their eyes," which I was told meant that God would explain why our loved ones were not with us and then help us forget them. The idea that I would miss my father, even in paradise, was acknowledged enough to create the horrifying concept of erasing his memory in order to bring me perfect peace and happiness, but that only created more fear and confusion. I didn't believe that even God could make me forget my dad or make me happy without him, but I had to believe in heaven.

My path to atheism starts with the most fundamental elements of my faith: reward and punishment, mercy and judgment, love and fear, but the path is only visible from this side. Start with me saying, "I don't believe in god." Go backward. See me struggling my best to believe. See me reading and reading, trying to find him, trying to fit him into the world I can see and touch. Go back. Follow the thread of doubt. See me crying in high school because I can't believe my prayers will be answered and knowing that my doubt undoes all my prayers. Go back further. Ask, "Where did the doubt come from?" See me learning early not to ask questions the Sabbath school teacher doesn't want to answer. Keep going back, and you find doubt at the very foundation of faith, so much a part of faith that it never demands much attention.

At the root of my childhood faith, there is sadness and rage, shame and defiance. There's love there, but there's also a hum in the background, like the sound a damaged eardrum makes, a little ringing or buzzing that only exists inside my head: the dissonance of believing two opposing ideas, of holding them in balance, of bringing one forward when I need it and then the other. *You will go to heaven and reunite with your sister. You will go to heaven and lose your father, a good man who is damned.* Alice didn't create that dissonance, but her birth brought it into focus, gave it meaning and urgency. She forced me to choose: the safety of the faith I knew, with all its love and comfort and intellectual dishonesty and cognitive dissonance, or the freedom of a new path I still can't see the end of and all the fear and uncertainty and possibility and truth we might discover together.

Alice is nine years old now. Like all parents, Alex and I are still learning how to be Mom and Dad. That we don't have a model for raising a child without religion is both a challenge and a joy. I don't always have comfort for her sorrows. I don't always have answers to her questions. I can't promise that she will always be safe, but I can promise her the freedom to find her own answers. In some ways, that's what Alice gave me. The spiritual crisis that led me to the painful yet fulfilling choice of atheism was a direct result of becoming her mother. Without her, I might still be in the church pew, dissatisfied but too cozy to get up and search for better answers. Our friends were right: she changed everything.

18

BORN SECULAR

Adrienne Filardo Fagan

Adrienne, twenty-five, is a grants specialist at the University of Florida in Gainesville, where she is also currently pursuing a master's degree in urban and regional planning.

As I write this, I am sitting in a Starbucks in Gainesville, Florida, next to a sharply dressed man in his late twenties. He is in pinstripes. It is a Sunday afternoon. This can mean only one thing in the South. This man, like millions of others around America, woke up and attended a weekly religious ceremony to honor a supernatural being that he has never met and with whom he has never spoken. Yet this man and the other millions across the country likely hope to yield all life decisions and prayers unto this being in order to receive guidance or maybe even favor.

To be clear, I in no way look down on or pity this man for choosing to live in theistic, pinstripe fashion. (Well maybe I do pity his waking up early on a Sunday every week.) I understand his motivations, because I once sought to be one of his kind.

One misconception that often I run into is that people almost always assume that atheists leave their faith in anger or disappointment. Perhaps some people do drop their faith because they feel that God is not helping them or the millions of starving children in the world. I was not molested by a clergy member nor did I have a flurry of bad Christian role models in my life. The path leading up to my self-discovery was in no way idyllic, but it played a remarkably minor role in my path to atheism.

My family is Puerto Rican, loud, and large in size, not to mention deeply and passionately religious. That is a lot of opinionated people to contend with. They are evangelical Christians, and although I don't follow their motivations, I do not begrudge the results of their faith. The vast majority of my family members are people who would give the shirts off their backs to help anyone who needed it; they tithe weekly in hopes of helping others through the work of their church, and they frequently take mission trips to the farthest ends of the earth to spread the gospel, because they truly believe it enriches the lives of all who hear it.

Most recently, my youngest sisters have traveled to South America for missionary work, and one is currently planning a jaunt to rural China. These trips usually entail fitting local children with climate appropriate apparel and distributing literature in the native tongue. But for every act of charity, there is also an act which reminds me where my family and I diverge on what we see as good deeds. In the past my family members have travelled to participate in Right to Life marches, which not only frustrate me but sadden me as my very own sisters do not seem to value their own reproductive rights. This was followed up by their proud participation in "I Support Chik-Fil-A Day," which occurred during the height of the fast food chain's antigay controversy.

The enthusiasm for God that exists in my family would be hard for some people to accept as genuine. Besides the missionary trips to Third World countries, nearly every moment of the day can somehow be spent thanking God or talking about the many blessings God has given them. Depression runs in my family, but my family uses God as Prozac. One consequence of this is that I feel that this disables them from holding themselves accountable for either their triumphs or their shortcomings. I suppose I wish they were more empowered to do things for themselves instead of waiting for a sign from God.

As a kid what I wanted more than a Barbie Dream House was to feel God the way that my family did. Looking back I now realize that this was my child self's desire to fit in. I attended Christian summer camp to pursue "the gifts of the spirit," which is the euphemism my family attributes to speaking in tongues. In my teenage years I hosted Bible study in my home, sang in the praise and worship band at church, and even delivered sermons for a short while in a more "progressive" service at my church, which was held after the normal Sunday worship.

Throughout my pursuit to feel and understand God, there was a persistent, gripping feeling that the laws of justification by faith, or the acknowledgment of any supernatural realm, were never going to make sense to me. The more I attempted to immerse myself in the discovery of a god, the more difficult it became to reconcile the laws of the universe and my personal value system with what was presented to me. At the age of seventeen, I began to entertain the notion that I may be an agnostic. When someone admits to being an agnostic, this is analogous to someone in a relationship saying "I think we should go on a break." A year later I could no longer keep fending off my own prying questions with admitting to only agnosticism. I had to be honest with myself and admit that I was an atheist.

With my background and the years of attempting to find God, it would be easy to assume that this moment was a harrowing and heartbreaking one. But instead came an amazing lightness. I had spent eighteen years being told that God makes us all whole. But my fruitless search for reconciliation never brought me closer to this. As soon as I admitted to myself what I really was, I finally felt the wholeness that I was searching for all along. I no longer felt as if there was something wrong with me or that I was missing out on this amazing gift of knowing God and having a personal relationship with Him. I realized that I was able to get everything I needed from the people around me, the causes I believed in, and the tangible world.

Relations between my family members and I have not changed as much as I thought they would. I can credit this to the gradual course that my coming out had taken. I think their suspicions were piqued when I started working on political campaigns for Democratic candidates. This resulted in prodding me for clarification on where I stood regarding the entire spectrum of social issues, which I know was their criteria for judging whether or not I was a good Christian. I think based upon those conversations they came to the conclusion that I was not. Although I know that there are many Christians who strongly align themselves with the Democratic Party, you would be hard pressed to tell that to my grandmother. From these conversations it became more and more obvious to them that I did not share their values.

But despite my status as a secular, feminist Democrat I am still welcome at family gatherings, and my grandmother still sends me birthday cards with Bible verses transcribed inside and prays for me whenever we end a telephone conversation. Except now in these interactions she asks if she can pray for me instead of just launching into an impassioned and lengthy blessing as she would typically do with anyone else. I always oblige as I know her inviting me into the presence of her Lord means more to her than getting off the phone three minutes sooner means to me.

They all kept their thoughts to themselves when I lived out of wedlock with my future husband. In fact I think they were all just thrilled that I wasn't a lesbian, as that would have been even more shameful to them than me being a Democrat. They also kept mum after they attended our wedding, which came and went without a single prayer or spiritual element. My grandmother did leave our wedding shortly after the ceremony, stating that she had a sudden-onset case of vertigo. I appreciated her taking the length to tell me a white lie on my wedding day, but her real reasons for leaving were obvious to me. The lack of reverence to God and the omission of "women submit to your husbands" was probably too much for her to bear. This was the confirmation of her fears that I may just be as confirmed an atheist as I had indicated to her in the past.

Recently it was confessed to me that the family was brought together to pray in tongues for my "godless marriage." I am in no way shocked or offended by this. I almost expected this prayer gathering to take place *during* my wedding reception, so I am pleased that it took months for them to get around to conducting this.

My husband and I do plan to have children. And I mean children, not child. Coming from a large family, I really do feel that there is value to having siblings, even if you grow up to have your ideological differences and will bicker during the holidays. My husband, also being an atheist, makes the prospect of childrearing much less daunting. It potentially removes at least one thing to butt heads on. We have toyed with the idea of allowing our hypothetical children to be taught in Catholic schools as my husband was and as my mother-in-law would probably like. I do appreciate most of the Judeo-Christian principles that I was raised with, and I do believe the concept of God is a useful tool to impress those principles on a child until they are mature enough to make good decisions on their own. But I know that it would be difficult for a young child to separate the information taught to them in school all day and what their mother tells them is reality. But I suppose we can cross that bridge when we get to it.

My family has always told me that they were praying for me; now it is just for different reasons. I know that they still love me, but I also know that there has been some impact on our relationships. My coming out as an atheist has now placed a lot of fear in the hearts of my family members. Not that they are afraid of the big, bad, "satanic" atheist, but that they are genuinely fearful for my salvation and what they believe lies ahead for me in the afterlife. They have never outwardly condemned me, but being that I was raised with their belief system, I am certain they look at me and know within their hearts that I am going to Hell. I am not nearly as bothered by this idea as I could or probably should be. The thing about faith is that it is irrational, and its sole job is to override your rational thought process. I suppose the toughest consequence of this is trying to have any of my political or social views taken seriously by them. Because God is not a factor in my thought process, they cannot consider any of my arguments. That is probably the hardest pill I will have to swallow.

Despite their very obvious concern, there are few people in my family that have taken the time to ask or listen to my perspective on things. I am convinced this is because they knew that if they did they would become fully aware of how strongly I feel about my belief system. God is central to every aspect of my family members' lives. The literal word of the Bible is consulted before making any kind of life decision, serious or otherwise. Because of this, I honestly believe it would be far too painful for them to hear me plainly say, "I do not believe there is a god."

Of everyone in my family, my father is probably the one person who has shown the most interest and invested the most time in speaking to me about my perspective. In one of the greater paradoxes of my life, my father the Pentecostal Puerto Rican is also a lifelong drug addict. Besides myself, he is the black sheep of the family. It is his personal faults and his recent openness to admitting them that has made it easier for him to hear my side. As a result of ongoing drug abuse, prescription pills being this decade's affliction, my father's memory is not what is used to be. In his younger years he was a guitar virtuoso with the ability to calculate compounding interest in his head. Now he struggles to remember how old he is, or he will frequently ask me when I graduate. He is now fifty-three, and my time as an undergrad concluded about three years ago. But you know one thing he absolutely remembers clear as day? The time of day, weather conditions, and probably what he was wearing when I told him that admitting my atheism to myself was the happiest day of my life. This has affirmed to me that, although my father and the rest of the family love me, I will always be seen as a soul that needs saving.

I am sure they would all be surprised that I find myself to be a reasonably moral person and that I am able to structure moral values without belief in a god. In a sense I do it the very same way that they do. Judeo-Christian values are based largely on the Big Ten. The Ten Commandments are admirable, as they are a great start on how to live a simple and uncomplicated life. Don't bed your neighbor's spouse, don't murder others, and don't steal—all great ways to keep things easy. The Ten Commandments are also a mirror of the social contract. How do we as a group of self-interested individuals continue to live together in a civil, functioning society? Aside from the obvious enforcement of these mores, we trust that those around us will honor the social contract of the Ten Commandments.

As much as I hate to feel this way—because it may seem to imply non-believer superiority—but there is something honorable in being an atheist. Although we have no fear that a higher power is looking down and taking notes on our every action and tallying up whether or not we win the eternal prize, we can still decide to live honestly. I believe that all we have is here and now. No forgiveness at the pearly gates, no valuable repentance as our last rites are read to us. We have one opportunity to make the right decisions for ourselves, our families, and our communities. This knowledge is what gives meaning to my life.

I have always been fascinated by the reasons people want to discover the supernatural. One thing I hear all of the time is that they want to know how the human race came to be. "Evolution" and "big bang" were dirty words when I was a kid since New Earth Creationism was all the rage with my family at the time. Despite my parents' best efforts, those dirty words are how I believe we got here. But in the end the "how" has never been as important to me. In fact, asking "how" we got here has always seemed a little egotistical. "How" we got here is not important; just being grateful that you are here is.

No one was dealt the perfect hand, but I am grateful every day for my life, my husband, career, dogs, roller derby, neighborhood, and hell, I am even grateful for my family that I disagree with on a daily basis. I love all of it. If I can wake up and feel this more days than not, then I will judge my life as a success.

PART 6

THE SEARCH FOR CONNECTION

Coming Out to Friends and Questing for Community

AMERICANS ARE TRULY "one nation under God," and this leaves little room for atheist individuals to exist openly. With this blanket assumption of religiosity, there is even less room for nonbelievers to safely organize, share thoughts, or build communities without facing backlash, fear, or skepticism.[1] For example, "why would people need to organize to discuss their *lack* of belief in God? They must be up to no good!" However, for all individuals there is something comforting and cathartic about gathering in groups of likeminded peers. In such spaces, people can be open, honest, and true to their beliefs. *Communities of practice*—defined as groups of individuals who share passions, concerns, or beliefs about something and want to gather regularly to follow this mutual pursuit and learn from one another—are a new and important avenue by which atheists congregate.[2] Stated with wit by Dale McGowan:

> The question that remains is how best to achieve the benefits of churchgoing, including a sense of community, for those people who would rather not sit through the supernatural stuff. . . . One experiment in this direction is religion that's built around something other than belief in God. At first, church without God may seem as silly as a restaurant without food. Isn't God the point? . . . Sure, God's name is on the shingle, and he's the one who

is sung and prayed to. But that's just one possible focus for a welcoming community that inspires its members to be better people.[3]

One option for this may be the Unitarian Universalists, 91 percent of whom identify as humanist and over half of whom are fully atheist. With core beliefs such as a free search for truth and meaning, justice and compassion, and the inherent worth of all people, it seems clear why the Unitarian faith may feel attractive to many atheists. But aside from a formal *religious group*, across the United States burgeoning groups of secular humanists are banding together to partake in fellowship, volunteering, learning, and connecting with others. As McGowan notes, there is something very powerful in finding a tribe or a smaller group of people who are like you in some meaningful way.

There are also many formal groups specifically for atheists, where individuals can go to conferences and meet other nonbelievers in a relaxed and welcoming environment. Often located in larger cities, these organizations will form smaller chapters that get together for local activities; for example, the New York City Atheists—a nonprofit, nonpartisan educational association open to believers and nonbelievers alike—will sometimes hold brunches, guest lectures, film screenings, or other social meet-ups. A few national and international organizations include:

> American Atheists, founded by Madalyn Murray O'Hair in 1963 and "dedicated to working for the civil rights of atheists, promoting separation of state and church, and providing information about atheism"
>
> The American Humanist Association, founded officially in 1941, which "strives to bring about a progressive society where being good without a god is an accepted way to live life"
>
> The Center for Inquiry, founded by Paul Kurtz, which runs the lively atheist journal *Free Inquiry*
>
> The United Coalition of Reason, a national organization that works to raise the visibility of local nontheistic groups all over America
>
> The Foundation Beyond Belief, comprising humanists who support charities and do community-based volunteer work

The Foundation from Religion Foundation, one of the largest organizations for atheists and agnostics in America, with a mission to "promote the constitutional principle of separation of state and church
and educate the public on matters relating to nontheism."

As with other marginalized groups in the United States, the Internet has
become a fruitful tool in stimulating dialogue, organizing events, and forming virtual and in-person communities for atheist individuals.[4] Websites
such as AtheistNexus, Reddit, and AtheistForums all link millions of atheist
people from across the world. There are also many bloggers and broadcast-
ers who give a more in-depth look into the opinions and personal lives of
atheist people (e.g., Greta Christina, Sikivu Hutchinson, Freethought Radio
with Dan Barker and Annie Laurie Gaylor). But although virtual connections may help assuage feelings of isolation, many atheist people still crave
in-person interactions with friends, neighbors, and family. As such, the following pieces explore how atheist people have undergone the difficult task
of finding likeminded peers and worked to establish their own communities
of practice. Though quite different in age, gender, and region of the country,
Justus, Brittany, and Pam all describe similar phenomena in their narratives:
awkward and sometimes painful processes of selectively hiding parts of their
identity to maintain friendships and community. Drawing from the review
of identity management strategies introduced at the start of this book, it is
plain to see how the authors used almost all of these approaches.

In many ways, Justus has a typical atheist identity development: he was
very Christian but in college became exposed to Darwin, Freud, and other
great thinkers, and he gradually realized that his beliefs no longer fit. From
having worked as a Christian camp counselor, most of his friends were very
religious. This lead Justus to feel disconnected and isolated, and he eventually
fell into a deep bout of clinical depression; as he poignantly states, "I felt like
I was lying to them about who I was, pretending to be someone I could no
longer be." He very slowly became more forthcoming about his beliefs (and
was not rejected by friends or family) and began regularly to utilize online
sources for connection and information, primarily the "Skeptics' Guide to the
Universe," a podcast focused on critical thought and a scientific worldview.

Further, his sister also experienced a deconversion at around the same time, and this allowed them to support each other. Justus, luckily, remains close to his religious friends and family to this day and is still devout in his nonbelief.

For Brittany, attending college in the Bible Belt has made being true to her atheist beliefs a challenge. She describes a complicated process of carefully weighing how honest she can be about her nonbelief with nearly everyone in her social network. Describing a mix of reactions from disgust to acceptance, Brittany expresses frustration that communication with potential friends has to be so challenging for her but not for religious people: "why should I have to hold back because it makes some people squirm?" And, indeed, she explains that she has been atheist for years but still has not told some of her closet friends for fear they will reject her. Pam, while in her sixties, describes similar irritation that she cannot be more forthcoming about her beliefs to friends and coworkers: "if it were accepted as a normal stop on the spectrum of life philosophies, atheists wouldn't have to be nonconformists to openly declare themselves." Pam described a number of avoidant techniques she used with acquaintances to avoid openly discussing her atheism. Most commonly, she would default to the "I'm just not that religious" position, one that is commonly accepted by liberal people in the United States. Pam, however, differs from Justus and Brittany in that she is very active in her local atheist community, Pennsylvania Nonbelievers. In this group, Pam expresses feeling totally at ease: able to make jokes, let down her guard, and bring all her identities to the table.

19

SLOW GROWTH

———————

Justus Humphrey

Justus, thirty-four, was born in a kitchen on an Alaskan island.

When I was eighteen, I filled out scholarship applications that often included essay components and prompts asking me to express who I was. Often some version of the same question was posed: What five words describe you? Like many, I chose variations on "funny" and "intelligent," alongside "quiet" or "relaxed." Maybe I threw in something like "reader" or "creative" too, but one term that inevitably showed up was "Christian." By the time I finished college four years later, that last word had dropped off my list, yet it would be nearly a decade more before I could comfortably apply the word "atheist" to identify myself.

My father is a Presbyterian pastor. As I grew up, church was central to my life. Not only did I attend church each Sunday morning, but also I was active in the youth group, volunteered to help out in the nursery, joined the hand bell choir, read Bible passages for the congregation as a liturgist during Sunday services, acted in church plays, taught vacation Bible school, and was ordained as a youth elder. Most of my closest friends were church friends rather than classmates at school. I went to church camp each summer and became a counselor once I was too old to attend as a camper. My first kiss occurred at a national Presbyterian youth event.

In college, however, things began to change. In my new university town, I sought out the local Presbyterian church and attended a few times but was disappointed that the pastor's sermons failed to equal my dad's. I soon gave up on finding a church to call home, but I tried attending some on-campus Christian group meetings, only to be equally disappointed. The groups seemed focused on the extroverted lifestyle that our culture holds up as ideal. Rather than engaging me with thoughtful, small group discussions or interesting talks by talented speakers, the groups blared unpleasant music and featured silly games. Within a year of being in college, my Christianity was still central to my internal sense of identity, but it did not affect my life in any way that an outside observer would be able to note.

I focused more of my efforts during this time on another criterion of my identity, intelligence. I aspired to nurture it and become a full-blown intellectual. I was a devoted student in the honors program at my college, and I loved to learn new facts and challenge myself with new concepts and approaches to the world. I spent hours at the school library. My freshman honors survey course focused on paradigms in conflict and began with readings about epistemology, the value of education in terms of shared points of knowledge, and the concept of cultural literacy; then it was on to different cultures' creation myths, Sophocles, Shakespeare, Rousseau, Darwin, Freud, and more.

In the next couple of years, my worldview continued to expand. I was majoring in theatre, and as the stereotype indicates, I spent my days and nights working, studying, and partying with more gay folks than I had ever previously known. My religious upbringing had been a thoughtful one, so I did not have the virulent antigay views of many religious folks. I had been taught, however, that homosexual acts were sinful and that, indeed, all sex outside of marriage or even lustful thoughts were sinful. As I was exposed to more and more decent, humane, kind individuals who happened to be homosexual, I started to wonder about the God who would create these people with a desire to love, only to label any actions on their desires as sin.

During the summers between my college years, I continued to counsel at the church camp I'd grown up attending, but I felt more and more uncertain in my role as a leader. I was supposed to be teaching youth about God, but I wasn't sure I knew what I was talking about. My fellow counselors who seemed most certain of themselves were the ones who seemed most absurd to me in the expression of their faith. I remember one prayer led by a friend, in which every sentence contained the word "Lord": "Thank you, Lord, for all you've given us. Lord, continue to bless us today. And allow us, Lord, to enjoy the beauty of your natural world around us." It struck me as ridiculous to proclaim on the one hand that we had personal relationships with God, that He was actually our friend, and then to interact with God in such a stilted manner. But my own prayers felt equally artificial when I would say, "Hey, God, thanks for the sunshine and the rain. We appreciate it." I felt like I was speaking to a great-grandfather I didn't really know or, worse, that I was acting the role of a character in a one-man play in which the actor and audience alike must suspend disbelief to accept that there is another character present.

In my third year of college I signed up for a biblical studies course, the first time I was going to study the Bible seriously. We began the class by learning about the history of how the Bible came to be the book (or books) that we have now, including amendments and interpolations—marginal notes made by monks transcribing by hand, which were later included in the text itself by other monks transcribing by hand. During that semester, I began wondering how every word could be divinely inspired if the document itself was adjusted and altered so much over time. If any one version of the Bible was God's perfected text, then all other versions must be flawed. It made no sense that any version could be right.

By the time I completed that class, I was no longer sure what label to apply to myself. I had decided the Bible was hopelessly flawed, with no way to know what God intended. Therefore, I needed to start from scratch. I did not intend to convert to atheism. I merely wanted to dump out all the junk that had accumulated in my faith drawer and put back only what belonged. I was confident that Jesus would still have a spot, but I needed to figure out how he would fit in and what exactly I made of him.

I counseled at camp again that summer but felt more and more like a fraud. I enjoyed spending time with my fellow counselors, some of whom had become my closest friends, but I felt like I was lying to them about who I was, pretending to be someone I could no longer be. One of the things I'd always loved about that camp was the feeling of a type of community that didn't exist in the rest of my world. I knew that if I walked up the trail to my cabin, a stranger would give me a hug if I asked for one. But that summer seemed different. That community still existed around me, but I was apart from it rather than a part of it.

Gathered on the back deck of the lodge, looking out at the meadow, my friends would comment on the beauty of God's creation; I saw only the natural world that had evolved over the millennia. I wasn't yet opposed to their worldview, but I saw myself less and less as a Christian and more and more as a questing agnostic, someone who didn't know the answers but was hoping to find them. I wanted to be convinced by my friends, to have them say something that would resonate with me to make me think, "Yes, it makes sense again. We're alike. That connection that bound us together is still there." Instead, they prayed, "Lord, thank you, Lord, for blessing us, Lord, with your presence, Lord," and I shook my head by myself.

In my final year of college, I began dating a woman with whom I'd had an ongoing flirtation for years but had never previously considered dating because of her Bahá'í faith. When I told my camp friends about my budding relationship, their first question was whether she was a Christian. My camp friends were spread across different cities and universities, so our communication was primarily through e-mail, and when I got the messages asking about my new girlfriend's religion, I froze. I didn't respond for a few days. I was afraid. I thought they would reject me, that I might end up not only losing my faith and that central component of my identity but also losing my closest friends. Yet I felt I needed to finally tell them the truth about who I was becoming.

I braced myself and tried to take comfort in thinking about the friendships I'd made in the theatre department at my college, about my new girlfriend and how she didn't care whether I believed in a god; however, those friendships weren't the same. No matter how many theatre parties I attended, those relationships still lacked something, the bond that had originally linked me to my Christian friends, except that bond didn't exist any longer with those friends either. Fortunately, my fears were unfounded, and when I told them my thinking in recent months, my friends supported my searching. They, like my parents, thought I would eventually find my way back to the faith we had shared for so long. That faith seemed to them so right and true; it was inevitable that, after some reflection, I would conclude the same.

In the year after graduating, I continued ongoing discussions with my father and with those camp friends, and I read some books they recommended. I was hoping for some sign to give me a clearer understanding about the truth but found all their thoughts unconvincing. I was also trying to figure out who I was as an adult. I was out of school, with a useless bachelor's degree in theatre. Still aspiring to be an intellectual, I applied to graduate school but, foolishly, only to three universities, all top programs. After quick rejections from two, I was selected as a finalist by the third. I interviewed with them, hoped, and weeks later received my final rejection.

I was admitted to graduate school the next year, this time to study a wider range of writing rather than just plays. After moving thousands of miles away, I lost all but sporadic contact with my dearest friends and family and sank deeper and deeper into a dark depression. My camp friends were busy with their lives, too busy to e-mail regularly. They were working full-time jobs, dating, starting families. And, as ever, they were attending church, counseling at camp, and leading youth group meetings.

One friend made the decision like I had to pursue a graduate degree, but hers was in youth ministry. Our grad school experiences were so different that we never managed to connect when the topic of coursework and studying came up. She, perhaps the most conservative of all my friends, was considered the liberal thinker among her grad school peers at her Christian college because she had decided against taking her husband's name when she married. Yet the university I attended felt in some ways as foreign to me as her description of her school. I had imagined grad school as a utopian world of intellectuals discussing great ideas, where I would make many close friends and maybe fall in love, but I was disappointed with the reality: my peers spent their Saturday nights getting drunk and their weekdays complaining about the students in the freshman composition courses we taught.

I walked through the hallways of the university feeling isolated, longing for the experience of being at camp and knowing a stranger would gladly hug me if I asked or being at church and passing the communion plate to my neighbor. But that world that had provided such community was no longer a part of my life, and I didn't know where to turn for that fulfillment.

My depression reached a breaking point one afternoon in the spring of my first year of grad school. I had attended a showing of an independent film on campus, partly because I love movies and partly in the hope that I would strike up a friendship with someone else there. After leaving the movie without speaking to anybody, I stood alone in my apartment and began to cry. I couldn't stop for an hour and a half. Later, I called my parents to seek their advice about what I should do. They suggested I set up an appointment with the counseling center on campus and see if I could get therapy and some antidepressant medication.

My dad called me the next day to tell me he had mentioned my struggles to a friend, who had offered some frequent flyer miles if my dad wanted to fly out to be with me for a few days while I got situated with a counselor; furthermore, his schedule was relaxed and flexible for the next week, so the timing would work out easily for him. He said he thought God had arranged it so he could fly out and be with me. I told my dad I would be fine alone. "If you change your mind, just call me," he said.

That afternoon, I was in my car driving to a store listening to an oldies station on the radio. I wondered whether I should ask for my dad to come visit, whether I was being foolish in trying to stay strong by myself when clearly I had already proven myself incapable of dealing with my depression alone. As I pondered what to do, the song "Lean on Me" came on the radio. The song is one that always reminds me of church camp since we regularly sang it during our morning chapel services. It felt like the song had been expressly delivered to me in this moment. The song ends with the words "Call me if you need a friend" and then the chanting repetition, "call me, call me, call me." I felt sure God was telling me to call my dad, so I could lean on him in my moment of need.

I did call, and my dad flew across the country to be with me. I cried in his arms and told him about the song, and he agreed that it was a sign from God. What are the chances, we both wondered, of that song being on the radio at that exact moment?

In the following year, I began a regime of antidepressant medication and counseling. My mood stabilized. Though I viewed myself as a theist again, I was unsure whether the label of Christian was appropriate, so I continued to debate with myself, with my father, and with some old camp friends about faith. But as I tried to determine how to identify myself, I kept returning to my conversion moment in the car. "Lean on Me" is a popular song that surely is played regularly on oldies stations. Furthermore, there are many songs that would have had a similar effect on me in that moment. Had I been listening to an alternative station, R.E.M.'s "Everybody Hurts" would have resonated with me. The other point that stood out to me was that my counselor and my parents both insisted that when I was in such a severe state of depression, my mind was not working rationally. My thoughts spiraled in negative directions, insisting my life would never improve, I would never have friends, I would never make anything of myself. Those were not rational thoughts, they said again and again. My brain was lying to itself. I couldn't trust my thinking. I accepted that there was some truth to this concept, but in order to be logically consistent, I needed to accept that just as my depressed, irrational brain had been incapable of imagining a future in which I would be happy, it was equally incapable of properly processing the significance of hearing "Lean on Me" in that moment. It was completely irrational for me to draw the conclusion I had drawn.

After that analysis, the last remnants of my newly rediscovered faith slowly faded. Over the following years, I became more and more interested in science and rationalism, regularly listening to the "Skeptics' Guide to the Universe," a podcast focused on critical thought and a scientific worldview. Though I've never met the hosts, I came to consider them almost like friends, members of my new community. I picked up skeptical magazines and books; I read more about evolution and logical fallacies and the willful blindness required to argue for some faith positions. My sister underwent a similar deconversion from faith during her mid-twenties, and along with her husband; we discussed these issues and formed our own small skeptics group.

I eventually concluded that the question of a god's existence is one that cannot be answered through logic and rational thought. There is not enough evidence to support the conclusion that there is a god. Any evidence that may suggest such a conclusion has other likelier explanations. Rather than a god sending me signs, it's reasonable to conclude that someone made a mistake and plugged my name into the wrong form letter and that a radio station happened to play a certain popular song on a certain afternoon during the twenty minutes I coincidentally listened to that station in my car.

Over the years, I also expanded my search for connections. As my depression eased during the later years of grad school, I made new friends who shared my interests in independent films or particular writers or various other issues. After grad school I taught at a college and met other teachers. We connected over approaches to reaching our students and particular pet peeves regarding grammar and usage. I joined Mensa and connected with fellow members in online discussions. I attended writers' conferences and enjoyed being in the presence of so many other people who love the written word.

Neither a common faith nor a lack of faith is now a factor for my friendships. Some of these new friends are religious; some aren't. It doesn't matter like it used to. When I shared the news with one friend that I had written an essay about losing my faith for a book about atheists in America, he expressed surprise to learn that I'm an atheist. Though we are both pastors' sons and we've discussed personal essays we've each written, the issue of our personal faiths or lack thereof had never explicitly come up before.

The other day, I happened to speak to my mom on the phone, and she asked what I label myself these days. She hoped I considered myself agnostic rather than atheist. I told her that either term was fine. "I'm an atheist," I said, "in the sense that I'm a nontheist. I'm agnostic in the sense that I think the question of a god's existence is unknowable. If you ask if I believe in a god, the answer is no, but that doesn't mean I believe there's definitely not a god." As she often does, she said she hoped I was keeping an open mind about it.

I suppose I am. It's not inconceivable to me that I would someday convert back to faith, but it strikes me as unlikely. The naïve eighteen-year-old I once was has become a much more critical adult thinker. Though I maintain friendships with those old camp buddies and remain close with my religious family, I cannot take the leap of faith to believe myself. My worldview now centers on reaching conclusions supported by evidence, and I don't see that there will ever be sufficient evidence for me to answer those key questions with a yes. I've been in the foxholes a couple times, and I suspect the next time I'm there, whether it's after a relationship's breakup or a lost job or the death of a parent, I will still be an atheist.

20

AN ATHEIST IN THE BIBLE BELT

Brittany Friedel

Brittany, twenty-one, lives in Kansas and is studying psychology at Baker University.

Growing up in the Bible Belt is the pits. If you're different in any way, people will find out and destroy any hope that still flickers inside of you. This is extraordinarily true when you're an atheist. I can only equate it to being a member of the LGBTQ community and the experiences that must happen with coming out. When a "good Christian" or conservative person finds out you're an atheist, they hate you, they want you dead, and suddenly you're on the same level of importance as dirt. There is real fear in "coming out" as an atheist that often leads to the loss of long-time friendships and physical harm.

Coming from Kansas I've realized that this must be one of the worst states to be an atheist in the nation. Churches in Kansas are like Starbucks around the rest of the country: they're everywhere, and everyone goes to them. When you first meet people it's not odd for them to ask which church you go to or what religion you are. As an atheist, I've often lied and said I was a Christian or that I didn't really belong to one church. This is out of pure survival. I just wanted to avoid the dirty looks and disgusted words that pour out of my new Christian acquaintance. Of course this doesn't happen every time. There have been many moments where I shared my beliefs and my new friend acted very Christlike. Those are the best encounters. I've been an atheist for quite a few years, and some of my closest friends still don't know. Telling my mom was easy since she actually practices what she preaches. She barely batted an eyelash when I told her. However, I still didn't tell her for a few years because I thought this might be the one thing she isn't cool with. Other family members are not as accepting. When I first came out to other members of my family I saw the flash of hatred on their faces. My favorite invalidating reaction was one of them saying that my atheism was a "phase."

Deciding when to disclose your true beliefs can be a daunting experience. When you begin to meet new people and befriend some of them, often personal views and experiences will be brought up. When you're an atheist, this can get uncomfortable very quickly. Sometimes you want to say, "I don't believe in God," and leave the situation at that. Yet you have to wonder: *How will they react?* Badly. *Is this the type of person that will hurt me?* Maybe? And ultimately decide: *This person may be a Bible-thumping Christian, so it's best to play it safe and keep your mouth shut.*

But why should I keep my mouth shut? Why do I have to keep my beliefs to myself? I haven't done anything wrong by thinking and feeling this way. They can spout their beliefs at the drop of the hat without any fear of retribution. Obviously not everyone will react negatively or violently when I tell them I'm an atheist and I don't believe in God. I have many Christian friends that harbor no ill will toward my beliefs or me for believing what I do. I currently attend a Methodist-based university in Kansas, and I have made friends with someone going to seminary in the fall. It's like a twisted episode of *The Odd Couple*, and I can imagine the dialogue: "Sorry, I accidently borrowed your Bible, thinking it was my copy of *God Is Not Great*." If only every person of the cloth held these same beliefs. I haven't always been an atheist, so there are plenty of people that I know that don't know my true beliefs. That is the most difficult situation to encounter. How do you tell someone that you have known for years that you feel everything they believe is a fantasy, a fairy tale they have to cling to get through the day? You certainly don't tell them their beliefs are a fairy tale. I don't want to be rude. There is a difference between sharing how you feel and being a total asshole. There is a comfort in finding a middle ground and knowing someone will accept you without hesitation for exactly who you are.

At Baker University I have met people who have reacted beautifully to my belief system. When I was first getting to know my friend Jake, I was considerably worried that he would not want anything to do with me or be offended by my lack of a god. I remember checking out his Twitter account, and his profile included "God loving." In my mind, this meant the end to a friendship that had barely started. My own selfish way of thinking had already decided he would not be interested in sharing the same space as a heathen destined for Hell. How wrong I was. I remember one night in particular. Jake was walking me to my car, after a class we shared, when the discussion of religion came into the conversation one way or another. I stated I was an atheist because I was not sure if he was aware, and Jake casually said, "Oh okay" and continued on with what he was saying. It felt amazing to say I did not believe in god, on a Methodist university's campus, in Kansas, to someone I wished to get to know further, and realize he could not care less. This conversation is probably not important if Jake remembers it, and I think that is a big "if." To me, it opened a door to acceptance that I still continue to experience on Baker's campus. Who knew the oldest university in Kansas that is Methodist-based could be a Mecca to someone like me? Similar experiences of approval toward me continue with my amazing professors and other students that I am becoming acquainted with. One of my favorite professors is also an ordained minister and nothing but warm and open to me and my lack-of-a-god lifestyle. I often think I must be in the Twilight Zone when I have conversations with her and know she does not think I will burn in Hell for eternity.

Baker University is not all sunshine and rainbows for an atheist. In one of my discussion-based classes, we have recently been discussing creationism and if it holds a candle to evolution and scientific theories (spoiler alert: it doesn't). My more conservative classmates like to view creationism as at least somewhat legitimate when you compare it to evolution. It disturbs me that perfectly intelligent individuals refuse to look at scientific evidence and dismiss Charles Darwin's amazing contribution to mankind. In this same classroom, topics of religion and belief systems are brought up. I remember one student telling me we were not going to discuss religion because it could offend some people, himself included. Challenge accepted. Why should I have to hold back because it makes some people squirm? If your religion cannot remain solid because I ask questions about evidence and proof, then maybe you need to rethink why you believe it.

There are still friends that I have known for years who do not know that I do not believe in god. Sometimes I think about telling them, but the fear of their rejections and reactions cripples my ability to be open with them. Perhaps we are not real friends. Why am I "friends" with someone I cannot be honest and open with? Because I am too cowardly to admit my real feelings and ideas to these "friends" and because I wish that something as simple, yet groundbreaking, as religion did not have to tear us apart. I think the situation I am in could be different if I lived in a less religious state or country, but I am stuck in Kansas. It makes me feel as if I am some sort of atheist pilgrim looking for a promised land that is not controlled by religious dogma.

When I start to think it is impossible for an atheist to make meaningful relationships, I think of my friend Carly. She is one of the best people I know on the planet. She is kind, giving, and supportive, spends her summers working at a Christian summer camp for underprivileged children, and is devoted to her faith. Carly is great because she is able to find humor in our unique friendship. During a communication class we share, Carly wanted to give her presentation on her summer camp experience and how it made her close to god (or something). She actually approached me about her topic to make sure it would not make me uncomfortable. I still feel touched by this kind (unnecessary) gesture. Before she gave her speech to our class I told her, "Don't worry, I won't 'Boo!' you if you say something I don't agree with." She laughed. Her presentation was flawless, and I was able to enjoy it too. As Carly went to sit down, I yelled some sort of heckle at her in a playful manner. This is what gives me hope for my future with friends that believe in god and those that share my atheism. Religion and atheism do not have to cause so much strife and turmoil with people. Both sides just need to be willing to let their hair down and joke with each other. I think if we can all just laugh at one another and with ourselves everything will be fine.

21

COMING OUT AND FINDING HOME

Pam Zerba

Pam is a sixty-three-year-old resident of York, Pennsylvania. She has been married to fellow atheist George for forty-one years, and they have one daughter, Jean, and a son-in-law, Brian (who are—surprise!—atheists, too).

I've been a public atheist for about twelve years. I was a semicloseted atheist for many years before that, from the early 1970s, when I was in my early twenties.

Atheists come from a wide variety of backgrounds and experiences. I've heard many atheists' stories, and there does not appear to be one consistent "conversion" narrative. Some had horrible experiences with organized religion, others had some terrible life event—death of a child, for example—that lead them to doubt the idea of an all-loving God. Some were born into nonbelieving families, and some thought that religion, and therefore God, rejected them, because they were gay or because they had an abortion.

I belong to an atheist group, Pennsylvania Nonbelievers, that has booths at fairs and festivals in conservative central Pennsylvania every summer. Religious people often come to our booths to argue with us, which can be fun. Often, though, a theist will approach the booth, look soulfully into our eyes, and ask, "What happened?"

Nothing happened to me. I was born into a religious Catholic family and am the product of sixteen years of Catholic education. I'm not rebelling against my parents or my family. I don't have horrifying nun stories or priest stories. (I actually taught in a Catholic grade school where one of the priest molested boys. By the time that happened, I was definitely not religious, although I would not then have described myself as an atheist.)

I was just religion resistant. When my friends described having a personal relationship with Jesus, when they talked about how much the Virgin Mary helped them, I couldn't imagine what they meant. I presumed something was wrong with me. It was like when I was six or seven and people would describe something they saw across the street. I couldn't make out what they said they could see, so I assumed they were just making stuff up. Eventually my parents caught on, got me glasses, and I could see what everyone else saw. I figured I just needed religion glasses and then I would understand religion, just like everyone else I knew.

Religion was interesting, a subject I enjoyed. The more I studied, though, the more questions I had. It didn't help that I went to a good high school, where we weren't afraid to question dogma or church rules. All too often, though, the answers weren't really answers; they just seemed rote, destined to be satisfying enough to shut us up.

In high school I was outspoken, not one who was afraid to challenge authority. Yet I never mentioned having any doubts to my friends, or sisters, or anybody else. I gradually realized that there were people, even other Catholics, even girls in my class, who didn't attend church. That was different; church was boring and inconvenient. Not wanting to go to church was one thing; not believing in religion, the Catholic religion, and finally God, was entirely different. I presumed that the people I knew who had given up on religion still believed in God. In any event, nobody bragged about staying away from church or even talked about it at all.

By the time I went to college in the late 1960s—a college with a first-class theology department—the Catholic Church was dealing with the turmoil of the Second Vatican Council, and the professors, priests, nuns, and laypeople were not interested in the fine points of Catholic theology. Hierarchy of belief, they would tell us: don't worry about Mary's being bodily assumed into heaven, or all the rules about sex. Some things are more important than others; don't sweat the stuff that strains credulity.

What was the point of a church whose precepts are optional? It had begun to seem to me that the Catholic Church was more of an interest group, or club, than a religion, and it was a club to which I no longer wanted to belong.

But I would stop myself when my mind started to wonder about the existence of God. I didn't want to be an atheist. Atheists were bad people, angry people, negative people. "Godless communists" was a standard description of the United States' enemies in the 1950s and 1960s. It was unpatriotic to be a nonbeliever. I realized that many of my friends didn't go church. And then I didn't go to church. It had nothing to do with believing in God; it had everything to do with having better, more interesting things to do than dozing off while attending a boring ritual. Nobody much cared.

My parents had insisted that if I went away to college, it had to be a Catholic college, because they didn't want me to marry a non-Catholic. In yet another example of how pointless it is for parents to try to control their kids' lives, I met my future husband, an atheist, my freshman year at my Catholic college. I had never met an atheist before, or at least anyone who admitted it out loud. He wasn't a bad, angry, unpatriotic person. He was smart, funny, and kind. We've now been married for forty years.

We were married in a Catholic ceremony (my parish church was beautiful, the perfect site for wedding pictures). My parents knew my husband was an atheist, had gathered that I was not regularly attending church, but they were not the kind of people to make scenes or draw lines in the sand. According to my sisters, they assumed I was going through some kind of phase and that I would get over it. Much to their surprise, my mother told me later, they found that they liked my husband.

I still was a nominal believer in God, continued to be a nominal believer, until one day in Atlanta in 1973. I was riding the bus home from work, and it stopped in front of a Catholic church. I guess that's my parish church, I thought. I hadn't attended mass in ages or bothered to find out where the nearest church was. My next thought rocked me: *You don't believe any of it.* And it was true. I didn't believe in Catholicism, but I hadn't for years. I didn't believe in God. I was an atheist.

I was stunned. "Atheist" still sounded ugly and harsh to me, despite my being married to a perfectly nice atheist. I knew what people would think if I told them. Actually, at that point in Atlanta, just being a Catholic was problematic. After I'd been hired, one of my co-workers told me that the manager, seeing Catholic schools on my resume, had been concerned about hiring a *Catholic*. Gee, I now thought. Let me put your mind at rest. I'm not a Catholic. I'm an atheist.

I didn't tell people, not then, not for years. If pressed, I would simply say that I wasn't religious. Most people didn't push very hard, and I became gifted at smoothly changing difficult subjects. My friends weren't interested in religion; they wouldn't have been my friends if they were. They simply didn't care about religion, didn't think about it. It was easy to maintain these friendships. I just had to censure myself a bit, not be too blunt when a religious figure interfered in politics or when a school board rewrote science books. My friends agreed with me about religion, but would they have been willing to go that extra step, not just no religion, but no God?

My husband has always been completely open about his atheism. He laughed at my squeamishness. But I worked for consulting firms and had clients who had to like and trust me. My husband's job was different, I told myself; he worked in medical collections, and nobody has to like a collector. Later on, I had jobs in human resources, where I wanted to influence management, wanted to get ahead. I know a lot about religion, especially the Catholic religion, enough to fake my way through religious references. It was a reasonable compromise, I thought; not really saying I was a churchgoer but not saying I was an atheist, either. I worried that I wouldn't get ahead if people knew I was an atheist.

Was that true? I don't know. We were living in Baltimore then, and there is enough of a mixture of people that religion simply doesn't come up much. It's possible that it would have caused me problems, would have made people uncomfortable about me, perhaps without them realizing why. That kind of prejudice is the hardest to fight. Nobody would have said, "you can't go to that client meeting, we can't promote you, you're an atheist." But what would they have thought about me? That I was disagreeable, potentially hard to get along with, someone who couldn't be trusted?

And atheists can't deny the truth of some of those concerns. If you are willing to come out as an atheist, by definition you are someone who is not overly concerned with what people think. That kind of person is less willing to go along to get along, work for consensus, than someone who keeps his unconventional opinion on religion to himself. The irony, of course, is that atheists are only iconoclasts because religionists brand atheism as evil. If it were accepted as a normal stop on the spectrum of life philosophies, atheists wouldn't have to be nonconformists to declare themselves openly.

As I've become more open about my atheism, religious and nominally religious people confide their doubts to me. One message that comes through constantly is that, even if they are repulsed by religion, even if they don't believe in the conventional Big Guy in the Sky picture of God, they don't want people to think of them as *atheists*. Atheists aren't nice. Atheism is vulgar. Atheists are the kind of people who delight in telling children there is no Santa Claus. Atheists live to stick their fingers in the eyes of people who are just minding their own business. Many times I've spoken with people who agree with everything I say but then begin to hem and haw when I mention that it doesn't sound as if they are just skeptics, it sounds as if they are atheists. Oh no, they will say, laughing nervously. Not really. Not *that*.

I came out as an atheist after my husband and I moved to York, Pennsylvania. We had lived most of our married life in Baltimore, a liberal, open-minded city where "what church do you go to?" was not the first or second question new acquaintances asked. In central Pennsylvania, a repairman asked if I wouldn't want to try his church, I worked with a woman whose parents distributed Bibles in public schools, and in my department there were two separate incidents of employees feuding over religious issues. We were thrilled to find Pennsylvania Nonbelievers, happy to verify that we hadn't been time-warped back to 1957. We had a community, friends, where we could say whatever we wanted without fear of offending, inadvertently or not. For example, people often say to us that they can't imagine living without God; life would be pointless and hopeless. The response I always want to give is that believing in Santa Claus may make Christmas more fun, but it doesn't mean that Santa Claus is real. Or people ask me if atheists worship Satan. No, I say. Not Satan, not Zeus, not Santa Claus, not the Easter Bunny.

Religious people can find the comparison of God to Santa Claus or the Easter Bunny insulting.

When I'm with Pennsylvania Nonbelievers I don't have to worry about that. I can laugh at Pat Robertson or Cardinal Dolan and not wonder if I should apologize or offer a disclaimer. People who join Pennsylvania Nonbelievers often talk about how free they feel, how wonderful it is not to have to edit what you say, to hear other people say all the things you've thought. When a politician makes a statement pandering to religion, when a religious figure inserts himself into a public issue, I can't wait to see what my fellow atheists think about it or to tell them my opinion. Not that we always agree: atheists are correctly identified as independent thinkers, but nobody is shocked or appalled by our discussions. It's not that we're obsessed about religion and can talk of nothing else. Even when we share stories about our kids, or swap recipes, that internal editor doesn't have to be switched on, and that is an enormous relief. It is our intellectual home, the place where we can be ourselves without apology.

One of the most distressing thing about being an atheist is that so many people, at least in central Pennsylvania, seem horrified by our very existence, angry even before we have the chance to say something they'll find offensive. People march past our booths at local fairs, glaring at us, swearing under their breath, making rude gestures. Just by being visible, we are somehow insulting them, threatening them. Pennsylvania Nonbelievers has a TV show on a local cable access station. Once someone called in to the show to ask why we wanted to be on TV, identifying ourselves as atheists. "I mean," the caller said, "there are people who like to drown puppies, but they don't go on TV." Atheists are the equivalent of puppy killers?

I've been on the board of the local Planned Parenthood affiliate. At one point, the board discussed forging alliances with other organizations with which we had something in common, to strengthen our ties to the community. Several of my atheist friends also volunteer at Planned Parenthood, so I started to say, "Well, Pennsylvania Nonbelievers would be willing to work with us—" but I stopped when I saw the expression on people's faces. An alliance with a bunch of atheists would not boost Planned Parenthood's popularity, I realized.

My official announcement to the people I worked with came when my husband and I attended the American Atheist Convention in San Francisco. "Why are you going to San Francisco?" people asked. "It's a beautiful city," I would answer, "lots of people go to San Francisco." Something in my manner must have seemed uncomfortable, though, because one person in particular wouldn't give up. "It's far away." "There are lots of nice vacation places closer to Pennsylvania." "Why are you really going?"

Finally, I said, "Okay, if you are sure you want to know, we're atheists, and we're going to the atheist convention." This extremely religious woman was stunned. (Of course, she had led a sheltered life. A few months before she had told me that until she met me, she hadn't thought liberals could be decent human beings. Thank you, I think.) A day or two later she asked me if I could give her copies of any handouts we got at the convention, which I agreed to do. I suspect I provided lesson plans for weeks of adult education at her church.

Did the people I work with treat me differently after I revealed my dark secret? Not that I could tell. They knew me already and had decided to like me, or not, before they found out about my atheism.

After one of my appearances on the Pennsylvania Nonbelievers TV show, I happened to be working on a project in a different department, where no one knew me. One of the women in the department mentioned the show the next day. "Why were you on that show?" she asked. "Because I'm an atheist, and I had something I wanted to talk about." "What's an atheist," one of the other women asked. I explained. "Why would you want to be on TV talking about that?"

"A lot of people are prejudiced about atheists," I answered. "In polls, people say they won't vote for atheists, that they don't trust atheists. I go on TV so people can see atheists aren't necessarily pure evil."

They thought about that for a minute. One of them said, "So it's a civil rights issue?" "Yes, I guess it is." They all nodded, and we went back to work. Were they bothered by working with an atheist? They didn't seem to be.

But to be honest, I'm not always so brave. I recently joined a writer's group here in central Pennsylvania. I don't know the other women well, but I know that they are religious. There are Christian references in their writing and in their conversations. They have noted that I'm not religious; for example, when they talk about a writer's conference for religious publications, one of them will say, "Well, that's not your type of writing."

So why don't I just say, "That's right, I'm an atheist?" I know their religions; they've casually mentioned them. We read one another's writing, comment, make suggestions. We have to trust one another to do that. Would they still trust me if they knew? Am I underestimating them? I will tell them eventually. Probably.

I still believe it's important that we come out. Just because it's harder to be prejudiced against homosexuals when you realized that the cousin who made family reunions bearable and the nice guy who always shoveled your walk were gay, when people realize that they have atheist friends, neighbors, and relatives, it will be harder to demonize atheists. It isn't easy for everybody. It isn't always easy for me, even though my family didn't disown me and I didn't face any work repercussions. I know people who have, who have no contact with their parents, whose fellow workers are put off by their atheism. But it won't get better until we start. People like me—people who are not likely to put all of their personal or professional lives in jeopardy—must take the lead and carve a path for others to follow. Atheists tend to be educated, thoughtful people, and we should not be cut out of public life. More important, though, we should not have to live our lives pretending to believe something that we do not.

PART 7

ATHEISM AT WORK

Tales of Coming Out to Coworkers
and Colleagues

T HERE IS A well-known formula for collegial harmony within the workplace: don't talk about sports, politics, or religion. Considering that
employers are the primary links to providing food, shelter, and material comfort for oneself or one's family, it's no wonder that many Americans
are perfectly content to, while on the job, keep quiet about any controversial
religious beliefs they may hold. However, growing movements that empha-
size being genuine and bringing "your whole identity" to work have begun to
shift these truisms. But in more conservative vocations, bringing your whole
person to work may not be welcome if part of your person includes atheist
beliefs. Hicks discusses that pressures for employees to be fully open about
their religiosity (or lack of) at work is "inconsistent if [employers] view spirituality as appropriate in the workplace, but exclude diverse employees' particular religious expressions from it."[1]

After over forty-five years, employers are still struggling to make sense of
and effectively deal with the ramifications of the Equal Employment Opportunity (EEO) laws. Though religion was addressed in the original laws, this
primarily focused on accommodations for spiritual practices outside of the
workplace.[2] While EEO commission guidelines do include "lack of religious
belief," it is difficult to define and describe what discrimination against atheist coworkers looks like, particularly considering the ubiquity of religious

belief in many parts of the world. Indeed, there is a very murky line between coworkers discussing personal religious beliefs and proselytizing in the workplace; this murky line obfuscates any clear definition of unlawful religious harassment.[3] For individuals who are atheist, their nonbelief may be largely invisible at work; however, beyond overt harassment that is documentable in the legal landscape, covert and implicit attitudes that being nonreligious is "not okay" can still be felt through stigmatizing coworker interactions. Thus, workplace stigma may be felt even by individuals who are not out or open about their identities.[4]

The following narratives capture how several employees have made the decision to be open as atheist in their workplaces, and they describe the ramifications of their coming out as nonreligious. Samuel, Camilo, and John are each middle-aged men who, by this point, have been atheist for more of their lives than not. Sam, an oncologist in rural Texas, describes the hardships of being a nonbeliever at work in such a conservative and religious state; for example, he describes that the town's atheist group only had six members. Most interesting, though, is the specific occupational hazards of being atheist as a medical doctor. When dealing with serious illness, chronic conditions, and death, it is no surprise that many patients and doctors turn to religious or spiritual beliefs as a coping mechanism. As such, in Texas, it is truly aberrant to be an outspoken atheist and a healthcare provider. But for Sam, the workplace strain on his identity goes further, as many patients would refuse state-of-the-art treatments such as chemotherapy or transfusions in deference to their religious beliefs. Navigating these difficult conversations with patients would be challenging for any doctor but even more challenging for one who cannot identify with the underlying drive to refuse life-saving treatments.

Related, in some ways, is Camilo's narrative. Surprisingly, though he is a psychology professor in one of the most liberal and atheist places in the country (New York City), Camilo still faces occasional backlash from coworkers for being an outspoken atheist at work. Ironically, he notes that his openness about disbelief has allowed other professors to express their own atheism quietly. If *academics in NYC* are not welcomed out of the "atheist closet" with open arms—that should paint a dismal picture for the climate toward atheists in the rest of the country! Camilo describes that the culture of his field (psychology) promotes closeting among students, professors, and practitioners; he states, "we are in a perpetual state of anxiety about offending anyone." Similar to observations from Austin Dacey's work (reviewed in the introduction), within psychology there is a great impetus to be multiculturally sensitive and respect all religious beliefs. With this drive comes the implicit assertion that you *cannot* be openly atheist, as such an expression is thought to demonstrate that you do not personally believe in or support others' religions. Though being out as a psychology professor may be an occupational hazard—in that, others may perceive you as multiculturally insensitive—Camilo remains out to serve as a role model for students who may be struggling with their own doubts about belief.

Finally, like Samuel and Camilo, John (who works at a multinational manufacturing company in Detroit) discusses the delicate decision-making processes of how to be open as atheist at work. All three authors highlight their intentions to be true to themselves but employ careful choreography not to offend or upset religious coworkers. Considering that U.S. adults spend the vast majority of their waking hours at work, maintaining these delicate collegial relationships is crucial. John highlights that one of his primary strategies has been to use humor—mostly of the self-deprecating variety—to discuss his atheism. Like Camilo, he also makes it a point to be out at work in order to show religious coworkers that he is normal, laid back, and kind; this deflects opinions that atheists are all immoral and challenges assertions that people have "never met an atheist."

22

IS THIS THE WAY TO AMARILLO?

Samuel W. Needleman

Samuel Needleman, MD, sixty-three, lives with his wife and three shelter dogs in Granbury, Texas, where he practices medical oncology part time.

I have practiced medical oncology in the Bible Belt, assisted by a physicians' assistant who is an African American woman. That's progress: an atheist Jew and a black woman would not have been permitted, much less welcomed, in Amarillo, Texas, in 1950.

And so I've watched scores of people die with neoplastic diseases, and I've been less directly involved with many others you would call "cancer deaths." In all, I've cured a few hundred, extended the lives of more than a thousand, and given pain relief to more than I can count.

Some deaths, despite the profound mercy of opiates, have been horrible. After thirty-five years, I am pretty well inured to this sort of thing, but occasionally a case will penetrate my defenses. I'm not sure I would want it otherwise, really. Most oncologists cope by escaping into the considerable intellectual challenges that the field demands. And many of my colleagues deal with the grief and tragedy through a combination of parrying, denying, and just plain avoiding it.

My wife is a Texan, and she has advised me never to speak of politics or religion at work. But alas, I can't help myself. They really get me going, when they rail at the government about their out-of-pocket expenses. Even in Texas, patients really want—and expect—the government to pay for their health care. Yet, almost in the same breath, they will vilify the president for "starting class warfare" with "Obamacare." And then follow it with my favorite, the Palinesque "I know how to spend my money better than BIG GOVERNMENT knows how to spend my money." It just strikes a nerve, and I seem to have to say: "*Then next election, vote Democrat. The free-market model does not work for health care.*" This was me, thinking I was being a good citizen and a patriotic American. Clearly, I hadn't realized how quickly this little exercise in democracy could come back to bite me in the ass. Or, in particular, how nicely it would synergize with the reaction that news of my atheism would generate.

So the stage was set when the nurse assigned to me resigned a few days after my profane and heretical outburst.

She made up a story about her scheduling. I learned the real reason that she had left the next day from one of the many people she had told that I was an atheist. I still wonder, though, that if being a "person of faith" were the profound, joyful, and comforting experience that she claimed, why did my blasphemy offend her so? If she were really secure in her love of god and basking in HIS love, wouldn't she just pity me and think, "Oh, Sam, you poor, dumb bastard!"?

And I have to wonder: why isn't theodicy a more pressing topic in the minds of the faithful and in our popular culture at large?

Anyways, the word spread quickly that I did not favor "simple hard-working American folks" and that neither was I "a man of faith." Then my referrals fell off rather dramatically, and my monthly spreadsheets began to reflect lower earnings. In fee-for-service medicine, that is the real measure of success, and soon enough I made plans to leave Amarillo.

In truth, the nurse did not reveal anything that I would not have stated freely soon enough: The idea that the creator of the universe would reproduce like a human being and have a son is laughable to me. The idea that the son's death would obliterate the sins of people who live centuries later is even more absurd. But most of all, the idea that recitation of portions of holy texts can cure cancer is not only absurd; it is dangerous and, dare I say—stupid. Clearly this all would have come out eventually—and probably in reasonably short order.

So I'm not complaining. Amarillo was oppressive. For example, I was a charter member of the Amarillo Atheists' Society: there were six of us, in a town of over one hundred thousand people and a university or two. With that name, we actually had difficulty booking meeting places, so we changed our name to Amarillo Pastafarians, and our problem was solved. Not surprisingly, I guess no one in Amarillo had heard of the Flying Spaghetti Monster or Bertrand Russell's teapot. And, to be honest, we kind of looked like Rastafarians. At least the other five atheists did. So I guess the reservations people thought we were Rasta men, who are, after all, men of faith, and we were then welcome in local restaurants, to have monthly meetings.

Every five or ten years, a patient will refuse to continue chemotherapy and will arrange a special prayer meeting at their local house of worship. Evidently, it has been reported that the recitation of an excerpt from the book of Deuteronomy (I think), when read by appropriately selected church elders, along with the afflicted, has miraculous healing powers. You'll hear about this sort of thing on the news occasionally, when such nonsense costs a young couple the life of their child. (Childhood cancer, by the way, in general is far more curable with chemotherapy than adult cancer.)

And more commonly, a Jehovah's Witness will refuse to have his life saved by transfusion, of all things—but under my care, more than half will finally give up this illegitimate idea when they actually get a glimpse of the grim reaper. The courts have ironed this out pretty clearly: you're free to kill yourself with such religious acts and thinking, but for your children, it is child abuse, and the state will take your child from you.

I would not interfere with any comfort people get from "faith," in these horrible circumstances. And I realize that it is my duty as a citizen to embrace the religious pluralism of Western democracy. But I'm not sure that there is all that much comfort from religion and prayer at the end of life, in any case, really. Prayer certainly has no measurable salubrious impact on the illness. This has actually been studied. Several times, in fact. Someone actually proposed this idea at a research conference with a straight face—and got it funded! And published!

But my observation is that the very personal god people pray to doesn't really ease much of the emotional and psychological suffering that cancer death most often causes. In fact, I have seen it actually make things worse, when the patient and family has been desperately banking on the literal text of the Bible—and it inevitably lets them down. Hard.

Seventy years ago, I would have been run out of Amarillo before anyone had found that I was godless. The fact that I do not accept Christ as the "Messiah" would have been reason enough back then. Now it seems that even the most fervent evangelical in Amarillo "likes Jews." (Or, at any rate, tolerates us.) Judging from my experience in Amarillo, I guess the Bible Belt also welcomes Hindus, Sikhs, and maybe even Muslims. And this is really impressive social progress.

It's bad form now—even in Texas—to persecute homosexual folks. In fact, I married into a cattle-dynasty family with several nieces who have same-gender mates, and one with a black husband. They were not upset that I was not Christian, and they welcome us all into the family. These couplings in my Texas family could not possibly have happened in 1950 without a great deal of acrimony.

So things are really improving, and I think that in two or three generations, we shall see similar evolution toward the acceptance of nonbelievers— and we shall see fewer "people of faith." But it will not happen quickly, and it will not come without bitter confrontation.

I'd like to think that I played a transformative role in the lives of the handful of "Witnesses" whom I saved with transfusion. Was my counsel to them unbiased? I will not insult your intelligence by claiming it to have been so. Did I violate their civil rights? I guess a constitutional lawyer might think so. But isn't it absurd to die from anemia by refusing blood transfusion? (It's one of the few diseases people do not have to die from today—almost ever.)

The passage that Witnesses cite in the Bible refers to eating or drinking blood; there was no transfusion of blood products addressed in any ancient, holy text. The ancient world's holy authors could not have *imagined* transfusion. There weren't plastic or rubber or metal tubes back then, much less sterilization or blood typing. And I strongly doubt that, holding forth today, the ancient sages would approve of this illogical interpretation of their document—one that costs the lives of their congregation needlessly. If an imam, or rabbi, or priest, or Bible author could travel in time and talk to a modern

cleric in the Witness clan about this, I'm pretty sure he'd say, "*Let him DIE???
Are you shitting me??! Are you insane??*"

And so, to play a role in this ongoing social revolution, let me suggest that
it is our moral obligation to identify magical thinking for what it is, even in
the Bible Belt—stupid and very dangerous. Progress will continue, but we
need to stop patronizing nonsense in the name of pluralism and tolerance.
Maybe they need to hear this most of all in places like Amarillo.

When a patient says to an oncologist, "I'm going to stop chemo and
heal myself with prayer," most of my Texas colleagues will humbly respond,
"I respect your opinion. It is your right, but I disagree." Or the always safe,
"I don't think that is god's will." But I think it has become our duty to say
politely and with sensitivity, but unequivocally, "That is just irrational!!"[1]

23

CRACKING OPEN THE CLOSET DOOR

Camilo Ortiz

Camilo, forty-one, lives in New York City and is an associate professor of clinical psychology at Long Island University, where he conducts research on parenting.

CAREY, A THIRD-YEAR doctoral student, peeked her head into my office in the clinical psychology department at Long Island University and nervously looked back into the hall to see if anyone was loitering nearby. When she saw the coast was clear, she stepped in and quietly shut the door behind her. She scurried into one of the two chairs facing my desk and excitedly whispered, "I'm already up to page ninety!" I whispered back, "Can you believe it?" And she said, "I know! I have so many thoughts running through my head, I don't know what to do!" She was referring to Sam Harris's tour de force, *The End of Faith*, which I had suggested she read a couple of weeks back. After years of hiding my atheistic beliefs at work, I was finally expressing them openly and suggesting to my students that they take a chance and see what had sparked my intellectual excitement.

The long journey to this point had many small but in hindsight inevitable steps. I think back and chuckle to myself about how nervous I felt becoming more open with my colleagues at work about my atheism. For instance, I remember how long I debated internally about whether I should change the blank "religion" field on my Facebook profile to "atheist." Some of my Facebook friends were also professors at LIU. There would be no going back once I hit the enter key.

This process of coming out began when I was hired as an assistant professor, only two years out of graduate school. "You shouldn't talk about religion at work. It might offend someone," my mother advised me. I listened because I didn't want to screw up this opportunity. After all, I was getting paid to think about ideas I found interesting and interact with impossibly smart people. It was a dream come true. Even though I was quickly coming to the conclusion that I wanted to leave the safety of agnosticism and begin referring to myself as an atheist, I begrudgingly listened to my mother's suggestion, managing not to discuss religion at work for the first nine years of my time at LIU. I was even awarded a research grant from the National Institutes of Health, and I earned tenure, two events that almost made me a believer, as they seemed impossible to explain logically.

Things began to change in earnest about two years ago. At that time I lived next door to my best friend Matt, whom I would describe as the smartest person I know. When my two kids got too tough to handle (even with my Ph.D. in clinical child psychology), I would temporarily retreat to my haven next door. We would play video games and drink exotic beers. He was my Cosmo Kramer, the comic relief to the monotony of my day as a responsible adult. One evening he handed me a book and nonchalantly suggested I read it. He had no idea it was going to change my life. The book was the aforementioned *The End of Faith*. For me, reading this book was like my own personal *Flowers for Algernon*, but with a happy ending. Much like the protagonist Charlie, who becomes the first human to undergo an experimental brain surgery that progressively makes him smarter, as I read the book, I felt like I was seeing the world more clearly with each passing day. I was elated and mesmerized by what I was reading. As I learned more, I felt as if I knew a secret that others didn't. At the same time, I berated myself for not previously seeing what now seemed so obvious. I felt as if I had been in a stupor for years and that Sam Harris had walked up to me and punched me in the face with a fistful of reason. It was a true awakening.

Still, I was confused about what to do with this newfound knowledge. I decided that I needed to tell other people about this book and others like it that I had started reading. I began with my wife. I breathlessly told her the many reasons why the concept of a personal god made little sense and how religion wasn't simply a collection of harmless beliefs but a serious threat to the progress of humanity. Her reaction was a polite shrug. She asked me if I had taken out the garbage. Undaunted, I decided to take my case to a different audience. I'd share my newly acquired knowledge with my professional colleagues and doctoral students. I could save them all from walking through life, as I had, with the well-meaning but misguided notion that while the existence of god was incredibly unlikely, one nonetheless should respect all religious beliefs and never, under any circumstances, question anyone's religious sensibilities.

For those of you who have never attended a graduate program in clinical psychology, I'm going to let you in on a little secret. While it is supposed to be a place of exciting new ideas and a forum for an open exchange of beliefs, it often is not, at least where religion is concerned. In this field, we are in a perpetual state of anxiety about offending anyone. As apprentices of this method, clinical psychology graduate students are asked to straddle a bizarre line of valuing the scientific method, which emphasizes the gathering of empirical, verifiable data, while at the same time being epistemic and moral relativists— that is to say someone who considers the truth unknowable and all points of view equally valid. Really! Imagine trying to understand human behavior—and in particular dysfunctional human behavior—and at the same time forcing oneself not to evaluate the validity of any patient's "culturally based" or religious beliefs. One particularly surreal result of this contradiction is that while we are trained to evaluate whether beliefs are delusional, in large part based on their level of bizarreness, religious beliefs, no matter how bizarre, are off limits.

To be fair, sometimes the ability to withhold judgment is quite useful. When one is working with a patient who is behaving destructively toward himself or another person, it is often not useful to think judgmentally or to express disapproval, as you will lose your empathic stance and thereby disrupt the therapeutic alliance. However, the convincing reasons for being nonjudgmental toward patients have infected *all* discourse that occurs within graduate programs in clinical psychology. In particular, this dynamic often makes questioning theistic beliefs practically impossible. One is likely to be accused of being intolerant if one questions the validity of religious epistemology. On the flip side, religious people get to assert their beliefs stridently (because religious beliefs are out of bounds for evaluation). This is often exacerbated by liberal secular colleagues who consistently side with the religious folks because they fear, more than anything, being labeled as prejudiced. My friend Peter Boghossian, a philosophy professor at Portland State University, had the audacity to give a lecture where he asserted (brace yourself) that there are better and worse ways of understanding the world and that faith, it seemed to him, was a less reliable way of understanding the world than was reason. Many of his colleagues pleaded with him to not give this talk—that it was offensive to say such things. This is precisely the work environment in which I decided to disclose my exciting new ideas.

As I read more on atheism (Richard Dawkins's *The God Delusion*, Sam Harris's *The Moral Landscape*, Christopher Hitchens's *God Is Not Great*), I decided to begin expressing my views somewhat timidly. I suggested *The God Delusion* to a student of mine named Alex, which I thought was a rather safe tactic for expressing my views since the words weren't coming out of my own mouth. Alex had grown up in an Orthodox Jewish home and was also struggling with what he had believed his whole life and what was becoming increasingly obvious to him. As I had hoped, the book hit him like a thunderbolt. We spent many hours discussing what we had read and musing about religious superstition, which we now saw everywhere. He taught me about Judaism, and we discussed whether there was any value in the cultural aspects of a religion if it was all based on a false set of premises. These conversations left me emboldened. While I certainly wasn't preaching or trying to convert students away from their faith traditions, I was no longer backing down when confronted with a faith-based factual claim. I wanted to be a role model for students who were doubting their religious beliefs: it was perfectly okay to say the words "I am an atheist" out loud. You would not be hauled away. You would not have your license to practice revoked. After one of my statistics classes, a student came up to me and whispered, "Are you an atheist?" Using a normal speaking volume, I stated that I was and that one needn't whisper these things. You would have thought I had outed him as a pedophile, from

his shrunken posture and full-body cringe. He pointed to a Christian fundamentalist student who was sitting nearby and whispered that we should be
careful since she might overhear our conversation. I found his reaction amus-
ing yet sad.

I have since discussed my beliefs with other professors and students, and
to my delight I have found many atheists, most of whom, unfortunately, were
closeted. Word seems to have gotten around that I am someone who can help
students take their first steps toward expressing long-suppressed beliefs. Several students have walked into my office, closed the door, and asked if I was
really an atheist. When I say yes, they invariably seem relieved and ask what
they can read. While it's no doubt a stretch, the feelings I get during these
interactions might be compared to what gay Americans went through in the
1960s and 1970s. I feel sad when I see religious dogma infect our public discourse, yet I feel excited and fortunate to be alive at a time when atheists are
beginning to assert themselves unapologetically and make themselves known.

24

MY FAVORITE ATHEIST

John Douma

John, fifty-one, is a proud father and dedicated husband who lives in the sprawling suburbs of Detroit.

I have been an atheist/agnostic since I was a teen. I have gone through many periods in my life regarding how I share my beliefs with my family, friends, and coworkers. There have been times when I have been a strident antireligionist, and there have been times when I have been apathetic about the topic. Now that I find myself in my fifth decade of life, I am trying to be honest and open with my beliefs while still trying to maintain a quality relationship with others. This is a bit tricky at times but can reap some rewards.

I currently work for a large multinational manufacturing company, and my coworkers are from very diverse backgrounds. My job has placed me in a rather small satellite office with just a dozen employees. Because of the small number of cohorts here I have been very cautious about sharing my beliefs. Even so, I try to be open and honest.

So when one of my employees says to me, "Well, God never gives you more than you can handle!" my reply is, "Do you really think so? I am not really religious. In any case, I have confidence in you, and I know you will succeed." This may sound a bit clunky at first, but it serves the purpose of expressing my confidence while still asserting I don't worship their god. Fortunately, the diverse setting at my office allows me to be fairly honest about my beliefs.

One of my coworkers is a very devout Christian. He has been a member of a church that is very literal in its interpretation of the Bible. He left this church because of a dispute over doctrine, and he has spent many years studying the Bible. He is fully committed to the idea that God speaks directly to people by evoking certain feelings and thoughts. He believes God has communicated directly with him. I will call him Peter, though this is not his real name.

Now, I am no slouch when it comes to the Bible. I was raised a Protestant and have read most of the Bible (many sections more than once). Of course, Peter knows his Bible very well. It was inevitable that we would somehow start a conversation about Bible interpretation. I just can't help myself, and neither can Peter. At first I was very concerned that we would have a knockdown, ugly fight, but I was determined to be honest and not judgmental. This can be very hard for me; I am known for being the sharp-tongued jerk in my social group.

As I recall, I think our discussions started out with politics. The state of the economy has a great deal to do with the success of our business, so it is common for us to discuss interest rates, inflation, and banking regulation. It was no surprise to me that Peter was a big fan of George W. Bush. I honestly believe he was one of the worst presidents in history. So here comes the tricky part. How can I talk about my opinions honestly and not get into a big fight? I think the trick is to frame your claims in a way that makes them personal and accurate but not universal.

An example of making a personal claim is to say, "I think George Bush was not a very effective president. He just didn't impress me with his decision making." Making a statement in this way allows someone to understand what you think but not be offended. I could have said "George Bush is a poor decision maker!" This claim is really no different than the first statement, but it makes a very big difference during a discussion. This second claim is very declarative. It states my opinion as a universal truth rather than simply being my personal judgment.

Well, at least in the case of Peter, this worked splendidly. He felt open to articulate his opinion and was rather polite. His claims were also framed as personal feelings and opinions, and he didn't feel any need to get defensive. Our initial conversation went smoothly, and we left feeling like we were informed but not disrespected. Of course, we knew that we would never agree on many topics. Perhaps we weren't trying to change each other . . . well, not intentionally at least.

For me, I found it much more comfortable to be honest with Peter. I can lie with the best of them, but lying is a burden. It makes me feel a bit knotted up inside, and there is always the risk of tripping up. I tend to avoid lying if at all possible. Being honest with Peter has allowed us to really share how we think and feel, which is far more satisfying than being guarded all the time.

And I really think I have made some kind of progress. Perhaps it is not a big thing, but I think Peter might see atheists a bit differently now. I really think he appreciates that I attack a problem in a different way than he does. He views me as a successful husband and father who has accomplished some good things using a naturalistic model of the universe.

Peter has had some serious turmoil in his life, and our open relationship has allowed him to share some of his problems with me. He sometimes seeks my advice about parenting and family issues. I have had a happy and fortunate family life. I have been married for decades and have two terrific children. My wife and I have a very honest relationship, we make decisions together, and we share many goals. I think many couples could have a better family life if they were more honest, open, caring, and dedicated.

I think Peter can see that things are working reasonably well for me. Perhaps he doesn't take my advice, but it must be of some value to him. Perhaps he just feels better sharing his problems, but I wonder if our conversations don't really help him solidify his own plans for how to tackle his problems.

Of course, we often talk about faith and the Bible. I have spent many years thinking about my beliefs and also reading about psychology, philosophy, ethics, religion, and the mind. I try to have a reasonable explanation for how I think the universe works and why I am not convinced by ideas of a supernatural power. It really helps to know why you believe what you believe. I am well equipped to explain my thoughts to anyone willing to listen. At the same time, it is important only to claim certainty when things are clearly certain. I never claim to know exactly what Jesus meant when he gave the Sermon on the Mount. I do have various opinions on the subject. I even think it is possible that Jesus never even existed. But really, it is okay to sometimes say you don't know and that you are still not convinced.

I suspect that everyone in my office knows I am an atheist. I don't go out of my way to talk about the topic, but I do give a few clues now and then. When the topic of Lent was discussed at a recent staff meeting, I exclaimed, "I am giving up sacrifice for Lent. I do it every year!" Most people get a chuckle out of this comment.

I also recall a time when I was on a phone call where my work team was trying to solve a difficult problem. Someone suggested we should all say a prayer in a joking manner. I replied, "Yeah, I have tried prayer, but I find it to be very unreliable." Most people chuckled about this. A little atheist humor is a good icebreaker. I am very cautious about this type of thing. It is clear that I cannot disrespect people or their beliefs, but I can pick on myself. Self-deprecating humor is a great tool and provides an opportunity to be honest but also not confrontational.

Just like most social experiences, we have to adjust our behavior based on the group. Every group is special, and coming out will look different in every situation. My coworkers and I have to get along, and our main purpose is to be productive. We will be far more productive if we can share our thoughts and cooperate. For example, work is not the right place to be strident and rail about the injustice caused by entanglements between churches and the government. At work, if a topic comes up, I will always share my thoughts and opinions, but I will do it in an open and personal way. It is a fine line to walk.

Over the years I have been accused of being immoral just because I am an atheist. I have had people claim I am only an atheist so I can do wicked things. I have been told that I am possessed by the devil or that I hate God. Of course, none of these ideas makes any sense. I think many people don't know an atheist that is "out of the closet." Just as people thought they didn't know any gays in the 1970s and 1980s, now people think they don't know any atheists. Perhaps I have at least allowed some of my coworkers to see that atheists are just normal people, like everyone else.

Lately Peter has given me a nickname. He recently popped into my office and said, "How is my favorite atheist?" I laughed and said, "You don't know any other atheists!" He replied, "Oh, I'm sure I do." Indeed, in this case he is correct. He does know other atheists, and they are just normal people like everyone else.

PART 8

ATHEISM AND AGING

The Challenges of Entering Older Adulthood
as a Nonbeliever

I F ASKED TO envision the weekly rituals of an elderly American, it is likely that one portion of the routine you might imagine would include participation in a religious service, or perhaps playing bingo in the meeting hall of a church or temple. While such assumptions about the religious activities of older adults are stereotypes, they are also rooted in some truth. Hands down, when considering levels of religious participation across the life span, older adults demonstrate the highest levels of religious engagement compared to any other age group.[1] Particularly compared to Millennials, over half of whom report disenchantment with religion today (noting they perceive it to be hypocritical, judgmental, and antigay), older adults remain invested in their faiths. National data from the 2010 General Social Survey demonstrates that roughly 40 percent of people aged seventy-five years or older attend religious services *at least* once a week; compare this to 12 percent of people eighteen to twenty-nine years old! On the flip side, only 13 percent of people aged fifty to sixty-nine are nonreligious, and only 7 percent of people over seventy are nonreligious.[2] Religious institutions often offer social, economic, and other forms of support to their elderly congregation members. And in truth, most social activities for older people (particularly in rural communities) are rooted in churches.

Though not uniformly, many studies find that religious beliefs have a salutatory impact on older adults' well-being. And beyond belief, congregational support—social support from fellow members of your religious community—is also posited to be at the root of some of the physical and mental health benefits of being religiously committed in older adulthood.[3] A strong commitment to religious beliefs may provide some older adults with a more resilient coat against the realities of the human condition—including the shifting of life roles (from being a caregiver, to requiring care), the loss of loved ones, and physical decline.[4] Indeed, many religions clearly offer answers to existential queries and articulate values about death and the afterlife—as such, they provide guidance in making meaning of one's life. However, contrary to the popular assumption that more religion equals more armor against the realities of being mortal, comparisons of highly religious individuals and committed atheists demonstrate that the two groups are similarly skilled at finding meaning in life and self-actualization.[5] Specific to older adults, recent research supports that a strong atheistic belief system can fulfill the same role as a religious belief system in that it provides the explanation, inspiration, support, and consolation to help elderly individuals cope with aging.[6]

In short, atheist older adults are likely not feeling as directionless and without meaning as scholars previously imagined. However, one reality of aging in the United States is the assumption that older adults will be actively engaged in religious communities and committed to a belief system. After all, what resources or social venues exist for elder individuals that are unaffiliated with religious institutions? The following narratives begin to shed light on how older atheist women and men have conquered their existential concerns, found purpose and meaning in life, and continued to have fun adventures as aging nonbelievers.

Chris, Betty, and Margaret are all older atheist women who have been nonbelievers for well over half of their long lives. While they are now reaching ages where loved ones are beginning to pass away and where their physical health is on the decline, each of their narratives depict a lively, active, and feisty approach to life. Chris, now almost eighty, does not shy away from examining the human condition. She writes, "to me it's a matter of luck if you survive and flourish," and "I have confronted my mortality with open eyes from the time I was a teenager, and when I can no longer be independent and feel I'm a burden to myself and others, I hope to find a way to exit this life on my own terms." Similarly, Margaret, who is seventy years old, reflects on the concept of heaven and how soothing it is for many of her older friends and relatives. She does not believe in an afterlife, and with acceptance explains, "difficult as it is to imagine not being here in some form, that's the only explanation that makes sense to me." Chris and Margaret both seem comfortable with embracing that their time on the earth may be all that there is. As they describe the lives that they have lived to this point, it becomes clear that most events have been enacted with a purposeful vigor of *carpe diem*.

However, it has not been entirely simple for these strong women. Betty, eighty-four years old, describes that her husband is now afflicted with dementia. As an atheist, she respectfully observes her friends and family praying for him but does not gain any solace from these actions. Indeed, being able to be open about disbelief in the face of loss seems like it would be a very important healing and uniting factor for older adults, yet many atheists are not able to experience this. Margaret laments that as she and her husband grow older they are beginning to feel the lack of a freethinking community. However, with age, she does not have the same level of energy that she used to and thinks that she cannot start a Humanist group for their town. These pains aside, it is clear from the narratives that Chris, Betty, and Margaret each have been able to enjoy "humanity at its naked best" as a result of their many years of nonbelief. As research suggests, they are still active, engaged, and creating purpose in their lives through scholarly pursuits, hobbies, and travel. Perhaps it *is* possible to grow old gracefully without god.

25

THE ROAD LESS TRAVELED

Ursula Raabe

Ulla, seventy-seven, and her husband are retired and live on the Gulf Coast.

At seventy-seven years of life it sort of comes naturally to look back and try to make sense of things. I've been a nonbeliever for more than fifty of those seventy-seven years.

I was born in Danzig, a famous Hanseatic League city on the Baltic, which is now called Gdansk and is part of Poland. This important little part of the world has an interesting history, sometimes being part of Germany, sometimes part of Poland, and more often a Free City. After the First World War, from 1919 to 1939 Danzig was again a Free City, but the Treaty of Versailles had granted the Polish government certain privileges in the city, one of which was a Polish Post Office. In 1933, elections were held in Danzig, and the Nazi Party won a majority of the Assembly seats, and two years later, during the next election, the Nazi Party consolidated its power. That's why in 1938 Hitler demanded that Danzig be made part of Germany again. The Germans used Poland's refusal as provocation for its attack on Poland on September 1, 1939.

I was born in 1935, right in the middle of what turned out to be the defining moment for my generation in Europe, the United States, as well as the rest of the world.

One of my earliest memories is watching the German ships anchored in the Bay of Danzig shooting salvos into the Polish port of Gdingen and the Polish batteries shooting back. My family had a safe vantage point on a bluff many miles away, and I can still remember the puffs of smoke from the ships' guns. For me, as a three-year-old, that was a fun spectacle. Little did I know where all of this would lead to and that what we were witnessing was the beginning of the Second World War.

As far as religion is concerned, I seem to have had a problem with it from way back in my childhood in Germany. Sitting in church with my parents and hearing about sin and sinners, I thought that my little disobediences like stealing cookies or being mean to my sister should hardly rate as something that would bring the wrath of God upon me. Interestingly, I remember that when I found out there was no Santa Claus I thought it would be just a matter of time before I was told there was no God. But it took me many years and lots of thinking about this matter before I came to that conclusion myself.

As a kid, what puzzled me about God was the unjustness I perceived in how the world was run by this god. There were the nations that practiced Christianity, where you had a chance to get to heaven, then there were other nations with other religions; what about those people? Of course, the church had explanations for all of my questions, none of which was satisfactory, as far as I was concerned. No matter how you sliced it, being born into a Christian environment gave you a tremendous advantage. I thought that was unfair of God.

At the age of fourteen, when I got ready to be confirmed in the Protestant Church in Germany, our Sunday school class had a visit from some church dignitary. He asked if anybody had a question about religion. I asked him: "Why do we proclaim in the Apostolic Creed that we believe in the resurrection of the body, when in fact we don't? We are taught that it is the soul that survives death, not the body." The dignitary had no answer to that, other than a lengthy explanation that made no sense to me at all. That moment was the beginning of my distrust of the teachings of the church.

In my teenage years I came to the conclusion that in order to do what God required, a person had to be living a life like Mother Theresa. It was around this time I decided I would follow my own instincts. I made my peace with the fact that I was not as smart as most people around me, but what I had was integrity. I could not in good conscience pretend to believe in God. However, when I was twenty-three I was married in the church because I wanted to have a pretty wedding gown, and I also didn't want to hurt my mother's feelings. She was religious and had a hard enough time letting me get married to an American, and moving to the United States, so I didn't need to make matters any harder for her by bucking tradition.

I immigrated to the United States and never joined any church, though I went to services a few times at a local Unitarian church. My husband wasn't religious either, and we had a good marriage for thirty-three years until he died of cancer. He died at home with the help of hospice. The idea that I would turn to the church or religion at that time never entered my mind. He had wanted direct cremation, and my sons and I picked up the ashes from the funeral home. We had a tearful and quiet family get-together where we played some classical music and talked about my husband and what he had meant to us. His ashes are in the office at my home waiting for my ashes to be scattered together under the magnificent oak tree we both loved.

As far as "coming out as an atheist," I never did that, per se. The term "atheist" carries too much baggage for me. I prefer to think of myself as a nonbeliever. I never made a big deal out of that fact. When religion comes up in the form of an invitation to attend a church I just say, "I'm not a religious person." That usually is enough to stop that conversation, other than getting a surprised, "Oh?" I can't recall any other particular response.

I joined a secular humanist group in our city and met very many fascinating and kind people who are fun to be with. Some I had met before at the Unitarian church I attended years before. It was the diverse group of people in that church that taught me a lot I needed to learn. The minister was gay, a brilliant speaker, Harvard Divinity School grad, divorced father of a son, and now living with a young man who was the director of the church choir. I had never met an openly gay person. At the university where my husband taught there were several faculty members who were rumored to be gay, and one was outed when he got arrested in a public restroom. These people didn't interest me; being gay had nothing to do with it. But it was a true revelation to meet the gay minister. There also was a woman, very kind and friendly, who was born a man. Again, I had never met anyone like her, and I was impressed with her personality. I no longer go to the Unitarian church, but I'll never forget her or the gay minister either.

As I get older, I find it more and more amazing that people can believe in God. I look at the pictures, for instance, sent back by the Hubble space telescope with the tremendous distances of the universe, the innumerable number of galaxies, with stars coming into existence and others dying, where time is inconceivable in human terms; I find it inconceivable that people believe that this force we are witnessing is God's creation, the same God who is interested in humans and their doings.

Or, picking up a beach stone, worn smooth by the ocean, looking at the layers in that rock, realizing that I hold in my hand part of a mountain. A mountain that in turn was made up of sediments, which at one time were mountains themselves that decayed and then got deposited over millions of years in layers, then thrust up to form the mountain my beach rock came from. That process took millions of years, then the mountain decayed over time, its rocks tumbled into streams, some of which eventually found their way into the ocean. Over a long period of time, they were made smooth and round and then tossed up on the beach for me to find and contemplate.

To me this is reverence for the forces we are part of. A very insignificant part, to be sure. Of course, having a brain, we humans can dream up a scenario in which our individual lives are very important to the forces that we are taught is called God.

But if a belief in any god gives some people a sense of direction, a reason to be moral, a way to deal with death, or other reasons, that is their choice. I have no desire to debate that with them as long as they don't try to dictate their beliefs to me and keep religion out of politics.

I do, however, find some actions of my Christian acquaintances bizarre. After Hurricane Katrina, when her house was flooded with several feet of water, one of them put a four-by-eight billboard in her yard with "THANK YOU, LORD" printed in foot-high letters. I would think, that with his all-powerful eyes, God would be able to read a smaller version, so I had to assume this was some sort of testimonial to all passersby that she didn't blame the Lord for this misery but, on the contrary, saw the flood as a gift and thanked

Him for it. What gift could that be? A cynic might surmise that she was looking forward to a big payoff from FEMA. I don't think that this was what she had in mind. She is well off, and besides, such crass materialism would be in bad taste. So what else could it be that caused her to proclaim her gratitude when everybody else was in such misery? Did she feel it was a test to her faith that the Lord sent, like what Job went through, perhaps? Or by destroying her valuables the Lord wanted to teach her that she still had Him to believe in, which, when all is said and done, is, I have been told, the most important thing in the world for a Christian? Or could it be that perhaps the flooding of her own house spurred her to help others in need, and she wanted the Lord to know that she appreciated to be reminded of her Christian duties? I have no idea what made her put out that four-by-eight sign, but whatever her motive was I found that sign baffling.

I recently went to the 101st birthday party of a close relative. The party was held in the nursing home where many of the extended family gathered. This formerly handsome and formidable woman is now helpless and mentally confused, kept alive 24/7 with help provided by her family and the nursing home staff. She spends her life sitting in a recliner with only the slightest realization of what is going on around her. One of her relatives who is very religious said to me during the birthday party, "To see her in this condition is so pathetic. Why would God do this?" I could only agree that it was a sad situation.

It's so much easier to be a nonbeliever. You don't have to conduct any kind of convoluted mental gymnastics to justify a benign and all-powerful God doing horrible things. To me it's a matter of luck if you survive and flourish. It's a matter of genes if you are born good looking, giving you a tremendous advantage in our society. If you're born healthy, your life can unfold as it is supposed to. If you're handicapped, your life and the lives of people all around you is made harder. If you're born to a loving family or in a developed country, you have a chance of a happy and productive life. If you're born in a part of the world where starvation or wars rage or disease and tyranny prevail, your life will be less than ideal. To me, as a nonbeliever, it is circumstances, not God's grace, that determines, to a large extent, what kind of life you'll have.

So how to deal with religious people if you're a nonbeliever? This is how I do it casually: I sneeze, somebody says, "God bless you." I say, "thank you."

Somebody sneezes, I say, "Gesundheit" (which means "good health" in German). It gets a little more personal when someone hears I have to have an operation and says, "I will pray for you." To that I reply, "I appreciate that you will be thinking of me," and I give them a big smile and/or a hug. However, when someone sends me an e-mail with a political message with the added request, "pray for America," I reply that I do not wish to receive any more messages with either political or religious sentiments.

I got remarried after sixteen years of widowhood. My new husband isn't religious either, so the two of us went to the Justice of the Peace to make it official. My husband's family is religious. One of his sisters used to send me religious e-mails. In the course of a conversation I mentioned to her that I was not religious. She has stopped sending me e-mails but still bombards my husband with the stuff.

My husband's other sister converted to Catholicism and sent me a card the other day saying that a Novena would be celebrated in my name. I thanked her and reminded her that I was not religious but that I appreciated the thought.

My husband's kids and grandkids come to visit, and all of them are religious. Of course the kids used to say the blessing before dinner. Knowing now that we are not religious, the parents have started to say a silent prayer, without much fanfare, and the kids start eating after we wish them "Guten Appetit."

That's the way it should be. When in Rome do as the Romans do. When we eat at their houses we respect their custom to pray. So in our families there is no animosity about being a nonbeliever or a believer, and that's the way it should be.

I am now seventy-seven years old. Looking back on my life, each different period has been a good one. How I became a nonbeliever can probably be traced to my life experiences in my childhood.

My early childhood was a happy one overall, despite the intermittent horror of being a little kid in a war zone. My parents were not Nazis, and moreover, they were members of the Bekennende Kirche, a group of Protestants opposed to Hitler but not necessarily vocal about it. I guess that sort of limited their social life. I never thought about it as a kid, since I myself never had a close friend at that time that I can recall now. My parents were well educated, good looking, and solidly middle class. As far as I was concerned, I had a happy childhood, unaware of the stresses my parents experienced during that time. I remember including Hitler in my nightly prayers, which must have galled my parents.

When I was nine years old we had to flee from the oncoming Russian Army. This started perhaps the hardest part of my life. My father had been hospitalized and shipped out with all the rest of the patients. We had no idea what had happened to him. My brother, sixteen years of age, was drafted into the German Army and stayed behind in Danzig as an antiaircraft recruit. My mother, my sister, and I fled by ship with only the clothes on our backs. From one day to the next we were dislodged from our comfortable and, as far as I was concerned, safe existence and found ourselves on an overcrowded, filthy ship, with no food, hardly any water, and everyone suffering from dysentery. Not till we had landed three days later did we find out that the rest of the ships that were part of the convoy leaving Danzig had been attacked by subs, and many had been sunk. I saw several drowned people floating among the debris in the harbor where we docked. These were the first dead people I ever saw.

While all of this was going on I can't recall any prayers my mother might have said. She might have done so, but I guess I even at that time didn't place much hope on getting any help from God. I must have realized even then that survival is a matter of luck, not divine intervention.

We were finally deposited, like so much chaff, in a village in northern Germany. The farmers were not happy having to quarter refugees, and they let us know it. For them we were Gypsies, and they treated us that way. Despite that fact, I found life on the farm a lot of fun, with cows, pigs, horses, chickens, ducks, and geese all around. We stayed at the farm for six months and then moved to the next little town. The war was over, and life was beginning to get better. In town, however, there was the same attitude toward the refugees that we had experienced at the farm. We were very poor. We had to live on welfare until we were eligible to receive my father's pension.

Looking back on that time, I guess it looks pretty grim from the outside, yet there were many satisfying experiences that shaped my life. I suspect my desire to rely on myself and my immediate family only stem from those experiences, both good and painful. Perhaps my skepticism towards religion was shaped by these experiences. I kept my own council and never felt that I was "one of the gang."

My life changed for the better when I won a one-year, all-expenses-paid scholarship to the United States as a high school exchange student. I switched from being a poor second-class refugee in a small German town to a person in the United States others were interested in. I was chosen as homecoming queen, though I still was not comfortable being "part of the gang" and invented the story of a boyfriend left behind in Germany to avoid the awkward dating ritual I was uncomfortable with. My foster parents were very religious, and I dutifully attended church services and Sunday school every week. By this time I knew that religion was not for me. Yet when Billy Graham came to town I went to the revival meeting with my foster parents, got caught up in the mass hysteria, and went forward to be blessed. This was a very temporary conversion. The other day I watched an interview with Billy Graham's daughter, who stated that you couldn't be wise unless you believe in God. In view of that, I'm doubly glad that her father's teachings had but a fleeting influence on me.

I have a good, happy, and fulfilling life without religion. Religion is something other people concern themselves with. Since I haven't been "one of the gang" all my life, there is no conflict with religious people.

After many years of widowhood, I got remarried. Having raised my children and retired, I was free to pursue some of the things I had always wanted to do. I went on several exciting trips with the Sierra Club. During the last ten years I got certified as a scuba diver and had a chance to go diving eighty-seven feet down to a World War II warship sunk at an atoll in the Pacific. Two years later, at sixty-eight years of age, I took up downhill skiing, and at seventy I got good enough to tackle a black diamond run without falling once (though I must admit, I was scared enough not to try that again). My husband and I went clear across the United States on his motorcycle and also toured New Zealand for three weeks on a Goldwing. While there I had a chance to go bungee jumping from the famous Kawarau Bridge and got a certificate from A. J. Hackett to prove it. Later that year we went sailing on the Adriatic for ten days. The last three years have been overshadowed by a botched hip replacement that has put a temporary, perhaps even permanent, halt to the vigorous physical activities I used to enjoy. But my husband and I are "High-pointers," and our goal is to visit the highest point in every state of the United States. This I can still do. We have visited seventeen Highpoints so far and counting, though of course the really difficult ones will elude us. I love to garden, and I'm raising amaryllis from seeds. It takes at least five years until the bulbs get big enough to bloom, so you have to be patient to do that. Next year my husband, who is a pilot, will teach me to land our small seaplane. Perhaps I will even learn to fly.

Life is great right now. But I have confronted my mortality with open eyes from the time I was a teenager, and when I can no longer be independent and feel I'm a burden to myself and others, I hope to find a way to exit this life on my own terms.

I am now in the last quarter of my existence. Looking back on a good and productive life, I'm glad I've lived it with integrity and without God.

26

A CONTRARIAN LIFE STORY

Elizabeth Malm Clemens

"Betty," age eighty-four, lives in Knoxville, but she returns to her "born and bred" city of New Orleans every chance she gets.

As I tread through my eighth decade of life here in Knoxville, I ponder how to complete my life journey among strangers who seem to misunderstand my personal and independent lifestyle. My husband and I left Louisiana in 2005 when Katrina washed away our entire community of St. Bernard Parish. Life-long friends were dispersed, neighbors of forty-seven years were no longer available, and we lost our home and its contents to the ravages of mold that followed the flooding. Here in Knoxville we find ourselves far removed from our pasts, facing a confused present and an incomprehensible future.

I have never been one who anticipated the light at the end of the tunnel— I assume I having "saw the light" on my travel down Mama's birth canal. As first-born, I was a Daddy's girl, immediately destined to inherit his love of science, life, and family. With strong influences from all three directions I was taking charge by my third birthday, seeking my life's purpose by elementary school and voted "most unique" in the senior high school baby picture contest. Perhaps unique is the most fitting lifelong description, as I followed my own dreams, usually not in concert with others but always ready to defend my stance.

My first decade of life dawned on Columbus Street in an urban setting. There were no closets, literal or figurative, in my childhood home in New Orleans, perhaps accounting for the open-mindedness with which I was raised. My German and Swedish heritage through my grandparents exposed me to Presbyterian Sunday church services and the traditional vacation Bible school. The former filled me with the fear that "God sees everything"; I cowered in the pew between hymns. I actually thought that the choir members, seated behind a curtained area in front of the huge brass pipe organ, were the Lord's spies checking on my behavior.

The latter consisted of daily summer marches up the fifty-eight steps of Third Presbyterian Church on Esplanade and North Broad. It was comforting singing with the group of children,

> Onward Christian soldiers,
> Marching as to war
> With the cross of Jesus
> Going on before

I felt strength in every marching footstep, as we purposely imitated the German soldier marches seen in movie news coverage of World War II. I also noted, with confusion, that my parents never attended church events. It seemed something for children only.

It was fun. It was exciting. It was erroneous, I soon learned. Especially my memory of

> Jesus loves the little children
> All the children of the world.
> Red and yellow, black and white,
> They are precious in his sight.
> Jesus loves the little children of the world.

I took this so seriously, and it was reinforced by the strangers Daddy would invite home to dinner: a Scot in his kilt playing the bagpipes; the guest who left a xylophone for us to assemble and play; the Swedish ship captain who brought his Schiperk dog, Toto, to live with us while he sailed away; all interesting characters; all good, caring people who seemed to follow the Ten Commandments I had been taught. The world seemed filled with good, generous people who would never see children differently than the song proposed. I would soon learn that few practiced that philosophy.

By age twelve I was openly questioning a religion that doomed Daddy to Hell because he had to work on Sundays as a motion picture projectionist. Daddy was my idol, having weaned me from fairy tales to classic comics, to *Wuthering Heights* and *Jane Eyre*, and to scientific inquiry that fueled my constant questioning, "Why?"

By age sixteen, I had explored my neighborhood friends' Lutheran, Catholic, and Greek churches, noting differences but feeling at home in each. I was now fascinated with cultural differences, attending public school with second-generation students whose parents were from Italy, Spain, Ireland, Greece, China, France, Germany, and Norway. Quite a smorgasbord of experiences that culminated with Sunday evening teen services that provided a pulpit for young questioners to address their own concerns. I loved selecting the topic, the hymns, and the biblical passages from the Bible. These were my "in love" years with religion. I dreamed of being married to a minister, but I do credit Third Church with inspiring and cultivating my personal leadership skills, which would have led to the ministry itself.

My third decade of development included meeting Harold and losing Mama in a DUI car accident, both of which would change my life forever. Mama's death in suburban St. Bernard Parish would portend later difficulties with that parish's politicians. Harold would introduce me to the Baptist church and suburbia.

When Harold was called into active naval service aboard a destroyer escort in Korea, I promised to wait for him for two years before we would announce our engagement and marriage. I planned to be a second-generation bride in Third Church.

I had now mourned the deaths of my grandmother, uncle, and mother, but with no prayer. I had tried to do lip service during church but expected a conversation. Prayer had not been a part of our dining experience growing up. We were never urged to pray for help through traumas. We were taught to make decisions and take responsibility for our actions. We were to accept consequences and move on. Invaluable lessons in a fun-loving, adventurous family environment.

But when Bill lost his Madeline, everything changed. Daddy became bitter over her death, wondering aloud why God had not split up the constantly arguing couple next door rather than deprive him of his adoring wife. The inventor, who had introduced me to his world of science through his patent applications, would no longer pursue his dream. All of his ideas generated in the movie projection booth while the reels spun their magic for the audience died with Mama. Suddenly home just became a house. It led me to explore the world beyond the Seventh Ward and spend my time waiting for Harold acting on local radio and in community theater productions.

Are you wondering where I am, religiously, at this point? We have moved to St. Bernard Parish, where I daily pass the spot where Mama was thrown through the windshield onto the neutral ground. This astounding coincidence is fueling my Presbyterian belief in predestination. But I hardly understand the purpose.

I had left Tulane University before completing my degree program in preparation for teaching English. This circular shift to St. Bernard eventually provides me with the opportunity to teach and return to college to study. A second baby completes my family, and we move further into the parish for Harold to build our "dream house" on Poydras Pond. We were still a young couple, accepting help from our new church friends to finish the house, and I was teaching Bible class.

This is when I made the decision to leave the church behind, for two reasons. First, I needed more family time on weekends, after teaching five full days a week and attending night classes to complete my degree. Second, I had graduated from the Bible study. I had the feeling of having finished a small section of a journey and not wanting to retrace my steps. My self-assurance in the classroom had peaked. The elementary lessons had been learned, and I was flying on my own.

So we became a nonreligious family in a community that boasted on billboards, "Jesus Is Lord in St. Bernard." Yet this parish was also the home of a Ku Klux Klan, noted for burning crosses to frighten blacks amid a history of animosity toward "outsiders." When school integration was ordered by the federal government in New Orleans, the local school board transported white students across parish lines to educate them, leaving little Ruby Bridges behind to fend for herself. Nothing destroys Christianity like badly behaving Christians.

When St. Bernard's turn came to integrate their public schools, the beloved superintendent devised a plan to separate genders at the high school level, anticipating problems. I would say we get what we anticipate in education. That seemed to be the white administrative mantra.

Classroom teachers need limitless expectations of student performance. Perhaps none of the problems would have developed had a Christian approach been applied. But no, there was us and there was them. Only an agnostic, or an atheist, could have led these students through the turmoil that resulted from prejudicial Christian leadership. But no one of substance, and sans faith, would ever have achieved that status of leadership in New Orleans, St. Bernard, or perhaps in any public school in America. We had moved, as a nation, from the "Little House on the Prairie" to a conglomerate nation of successful entrepreneurs and corporations, but we were still operating our school systems like hand-me-down clothing. I chose to wear the metal of a warrior and to fight the intellectual battle for my students, but I soon learned that David only wins in the biblical story.

The battleground turned into a war. The Christian superintendent, who had used me to fill a post at an isolated elementary school where three teachers had already left in October 1957, was now determined to strip me of the fellowship experience that had prepared me as a reading specialist. Somehow, being chosen to attend based solely on my application had upset him. I shall never understand whether he wanted someone else to represent St. Bernard Parish or if he just wanted my obligation to him. Favors granted, favors owed kind of thing. I suspected the latter, as his school principal appointments included many closeted gays. I was too strong to be closeted for any reason.

So I left the system, withdrew my retirement garnered over fifteen years, and opened my own school for underachieving students. Utilizing my clinical training of diagnosis, remediation, and evaluation learned in my graduate studies at Loyola University; keeping class size down to ten; and accessing a goal-setting approach, we returned hundreds of academically overhauled students to public schools. We used the California Achievement Test for skill area measurement. I was elatedly using this small experience simply to prove that all students can learn, if their needs are properly met.

I had defied the labeling of "learning disabled." We had worked successfully with students deprived of a public school education for vandalism, arson, and substance abuse. In my decade of applied research, I had learned that reading skills not mastered by third grade meant failure at fifth and school dropout at seventh. So my next step was to introduce a preacademic program for three-, four-, and five-year-olds as a preventive measure. We successfully turned out accelerated first grade students to matriculate at public or private schools of the parents' choice. After a decade of success in the private sector I closed those school doors and devoted years to working with the New Orleans business community to lobby for educational change in Louisiana.

I still worked in the urban school setting that had educated me. I served as external consultant, trained principals, and retreated daily to my Poydras Pond to reflect on public education with my sole support, Harold. There were no prayers to help, no Gods to oversee what was happening in my beloved city. A return to my elementary and high schools displayed graffiti, lack of instruction, and no regard for school history. It was not a black doing, it was a lack of leadership that should have welcomed black students into a structured learning environment back in 1960, and the city was now paying the price.

In 2004, I was still successfully teaching a predominately black student population at the community college level, my forty-eighth year in education. The twenty-five years of hosting foreign students from Italy, Sweden, Germany, China, Serbia, Japan, and Korea had opened our home and our hearts to so many cultures and religions that Harold and I were now internationally flavored. Nothing informs more than exposure. When the German boy put his foot through our ceiling in Poydras, Harold got him to help with the repair. When our septic tank backed up and had to be emptied, Harold and I chuckled to find that the Italian student had flushed his fancy underwear down the toilet rather than hand it to me for washing. Sometimes, you just have to laugh. No restraints. No walls. Just humanity at its naked best.

Perhaps these growth cycles are needed to explore exactly who we are. I just know that my family provided me that extra spurt toward individuality. The current social culture may slow down the process, but I have always been enamored with Ayn Rand's take on the power of the individual. Ideas, I believe, are sparked by an independent mind. It may take teams to develop, manufacture, and market it, but the seed is nurtured in a sole brain. This observation leads me to the final decade of my story.

In 2005, we moved here to Knoxville and through post-traumatic stress, we tried to relearn who we were. We had suffered loss beyond comprehension: our past, our present, and our future. Through therapy sessions at the University of Tennessee, I dealt with my role with Harold. We were virtually lost, clinging to each other for mutual support, even returning to the Presbyterian church for lost memories. Harold had seen me through Mama's violent death and Daddy's easy one. Daddy's heart had just stopped beating on a return flight from Atlanta. His last thoughts were probably anticipation for his planned business opening back in New Orleans. I was happy to know that he had been spared the loss of that city's downtown, which we both adored.

Harold had driven me up here and, from Knoxville, had made repeated trips down to St. Bernard to sift through the house contents and move all of our belongings into several huge piles of trash higher than the house. He tried to rescue his beloved tools from his destroyed workshop. But it had all been too much.

Dementia has destroyed his thinking over the seven years we have been here. It bears many labels, Alzheimer's, Parkinson's, Lewy Body. But I do not recognize labels. I still research, diagnose, and try to help my husband of fifty-eight years deal. Everyone prays for him. I guess that is all they have to offer. And that is fine with me. I accept their prayers as well intended. But my bookcase holds copies of the Nag and the Quran next to the Holy Bible. I am a literary person who reads and thinks. My thinking these days focuses on comparing my earlier research in education with my current research efforts in medicine.

The comparison is astounding. When I sought truths in education, I opened a school to prove a point. Now that I seek truths about the brain, I am attempting to work with residential administrators to develop better options for the aged in their last decade of life. There are too many unknowns; too many poorly trained assistants, nurses, and administrators; and too much marketing. We are all being shuffled into one-size-fits-all containers. I have never allowed myself to be squeezed where I did not fit and neither has Harold.

I visit him in Memory Care daily, but it is during the trips away from the facility that he comes alive. I only wish that I could take all of the residents on our "dates" for mental exposure before their brains shrivel up and die. I remember a song from our dating days, "Don't Fence Me In." Having lost faith in earlier refrains that proved unworthy, I choose this one to end my time on this fascinating planet. My journey has left me well traveled and appreciative of the opportunity to share with others. It has been a worthwhile trip . . . and, at age eighty-four, I am still tripping!

27

DARK MATTER AND
MISSING SOCKS

Margaret M. Bennett

Margaret, seventy, lives in Londonderry, New Hampshire. She and her husband, Malcolm, have been married for nearly forty-nine years. They have two daughters and two granddaughters. Prior to her retirement, Margaret worked for many years in the finance office of Pinkerton Academy in Derry, New Hampshire.

I am seventy years old, and I have been an avowed atheist for more than half that time. I have been a doubter for even longer than that, as I began questioning the veracity of religious beliefs at the age of sixteen.

I was brought up in a religious household. In fact, my father was a Congregational minister, though in many ways he was not a typical clergyman. He was a skeptic about most things. He didn't believe in ghosts, extraterrestrials, and ESP. He didn't even believe in angels or demons, and I'm not sure that he believed in the actual existence of Satan. He did believe, though, that Jesus was the son of God (though he had some doubts about the virgin birth) and that there was a Resurrection. He also believed in the reality of an afterlife, though his views on Heaven and Hell differed somewhat from conventional Christianity. He was a Universalist in that he thought that most people who lived reasonably moral lives would go to Heaven, even if they weren't Christian, and that Hell was reserved for truly evil people, such as Hitler. He also thought that people should find their own paths, so he was not at all authoritarian in his preaching. He would say, "This is what I believe; you don't have to agree with me." A few members of his congregation criticized him for that approach and wanted him to be more authoritative and to preach more about sin and damnation, but that wasn't his style.

My mother was even less conventional in her beliefs. She had been brought up in a Methodist family in Kansas and in fact was a deaconess. Her motivation in becoming a deaconess, though, was that it was a route to becoming a social worker in a settlement house, which was what she really wanted to do. She didn't believe in the divinity of Jesus but just thought that he was a very good and wise man. She also didn't believe in an afterlife and once told me that when she and my father were dating they would have discussions in which he would say that she would be surprised when she died and found out that she was going somewhere, and she would respond that he would be surprised that he wasn't. However, she never talked much about her personal beliefs when I was growing up; perhaps she didn't want to confuse me. I do remember one occasion, though, when she let something slip. We were standing outside church one Sunday morning after the service, and one of the church ladies came up to us. The lady began regaling us with details about a trip she had recently made to the Cathedral of the Pines (an outdoor venue in New Hampshire where various groups hold religious services) and what a wonderful spiritual experience it had been. Mom listened politely and made appropriate remarks, but on the way home she turned to me and said, "What do you think that nice lady would have done if the minister's wife had said 'Bullshit!'"

When I was growing up there were four churches in our town: Congregational, Methodist, Episcopal, and Roman Catholic. Almost everyone I knew went to one or the other of those churches. I never encountered an atheist or agnostic—or at least anyone who admitted to being one—until I went to college. I believed in God simply because everyone around me did, and I never really gave it much thought. In high school I had a friend who would go into a trancelike state from time to time. Afterward, she would say that she had a physical experience of God's presence. At the time I rather uncharitably assumed that she was putting on an act, but I understand that studies of the brain have shown that some people do have physiological changes when they pray or meditate. If there is such a thing as a "God module," though, I don't have it.

As I mentioned earlier, I was sixteen when I began questioning what I had been taught about Christianity. The possibility that God might not exist caused me a great deal of anxiety. The Cold War was at its height then, and the realization that there might not be a God who would protect us from a nuclear attack was frightening. When I told my father about my concerns, he said, "Everyone goes through a period of doubt. Usually they come out of it with a stronger faith than before." My mother's advice was to "keep an open mind."

When I went to college I became involved in the peace and civil rights movements, and for the first time I encountered people who were atheist or agnostic. Looking back, I find it ironic that so many of the peace and human rights activists were nonbelievers while many professed Christians were hawkish about war and viewed those fighting for civil rights as communists and rabble rousers. At the time, though, I still wasn't quite ready to give up my religious belief. During my college years I often attended a Society of Friends meeting. I never fully understood the Friends' view of theology, but I liked their ideology. I would also ask religious people, such as members of the Friends meeting or devout classmates, what was the basis for their belief. The answers I usually got were, "You have to have faith," or "I just know it's true."

I met my husband, Malcolm, the summer between my junior and senior years of college. I was working in Boston that summer. I had some acquaintances who were members of a Unitarian group called Liberal Religious Students, and I met Mal through them. He was brought up in a reform Jewish household. His family attended services on holy days, and Mal was sent to Hebrew School and had a bar mitzvah, but that was more out of the desire to appease relatives than religious conviction. Mal says that he can't remember ever really believing in God.

Mal and I were married shortly after I graduated from college, and we will soon be celebrating our forty-ninth anniversary. For several years after my marriage I continued in my uncertain state concerning religion. For a while after we moved to New Hampshire in 1975, I attended a Congregational church, more because I thought it would be a good way to meet people than out of religious conviction. The church was quite liberal when I first started going there, but gradually a group of fundamentalists began taking over. When they started talking about ending the teaching of evolution in public schools, I stopped going.

Is it easy being an atheist in a nation of believers? No, not always. There is a sense of being an outsider, of not quite belonging. Our neighbors don't gather on our lawn with torches and pitchforks, but when we tell people we are nonbelievers we are often greeted with a noticeable coolness or sometimes pity. There is a misconception that nonbelievers became that way as a result of some terrible calamity or a dysfunctional childhood, instead of education and reason, and that they are basically unhappy individuals. That is the message on two popular television shows, *House* and *Bones*, where the protagonists are atheists. Dr. Gregory House, although a brilliant diagnostician, is a bitter, unhappy man incapable of forming normal relationships. Temperance Brennan, aka Bones, is a forensic anthropologist more comfortable with the dead than the living. Though she is a more sympathetic character than Dr. House, she also has difficulty with emotions and relationships.

A few years ago, before he retired, my husband had a coworker who was a born-again Christian. When he found out that we are atheists, he apparently decided to take us on as his project. He began showing up at our house unannounced, bearing religious tracts and booklets. Upon learning that my father had been a minister, he became very sympathetic. "I understand now," he said. "Your father must have been a very strict man. You were probably forced to go to church." I could see that he expected the conversation to lead to a literal "come to Jesus" moment, in which I realized that my nonbelief was nothing more than a reaction to having been forced to attend church. I admit that it gave me great pleasure to assure him that this was not the case.

Although New Hampshire is supposed to be one of the least religious states in the country, the area where we live apparently didn't get that memo. Our home is on a stretch of road which runs eleven miles between the southern and northern borders of our town. Along that road there are two Roman Catholic churches, two Baptist churches, a Methodist church, a Presbyterian church, and an independent nondenominational church. There are also at least three independent churches that hold services at the public schools. In what seems to be a bit of overkill, there was a schism in the Presbyterian Church, so a second church of that denomination will soon be built practically next door to the original one. In other parts of town there are a Korean Christian church, a Kingdom Hall of Jehovah's Witnesses, and a Pentecostal church. Neighboring communities have a similar variety of places to worship. My point is that in southern New Hampshire there is no lack of religious choices, yet to hear people talk there is imminent danger of the area being overrun by godless zombies.

As we grow older, Mal and I both feel the lack of a community of like-minded people. It's harder for Mal than it is for me because he grew up in a large, noisy family where get-togethers always involved lively discussions of politics and religion. We do have friends who are nonbelievers, but we don't get together on a regular basis. Also, even among those who agree with us on religion, there is, for some reason, a reluctance to discuss the subject. One acquaintance described himself as an "ignostic." When asked what that meant, he responded, "It means I don't want to discuss it." There is a humanist group in Cambridge, Massachusetts, that we attend on occasion (and I am currently the editor of the group's newsletter), but it isn't always convenient for us to get down there. For several years I ran a humanist group in our area, but I had to give it up when my parents became ill and I needed to make frequent trips to Connecticut, where they were living. My parents are both gone now, but I'm not sure I have the energy to start a new group from scratch. I'd be willing to work in cooperation with someone else, but no one seems to be interested. In recent years, Mal has developed an interest in learning more about his Jewish heritage, and he would like to find a humanistic Jewish group, but there doesn't seem to be one in our area. A couple of years ago we attended an adult education program at a synagogue in a neighboring town, and we enjoyed it very much. However, so far the synagogue hasn't planned another one. Our sense of isolation has increased in recent months. Mal was diagnosed with macular degeneration and is no longer able to drive at all. My night vision isn't very good, so I tend to avoid driving to unfamiliar locations after dark. Consequently, even when there are gatherings of like-minded people we are usually unable to attend.

At my age, of course, one thinks more often of death. In the past year I have attended several funerals of friends and colleagues, most of whom were younger than I am. I'm not afraid of death since I don't believe in an afterlife; I'm just not ready to go yet. There are still a lot of things I wish to accomplish.

I have a cousin whose wife passed away a couple of years ago. After her death he wrote to tell me that he had been in contact with her! He said that she was very happy in heaven, working as a social worker (that had been her profession in life). She had reunited with her sister, who had died several years earlier, and they lived together in a big colonial house (something she had always wanted). She got together frequently with my parents, and my father had taken up a new hobby: playing bagpipes!

I like my cousin's version of heaven better than the traditional ones, such as flying around playing harps or worshiping at the feet of a deity. I'm not sure about the big colonial house bit, though. Having to do housework for eternity isn't my idea of heaven. If there were an afterlife, I'd like it to be one where all one's questions would be answered. What is dark matter? Where do all the missing socks go? (Maybe dark matter is made up of missing socks.) Difficult as it is to imagine not being here in some form, that's the only explanation that makes sense to me.

As far as the future is concerned, I am somewhat encouraged by the fact that some of the more extreme, religious-right candidates didn't get elected this time. While I'm not convinced that they are gone for good, there is hope that rationality will eventually prevail. I would like to see a time when it will be no more unusual to be an atheist or agnostic than it is to be a Catholic or a Baptist and when nonbelievers can freely run for public office.

CONCLUDING THOUGHTS

The Open Door

THE NARRATIVES PRESENTED in *Atheists in America* help clarify some of the complexities of the current sociopolitical landscape for nonbelievers in the United States and the ramifications of this landscape for personal experience. Just as religious beliefs permeate and intersect with most dimensions of life, identifying as atheist is also a significant component of self for many individuals. Beginning with "Leaving Faith" (part 1), it is clear that the act of deciding to step away from religious belief (formally, as in leaving a church community, or informally, as in making the decision to no longer adhere to specific religious doctrines) can have serious social, personal, and existential ramifications. Many authors wondered how they would make meaning in life without the uniform guidance of their religious communities; others expressed feelings of relief and freedom from having shed the constraints of a formal belief system.

Importantly, claiming an atheist identity clearly does not exist in isolation of other dimensions of the self. Without belief in a God/gods, individuals are still active in their varied roles as employees and employers, parents, teachers, retirees, students, artists, and scientists. The authors of the narratives collected here came from all walks of life and represented a wide array of geographic locations within the United States. Authors also greatly ranged in age, socioeconomic status, race, sexual orientation, gender identity, and firmness in their irreligiosity. Thus *Atheists in America* begins to chip away at common demographic assumptions about atheists as a monolithic group: economically advantaged white men from the Northeast and Northwest. This is simply not true. Anyone can be atheist, and atheists are everywhere.

Throughout the narratives, authors reported their hesitancies around coming out as atheist. Even those who were quite firm in their nonbelief (for example, strong atheists) reported some amount of anxiety—coupled with hemming and hawing about *whens* and *how tos*—in weighing the prospect of disclosing their atheist identity to specific individuals in their lives (for example, grandmothers, romantic partners). And even the authors who resided in metropolitan and historically liberal regions of the United States still encountered some stigma and skepticism from members of religious communities upon coming out. Stepping out of the closet was not always a positive or liberating experience.

However, once atheism was truly realized, embraced, and verbalized, many authors did begin to rebuild their social networks and communities. As is often discussed in LGBTQ literature, several narratives indirectly broached the topic of *families of choice* and *communities of choice* or of finding likeminded individuals who supported and honored the authors' beliefs. These communities (for example, humanist groups or online freethought forums) gradually replaced support that was garnered previously from religious organizations. And, for the most part, even when authors disclosed their atheism to very religious friends and family members, they were typically not met with violence, ultimatums, or alarming disrespect—mostly just sadness that nonbelief might put a wedge in their connections or hinder the depth of their relationships.

I hope that this book represents a step toward recognizing that nonbelievers, while an invisible minority, do not need to exist in isolation. There are shared experiences and narratives among atheists in the United States. And while coming out may not always be an option (or necessary, or desired), the authors of these stories have begun to lay gravel for a future well-worn path of being known, acknowledged, and heard. They have cracked open the closet door.

NOTES

INTRODUCTION: THE OTHER CLOSET

1. Jamie Doward, "Atheists Top Book Charts by Deconstructing God: In the Wake of One Religious Sensation, *The Da Vinci Code*, Publishers Are Scoring a Second Success with Sceptics," *The Guardian* (October 29, 2006).

2. Richard Dawkins, "The God Delusion—Back on the *Times* Extended List at No. 24," RichardDawkins.net (2010).

3. "Hardcover Nonfiction," *New York Times* (December 2, 2006).

4. Victor J. Stenger, *The New Atheism* (n.p.: Prometheus, 2009), 25.

5. Seth Andrews, *Deconverted: A Journey from Religion to Reason* (Parker, Colo.: Outskirts, 2013), 72.

6. Livia M. D'Andrea and Johann Sprenger, "Atheism and Nonspirituality as Diversity Issues in Counseling," *Counseling and Values* 51 (2007): 149–158; Brian Davies, "The New Atheism: Its Virtues and Its Vices," *New Blackfriars* 92, no. 1037 (2010): 18–34; Philip Kitcher, "Militant Modern Atheism," *Journal of Applied Philosophy* 28, no. 1 (2011): 1–13.

7. Ned Curthoys, "Against the New Atheism," *Overland* 192 (Spring 2008): 40–43.

8. Melanie Brewster, "Atheism, Gender, and Sexuality," in *The Oxford Handbook of Atheism*, ed. S. Bullivant and M. Ruse (Oxford: Oxford University Press, in press).

9. C. Mooney, "The Future of Irreligion, Part 2: A Conversation with Barry A. Kosmin," *Free Inquiry* 31, no. 8 (2011): 44.

10. D'Andrea and Sprenger, "Atheism and Nonspirituality."

11. Emily A. Greenfield, George E. Vaillant, and Nadine F. Marks, "Do Formal Religious Participation and Spiritual Perceptions Have Independent Linkages with Diverse Dimensions of Psychological Well-Being?" *Journal of Health and Social Behaviour* 50 (2009): 196–212; Teresa E. Seeman, Linda Fagan Dublin, and Melvin Seeman, "Religiosity/Spirituality and Health: A Critical Review of the Evidence for Biological Pathways," *American*

Psychologist 58 (2003): 53; H. F. Unterrainer et al., "Dimensions of Religious/Spiritual Well-Being and Their Relation to Personality and Psychological Well-Being," *Personality and Individual Differences* 49 (2010): 192–197.

12. Frederick J. Kier and Donna S. Davenport, "Unaddressed Problems in the Study of Spirituality and Health," *American Psychologist* 559 (2004): 54.

13. Stephen G. Weinrach and Kenneth R. Thomas, "The Counseling Profession's Commitment to Diversity-Sensitive Counseling: A Critical Reassessment," *Journal of Counseling and Development* 74 (1996): 472–477.

14. Barry Kosmin and Ariela Keysar, "America Religious Identification Survey, Summary Report," Trinity College, 2009, http://www.americanreligionsurvey-aris.org; Phil Zuckerman, "Atheism: Contemporary Numbers and Patterns," in *The Cambridge Companion to Atheism*, ed. Michael Martin (New York: Cambridge University Press, 2007), 47–65; Phil Zuckerman, "Atheism, Secularity, and Well-Being: How the Findings of Social Science Counter Negative Stereotypes and Assumptions," *Sociology Compass* 3 (2009): 949–971.

15. Laura A. Hunter, "Explaining Atheism: Testing the Secondary Compensator Model and Proposing an Alternative," *Interdisciplinary Journal of Research on Religion* 6 (2010): 6; Karen Hwang, Joseph H. Hammer, and Ryan T. Cragun, "Extending Religion-Health Research to Secular Minorities: Issues and Concerns," *Journal of Religion and Health* 50 (2011): 608–22; Kosmin and Keysar, "America Religious Identification Survey."

16. J. L. Miller and R. M. House, "Counseling Gay, Lesbian, and Bisexual Clients," in *Introduction to the Counseling Profession*, ed. David Capuzzi and Douglas R. Gross (Boston: Allyn & Bacon, 2001), 386–414.

17. United States Census Bureau, "The Asian Population in the United States," 2011. http://www.census.gov/population/race/data/asian.html; United States Census Bureau, "The Black Population in the United States," 2011. http://www.census.gov/population/race/data/black.html.

18. Stephen Bullivant, "Defining 'Atheism,'" in *The Oxford Handbook of Atheism*, ed. Stephen Bullivant and Michael Ruse (Oxford: Oxford University Press, in press).

19. Julian Baggini, *Atheism: A Short Introduction* (New York: Oxford University Press, 2003); Stenger, *The New Atheism*.

20. Alister McGrath, *The Twilight of Atheism: The Rise and Fall of Disbelief in the Modern World* (New York: Galilee Trade/Random House, 2004), 175.

21. Michael Martin, "Atheism and Religion," in *The Cambridge Companion to Atheism*, ed. Michael Martin (New York: Cambridge University Press, 2007), 217–232.

22. Dale McGowan, *Atheism for Dummies* (Mississauga, Ont.: Wiley, 2013), 147.

23. Stenger, "The New Atheism," 15.

24. Sarah Hoyes "Prosecutor: Parents' Belief in Faith Healing Led to Infant's Death," *Belief Blog*, May 24, 2013, http://religion.blogs.cnn.com/2013/05/24/prosecutor-parents-refusal-to-seek-medical-attention-led-to-infants-death/?hpt=hp_t5.

25. Darrell W. Ray, *The God Virus: How Religion Infects Our Lives and Culture* (Bonner Springs, Kan.: IPC, 2009), likens religious belief to a dangerous virus that infects the minds of humans and triggers irrationality.

26. A. C. Grayling, *The God Argument: The Case Against Religion and for Humanism* (New York: Bloomsbury, 2013), 140.

27. A response by some members of marginalized groups to go "above and beyond" the required norms of success in order to assimilate into the dominant culture.

28. Anthony B. Pinn, *The End of God-Talk: An African American Humanist Theology* (New York: Oxford University Press, 2011), 114.

29. Austin Dacey, *The Secular Conscience: Why Belief Belongs in Public Life* (New York: Prometheus, 2008).

30. Ibid., 211.

31. William S. Bainbridge, "Atheism," *Interdisciplinary Journal of Research on Religion* 1 (2005): 11–24; Luke W. Galen, "Profiles of the Godless," *Free Inquiry* 29 (2009): 41–45; Kosmin and Keysar, "America Religious Identification Survey"; Darren E. Sherkat, "Beyond Belief: Atheism, Agnosticism, and Theistic Certainty in the United States," *Sociological Spectrum* 28 (2008): 438–459; Zuckerman, "Atheism, Secularity, and Well-Being" 949–971.

32. Bruce Hunsberger and Bob Altemeyer, *Atheists: A Groundbreaking Study of America's Nonbelievers* (n.p.: Prometheus, 2006); Hunter, "Explaining Atheism," 6; Zuckerman, "Atheism: Contemporary Numbers and Patterns," 47–65.

33. Madonna G. Constantine et al., "Religious Participation, Spirituality, and Coping Among African American College Students," *Journal of College Student Development* 43 (2002): 605–613.

34. Greta Christina, "Getting It Right Early: Why Atheists Need to Act Now on Gender and Race," September 9, 2009, http://gretachristina.typepad.com/greta_christinas_weblog/2009/09/race-sex-atheism.html.

35. Frederick Douglass, oration delivered in Corinthian Hall, Rochester, July 5, 1852, University of Rochester Frederick Douglass Project, http://www.lib.rochester.edu/index.cfm?page=2945.

36. Hunsberger and Altemeyer, *Atheists*.

37. John D. Barbour, *Versions of Deconversion: Autobiography and the Loss of Faith* (Charlottesville: University of Virginia Press, 1994), 35.

38. Helen Rose Fuchs Ebaugh, *Out of the Cloister: An Organizational Study of Dilemmas* (Austin: University of Texas Press, 1977).

39. Heinz Streib et al., *Deconversion: Qualitative and Quantitative Results from Cross-Cultural Research in Germany and the United States of America* (Göttingen: Vandenhoeck & Ruprecht, 2013).

40. Andrews, *Deconverted*, 97.

41. Robert G. Ingersoll, "Why Am I an Agnostic? Part I," *North American Review* 149 (December 1889): 397.

42. Hunsberger and Altemeyer, *Atheists*; Michael Argyle, *The Psychology of Religious Behaviour, Belief, and Experience* (n.p.: Routledge, 1997); Bainbridge, "Atheism," 11–24.

43. Pew Forum on Religion and Public Life, *U.S. Religious Landscape Survey: Religious Affiliation: Diverse and Dynamic* (Washington, D.C.: Pew Research Center, 2008).

44. Pamela Ebstyne King and James L. Furrow, "Religion as a Resource for Positive Youth Development: Religion, Social Capital, and Moral Outcomes," *Developmental Psychology* 40, no. 5 (2004): 703–713.

45. Michael Hout and Claude Fischer, "Why More Americans Have No Religious Preference: Politics and Generations," *American Sociological Review* 67 (2002): 165–190.

46. Gallup Poll, "Atheists, Muslims See Most Bias as Presidential Candidates: Two-Thirds Would Vote for Gay or Lesbian," June 7–12, 2012, http://www.gallup.com/poll/155285/atheists-muslims-bias-presidential-candidates.aspx.

47. Will M. Gervais, Azim F. Shariff, and Ara Norenzayan, "Do You Believe in Atheists? Distrust Is Central to Anti-Atheist Prejudice," *Journal of Personality and Social Psychology* 101 (2011): 1189–1206.

48. Penny Edgell, Joseph Gerteis, and Douglas Hartmann, "Atheists as 'Other': Moral Boundaries and Cultural Membership in American Society," *American Sociological Review* 71 (2006): 211–34.

49. Robert J. Nash, "Inviting Atheists to the Table: A Modest Proposal for Higher Education," *Religion and Education* 30, no. 1 (2003): 1–23.

50. McGowan, *Atheism for Dummies*, 263.

51. Margaret Downey, "Discrimination Against Atheists: The Facts," *Free Inquiry* 24 (2004): 41–43; Lawton K. Swan and Martin Heesacker, "Anti-Atheist Bias in the United States: Testing Two Critical Assumptions," *Secularism and Nonreligion* 1 (2012): 32–42.

52. Austin Dacey, *The Future of Blasphemy: Speaking of the Sacred in an Age of Human Rights* (London: Continuum, 2012).

53. McGowan, *Atheism for Dummies*, 156.

54. Ibid.

55. Arkansas, Mississippi, Tennessee, South Carolina, Pennsylvania, Texas, and Maryland.

56. IHUE, "Freedom of Thought 2012: A Global Report on Discrimination Against Humanists, Atheists and the Nonreligious," International Humanist and Ethical Union, 2012, http://www.iheu.org/files/IHEU%20Freedom%20of%20Thought%202012.pdf.

57. Virginia R. Brooks, *Minority Stress and Lesbian Women* (Lexington, Mass.: Lexington Books, 1981); Ilan H. Meyer, "Prejudice, Social Stress, and Mental Health in Lesbian, Gay, and Bisexual Populations: Conceptual Issues and Research Evidence," *Psychological Bulletin* 129 (2003): 674.

58. D'Andrea and Sprenger, "Atheism and Nonspirituality," 149–158; Rob Whitley, "Atheism and Mental Health," *Harvard Review of Psychiatry* 18 (2010): 190–194.

59. Emily Brennan, "The Unbelievers," *New York Times* (November 25, 2011).

60. AHA, "Atheists Give $10,000 to Oklahoma Tornado Victim Rebecca Vitsum After CNN Appearance," http://www.americanhumanist.org/news/details/2013-05-atheists-give-10000-to-oklahoma-tornado-victim-rebec.

61. Atheists Unite Indiegogo campaign, http://www.indiegogo.com/projects/atheists-unite. Indiegogo is a website that hosts fundraising campaigns.

62. Samuel E. Siner, "A Theory of Atheist Student Identity Development," *Journal of the Indiana University Student Personnel Association* (2011): 14–21; M. E. Brewster, "Atheism, Gen-

der, and Sexuality," in *The Oxford Handbook of Atheism*, ed. Stephen Bullivant and Michael Ruse (Oxford: Oxford University Press, in press).

63. Gregory M. Herek, "Hate Crimes and Stigma-Related Experiences Among Sexual Minority Adults in the United States: Prevalence Estimates from a National Probability Sample," *Journal of Interpersonal Violence* 24, no. 1 (2009): 54–74.

64. Edgell, Gerteis, and Hartmann, "Atheists as 'Other,'" 211–234.

65. Ibid.; Siner, "A Theory of Atheist Student Identity Development," 14–21.

66. Richard Cimino and Christopher Smith, "The New Atheism and the Formation of the Imagined Secularist Community," *Journal of Media and Religion* 10 (2011): 24–38.

67. Richard Dawkins, *The God Delusion* (London: Bantam, 2006); Christopher Hitchens, *God Is Not Great: How Religion Poisons Everything* (n.p.: McClelland & Stewart, 2007).

68. Curthoys, "Against the New Atheism," 40–43; Paul Kurtz, "A Neo-Humanist Statement," *Free Inquiry* 30 (2010): 5–6.

69. Edgell, Gerteis, and Hartmann, "Atheists as 'Other,'" 211–234.

70. Brewster, "Atheism, Gender, and Sexuality."

71. Thomas Linneman and Margaret Clendenen, "Sexuality and the Secular," in *Atheism and Secularity: Issues, Concepts, and Definitions*, ed. Phil Zuckerman (Westport, Conn.: Praeger Perspectives, 2010), 89–112.

72. Scott B. Button, "Identity Management Strategies Utilized by Lesbian and Gay Employees: A Quantitative Investigation." *Group and Organization Management* 29, no. 4 (2004): 470–494.

73. Siner, "A Theory of Atheist Student Identity Development," 14–21.

PART 1. LEAVING FAITH: ARRIVING AT ATHEIST IDENTITY FROM RELIGIOUS BACKGROUNDS

1. Mark Chaves and Dianne Hagaman, "Abiding Faith," *Contexts* 1 (2002): 19–26.

2. Jesse M. Smith, "Becoming an Atheist in America: Constructing Identity and Meaning from the Rejection of Theism," *Sociology of Religion* 72 (2011): 215–237.

3. A. S. Miller and J. P. Hoffmann, "Risk and Religion: An Explanation of Gender Differences in Religiosity," *Journal for the Scientific Study of Religion* 34 (1995): 63–75.

4. Seth Andrews, *Deconverted: A Journey from Religion to Reason* (Parker, Colo.: Outskirts, 2013), 22.

5. Bruce Hunsberger and Bob Altemeyer, *Atheists: A Groundbreaking Study of America's Nonbelievers* (n.p.: Prometheus, 2006); Smith, "Becoming an Atheist in America," 215–237.

6. Bruce Hunsberger, "Swimming Against the Current: Cases of Apostates and Converts," in *Joining and Leaving Religion: Research Perspectives*, ed. L. J. Francis and Y. J. Katz (Leominster: England), 233–248.

7. Phil Zuckerman, *Faith No More: Why People Reject Religion* (New York: Oxford University Press, 2012), 153.

8. Heinz Streib, Ralph Hood, Barbara Keller, Rosina-Martha Csoff, and Christopher Silver, *Deconversion: Qualitative and Quantitative Results from Cross-Cultural Research in Germany and the United States of America* (Göttingen: Vandenhoeck & Ruprecht, 2009), 97.

4. EX-MORMON, CORA JUDD

1. Within the Church of Jesus Christ of Latter-Day Saints (LDS), the word "testimony" is used by members to mean that they have confident knowledge that principles or doctrines of the faith are true because a spiritual witness was given to them by the Holy Ghost.

2. In 1857, several large groups of emigrants (called the Baker-Fancher party) from Arkansas were making their way to California, through primarily LDS-populated regions of Utah. The emigrants were encouraged by LDS officials to restock their supplies and rest at Mountain Meadows in southern Utah. During their rest, LDS-backed militia and Mormon settlers disguised as Native Americans slaughtered the party (over 120 women, men, and children) and took their supplies.

3. Instituted in the 1840s by Joseph Smith, *blood oaths* are practiced during Endowment ceremonies in the LDS faith. An endowment ceremony prepares a person to be a "worthy Mormon" before going on a mission or having a celestial marriage. They require the participant to swear never to reveal certain key symbols of the Endowment ceremony, including the penalty itself, while symbolically enacting ways in which a person may be executed if they do break the oath (e.g., gesturing that a throat would be slit).

PART 2. CULTURAL CONTEXTS IN COMING OUT AS ATHEIST

1. Sikivu Hutchinson, *Moral Combat: Black Atheists, Gender Politics, and the Value Wars* (n.p.: Infidel, 2011), 2.

2. Kelley Newlin, Kathleen Knafl, and Gail D'Eramo Melkus, "African-American Spirituality: A Concept Analysis," *Advances in Nursing Science* 25, no. 2 (2002): 57.

3. Jacqueline S. Mattis, "Religion and Spirituality in the Meaning-Making and Coping Experiences of African American Women: A Qualitative Analysis," *Psychology of Women Quarterly* 26, no. 4 (2002): 309–321.

4. Hank Fox, *Red Neck, Blue Collar, Atheist: Simple Thoughts About Reason, Gods, and Faith* (n.p.: Hank Fox, 2010).

5. Jacqueline S. Mattis and Robert J. Jagers, "A Relational Framework for the Study of Religiosity and Spirituality in the Lives of African Americans," *Journal of Community Psychology* 29, no. 5 (2001): 519–539.

6. "How the Faith of African Americans Has Changed," Barna Group, 2009. http://www.barna.org/culture-articles/286-how-the-faith-of-african-americans-has-changed.

7. Mattis, "Religion and Spirituality."

8. Hutchinson, *Moral Combat*, 4.

9. Donald R. Barbera, *Black and Not Baptist: Nonbelief and Freethought in the Black Community* (n.p.: iUniverse, 2003).

10. Anthony Pinn, *The End of God-Talk: An African American Humanist Theology* (New York: Oxford University Press, 2012), 149–150.

11. Norm Allen, *African American Humanism* (n.p.: Prometheus, 1991).

12. Hutchinson, *Moral Combat*, 43.

PART 3. TWO CLOSETS? IDENTIFYING AS BOTH LGBTQ AND ATHEIST

1. Jodi O'Brien, "Wrestling the Angel of Contradiction: Queer Christian Identities," *Culture and Religion* 5 (2004): 180.

2. Melinda Buchanan et al., "Challenges of Being Simultaneously Gay or Lesbian and Spiritual and/or Religious: A Narrative Perspective," *American Journal of Family Therapy* 29 (2001): 435–449; Bernadette Barton, "Abomination: Life as a Bible Belt Gay," *Journal of Homosexuality* 57 (2010): 435–484; Yoel Kahn, "The Liturgy of Gay and Lesbian Jews," in *Twice Blessed: On Being Lesbian, Gay, and Jewish*, ed. Christie Balka and Andy Rose (Boston: Beacon, 1989), 182–197; Brenda Cooper and Edward C. Pease, "The Mormons Versus the 'Armies of Satan': Competing Frames of Morality in the *Brokeback Mountain* Controversy in Utah Newspapers," *Western Journal of Communication* 73 (2009): 134–156; Tom Boellstorff, "Between Religion and Desire: Being Muslim and Gay in Indonesia," *American Anthropologist* 10 (2005): 575–585.

3. Barton, "Abomination," 472.

4. Patrick Califia, *Speaking Sex to Power: The Politics of Queer Sex* (n.p.: Cleis, 2002); Mitchell Gold and Mindy Drucker, *Crisis: Forty Stories Revealing the Personal, Social, and Religious Pain and Trauma of Growing Up Gay in America* (n.p.: Greenleaf, 2008).

5. E. Ozorak, "The Power, but Not the Glory: How Women Empower Themselves Through Religion," *Journal for the Scientific Study of Religion* 35 (1996): 17–19.

6. Thomas Linneman and Margaret Clendenen, "Sexuality and the Secular," in *Atheism and Secularity: Issues, Concepts, and Definitions*, ed. Phil Zuckerman (Westport, Conn.: Praeger, 2010), 89–112.

7. O'Brien, "Wrestling the Angel of Contradiction," 184.

8. Barton, "Abomination," 435–484.

9. Linneman, "Sexuality and the Secular," 89–112.

11. FAR FROM HOME, DAVID PHILIP NORRIS

1. Directly from Awana.org: "Awana helps churches and parents work together to develop spiritually strong children and youth who faithfully follow Jesus Christ. Our programs offer a proven approach for evangelizing and discipling kids in the church and community."

PART 4. AIN'T NO MOUNTAIN HIGH ENOUGH: NAVIGATING ROMANTIC RELATIONSHIPS AS AN ATHEIST

1. Christopher G. Elison, Amy M. Burdette, and W. Bradford Wilcox, "The Couple That Prays Together: Race and Ethnicity, Religion, and Relationship Quality Among Working-Age Adults," *Journal of Marriage and Family* 72, no. 4 (2010): 963–975.

2. David G. Schramm et al., "Religiosity, Homogamy, and Marital Adjustment," *Journal of Family Issues* 33, no. 2 (2012): 246–268.

3. Darrel Ray, *Sex and God: How Religion Distorts Sexuality* (n.p.: IPC, 2012).

4. AtheistPassions.com has roughly 6,000 members, whereas FreeThinkerMatch.com has about 17,000 (predominately men).

5. Chloe Logan, "Atheist Looking for Love? Stay Away from EHarmony.com," http://voices .yahoo.com/atheist-looking-love-189258.html?cat=41.

6. Kimberly Winston, "At OKcupid, Being an Atheist Is a Datemaker, Not a Dealbreaker," http://archives.religionnews.com/culture/entertainment-and-pop-culture/At-OKcupid -being-an-atheist-is-a-date-maker-not-a-deal-breaker.

PART 5. FAMILY LIFE AND ATHEIST PARENTING

1. Christel Manning, "Atheism, Secularity, Family, and the Children," in *Atheism and Secularity: Issues, Concepts, and Definitions*, ed. Phil Zuckerman (Westport, Conn.: Praeger Perspectives, 2010), 19–42.

2. Jesse M. Smith, "Becoming an Atheist in America: Constructing Identity and Meaning from the Rejection of Theism," *Sociology of Religion* 72 (2011): 221.

3. Manning, "Atheism, Secularity, Family, and the Children," 19–42.

4. Douglas J. Davies, "An Introduction to Mormonism," *Nova Religio* 8 (2004): 133–134.

5. Dale McGowan, *Parenting Beyond Belief* (New York: Amacon, 2007), x.

6. http://parentingbeyondbelief.com/MediaKit.pdf

7. Dale McGowan et al., *Raising Freethinkers: A Practical Guide for Parenting Beyond Belief* (n.p.: Amacon/American Management Association, 2009).

8. Greg Epstein, *Good Without God: What a Billion Nonreligious People Do Believe* (n.p.: William Morrow, 2009).

PART 6. THE SEARCH FOR CONNECTION: COMING OUT TO FRIENDS AND QUESTING FOR COMMUNITY

1. Kathleen M. Goodman and John A. Mueller, "Invisible, Marginalized, and Stigmatized: Understanding and Addressing the Needs of Atheist Students," *New Directions for Student Services* 125 (2009): 55–63.

2. Jeff Ritchey, "'One Nation Under God': Identity and Resistance in a Rural Atheist Organization," *Journal of Religion and Popular Culture* 21 (2009): 2.

3. Dale McGowan, *Atheism for Dummies* (Mississauga, Ont.: Wiley, 2013), 313–314.

4. Richard Cimino and Christopher Smith, "The New Atheism and the Formation of the Imagined Secularist Community," *Journal of Media and Religion* 10 (2011): 24–38.

PART 7. ATHEISM AT WORK: TALES OF COMING OUT TO COWORKERS AND COLLEAGUES

1. Douglas A. Hicks, "Spiritual and Religious Diversity in the Workplace: Implications for Leadership," *Leadership Quarterly* 13 (2002): 379.

2. Karen C. Cash and George R. Gray, "A Framework for Accommodating Religion and Spirituality in the Workplace," *Academy of Management Executive* 14, no.3 (2000): 124–33.

3. Josh Schopf, "Religious Activity and Proselytization in the Workplace: The Murky Line Between Healthy Expression and Unlawful Harassment," *Columbia Journal of Law and Social Problems* 31 (1997): 39.

4. Joy E. Beatty and Susan L. Kirby, "Beyond the Legal Environment: How Stigma Influences Invisible Identity Groups in the Workplace," *Employee Responsibilities and Rights Journal* 18 (2006): 29–44.

22. IS THIS THE WAY TO AMARILLO? SAMUEL W. NEEDLEMAN

1. In Texas, calling "bullshit" wouldn't make any sense—while the word is occasionally used as a symbol for profit derived from the beef industry, it isn't a commonly recognized metaphor for nonsense.

PART 8. ATHEISM AND AGING: THE CHALLENGES OF ENTERING OLDER ADULTHOOD AS A NONBELIEVER

1. Susan H. McFadden, "Religion and Well-Being in Aging Persons in an Aging Society," *Journal of Social Issues* 51 (2010): 161–175.

2. Barry Kosmin and Ariela Keysar, "American Nonreligious Identification Survey" (2008), http://commons.trincoll.edu/aris/.

3. R. David Hayward and Neal Krause, "Trajectories of Disability in Older Adulthood and Social Support from a Religious Congregation: A Growth Curve Analysis," *Journal of Behavioral Medicine* (2012): 1–7.

4. McFadden, "Religion and Well-Being," 161–175.

5. Tatjana Schnell and William J. F. Keenan, "Meaning-Making in an Atheist World," *Archive for the Psychology of Religion* 33 (2011): 55–78.

6. Peter J. Wilkinson and Peter G. Coleman, "Strong Beliefs and Coping in Old Age: A Case-Based Comparison of Atheism and Religious Faith," *Ageing and Society* 30 (2010): 337.

BIBLIOGRAPHY

Argyle, Michael. *The Psychology of Religious Behaviour, Belief, and Experience*. N.p.: Routledge, 1997.

Bagghil, Julian. *Atheism. A Short Introduction*. New York: Oxford University Press, 2003.

Bainbridge, William S. "Atheism." *Interdisciplinary Journal of Research on Religion* 1 (2005): 11–24.

Barbera, Donald R. *Black and Not Baptist: Nonbelief and Freethought in the Black Community*. N.p.: iUniverse, 2003.

Barton, Bernadette. "Abomination: Life as a Bible Belt Gay." *Journal of Homosexuality* 57 (2010): 465–484.

Beatty, Joy E., and Susan L. Kirby. "Beyond the Legal Environment: How Stigma Influences Invisible Identity Groups in the Workplace." *Employee Responsibilities and Rights Journal* 18 (2006): 29–44.

Boellstorff, Tom. "Between Religion and Desire: Being Muslim and Gay in Indonesia." *American Anthropologist* 10 (2005): 575–585.

Brewster, M. E. "Atheism, Gender, and Sexuality." In *The Oxford Handbook of Atheism*, ed. Stephen Bullivant and Michael Ruse. Oxford: Oxford University Press, forthcoming.

Brooks, Virginia R. *Minority Stress and Lesbian Women*. Lexington, Mass.: Lexington, 1981.

Buchanan, Melinda, Kristina Dzelme, Dale Harris, and Lorna Hecker. "Challenges of Being Simultaneously Gay or Lesbian and Spiritual and/or Religious: A Narrative Perspective." *American Journal of Family Therapy* 29 (2001): 435–449.

Bullivant, Stephen. "Defining 'Atheism.'" In *The Oxford Handbook of Atheism*, ed. Stephen Bullivant and Michael Ruse. Oxford: Oxford University Press, forthcoming.

Califia, Patrick. *Speaking Sex to Power: The Politics of Queer Sex*. N.p.: Cleis, 2002.

Cash, Karen C., and George R. Gray. "A Framework for Accommodating Religion and Spirituality in the Workplace." *Academy of Management Executive* 14, no. 3 (2000): 124–133.

Chaves, Mark, and Dianne Hagaman. "Abiding Faith." *Contexts* 1 (2002): 19–26.

Cimino, Richard, and Christopher Smith. "The New Atheism and the Formation of the Imagined Secularist Community." *Journal of Media and Religion* 10 (2011): 24–38.

Constantine, Madonna G., Leo Wilton, Kathy A. Gainor, and Erica L. Lewis. "Religious Participation, Spirituality, and Coping Among African American College Students." *Journal of College Student Development* 43 (2002): 605–613.

Cooper, Brenda, and Edward C. Pease. "The Mormons Versus the 'Armies of Satan': Competing Frames of Morality in the *Brokeback Mountain* Controversy in Utah Newspapers." *Western Journal of Communication* 73 (2009): 134–156.

Curthoys, N. "Against the New Atheism." *Overland* 192 (2008): 40–43.

Dacey, Austin. *The Future of Blasphemy: Speaking of the Sacred in an Age of Human Rights*. London: Continuum, 2012.

D'Andrea, Livia M., and Johann Sprenger. "Atheism and Nonspirituality as Diversity Issues in Counseling." *Counseling and Values* 51 (2007): 149–158.

Davies, Brian. "The New Atheism: Its Virtues and its Vices." *New Blackfriars* 92, no. 1037 (2010): 18–34.

Davies, Douglas J. "An Introduction to Mormonism." *Nova Religio* 8 (2004): 133–134.

Dawkins, Richard. *The God Delusion*. London: Bantam, 2006.

Downey, Margaret. "Discrimination Against Atheists: The Facts." *Free Inquiry* 24 (2004): 41–43.

Edgell, Penny, Joseph Gerteis, and Douglas Hartmann. "Atheists as 'Other': Moral Boundaries and Cultural Membership in American Society." *American Sociological Review* 71 (2006): 211–134.

Elison, Christopher G., Amy M. Burdette, and W. Bradford Wilcox. "The Couple That Prays Together: Race and Ethnicity, Religion, and Relationship Quality Among Working-Age Adults." *Journal of Marriage and Family* 72, no. 4 (2010): 963–975.

Epstein, Greg. *Good Without God: What a Billion Nonreligious People Do Believe*. N.p.: William Morrow, 2009.

Fox, Hank. *Red Neck, Blue Collar, Atheist: Simple Thoughts About Reason, Gods and Faith*. N.p.: Hank Fox, 2010.

Galen, Luke W. "Profiles of the Godless." *Free Inquiry* 29 (2009): 41–45.

Gallup. "Atheists, Muslims See Most Bias as Presidential Candidates: Two-Thirds Would Vote for Gay or Lesbian." June 7–12, 2012. http://www.gallup.com/poll/155285/atheists-muslims-bias-presidential-candidates.aspx.

Gervais, Will M., Azim F. Shariff, and Ara Norenzayan. "Do You Believe in Atheists? Distrust Is Central to Anti-Atheist Prejudice." *Journal of Personality and Social Psychology* 101 (2011): 1189–1206.

Gold, Mitchell, and Mindy Drucker. *Crisis: Forty Stories Revealing the Personal, Social, and Religious Pain and Trauma of Growing Up Gay in America*. N.p.: Greenleaf, 2008.

Goodman, Kathleen M., and John A. Mueller. "Invisible, Marginalized, and Stigmatized: Understanding and Addressing the Needs of Atheist Students." *New Directions for Student Services* 2009, no. 125 (2009): 55–63.

Greenfield, Emily A., George E. Vaillant, and Nadine F. Marks. "Do Formal Religious Participation and Spiritual Perceptions Have Independent Linkages with Diverse Dimensions of Psychological Well-Being?" *Journal of Health and Social Behavior* 50 (2009): 196–212.

Hayward, R. David, and Neal Krause. "Trajectories of Disability in Older Adulthood and Social Support from a Religious Congregation: A Growth Curve Analysis." *Journal of Behavioral Medicine* (2012): 1–7.

Herek, Gregory M. "Hate Crimes and Stigma-Related Experiences Among Sexual Minority Adults in the United States. Prevalence Estimates From a National Probability Sample." *Journal of Interpersonal Violence* 24, no. 1 (2009): 54–74.

Hicks, Douglas A. "Spiritual and Religious Diversity in the Workplace: Implications for Leadership." *Leadership Quarterly* 13 (2002): 379–396.

Hitchens, Christopher. *God Is Not Great: How Religion Poisons Everything.* N.p.. McClelland & Stewart, 2007.

Hout, Michael, and Claude Fischer. "Why More Americans Have No Religious Preference: Politics and Generations." *American Sociological Review* 67 (2002): 165–190.

Hunsberger, Bruce. "Swimming Against the Current: Cases of Apostates and Converts." In *Joining and Leaving Religion: Research Perspectives*, ed. L. J. Francis and Y. J. Katz, 233–248. Leominster, England.

Hunsberger, Bruce, and Bob Altemeyer. *Atheists: A Groundbreaking Study of America's Nonbelievers.* N.p.: Prometheus, 2006.

Hunter, Laura A. "Explaining Atheism: Testing the Secondary Compensator Model and Proposing an Alternative." *Interdisciplinary Journal of Research on Religion* 6 (2010): 6.

Hutchinson, Sikivu. *Moral Combat: Black Atheists, Gender Politics, and the Value Wars.* N.p.: Infidel, 2011.

Hwang, Karen, Joseph H. Hammer, and Ryan T. Cragun. "Extending Religion-Health Research to Secular Minorities: Issues and Concerns." *Journal of Religion and Health* 50 (2011): 608–622.

IHEU. "Freedom of Thought 2012: A Global Report on Discrimination Against Humanists, Atheists and the Nonreligious." International Humanist and Ethical Union (IHEU), 2012. http://www.iheu.org/files/IHEU%20Freedom%20of%20Thought%202012.pdf.

Kahn, Yoel. "The Liturgy of Gay and Lesbian Jews." In *Twice Blessed: On Being Lesbian, Gay, and Jewish*, ed. Christie Balka and Andy Rose, 182–197. Boston: Beacon, 1989.

Kier, Frederick J., and Donna S. Davenport. "Unaddressed Problems in the Study of Spirituality and Health." *American Psychologist* 59 (2004): 54.

King, Pamela Ebstyne, and James L. Furrow. "Religion as a Resource for Positive Youth Development: Religion, Social Capital, and Moral Outcomes." *Developmental Psychology* 40, no. 5 (2004): 703–713.

Kitcher, Philip. "Militant Modern Atheism." *Journal of Applied Philosophy* 28, no. 1 (2011): 1–13.

Kosmin, Barry, and Ariela Keysar. "America Religious Identification Survey, Summary Report." Trinity College, Hartford, Conn., 2009. http://www.americanreligionsurvey-aris.org/.

Kurtz, Paul. "A Neo-Humanist Statement." *Free Inquiry* 30 (2010): 5–6.

Linneman, Thomas, and Margaret Clendenen. "Sexuality and the Secular." In *Atheism and Secularity: Issues, Concepts, and Definitions*, ed. Phil Zuckerman, 89–112. Westport, Conn.: Praeger, 2010.

Logan, Chloe. "Atheist Looking for Love? Stay Away from EHarmony.com." http://voices.yahoo
.com/atheist-looking-love-189258.html?cat=41.

Manning, Christel. "Atheism, Secularity, Family, and the Children." In *Atheism and Secularity: Issues, Concepts, and Definitions*, ed. Phil Zuckerman, 19–42. Westport, Conn.: Praeger, 2010.

Martin, Michael. "Atheism and Religion." In *The Cambridge Companion to Atheism*, ed. Michael Martin, 217–232. New York: Cambridge University Press, 2007.

Mattis, Jacqueline S. "Religion and Spirituality in the Meaning-Making and Coping Experiences of African American Women: A Qualitative Analysis." *Psychology of Women Quarterly* 26, no. 4 (2002): 309–321.

Mattis, Jacqueline S., and Robert J. Jagers. "A Relational Framework for the Study of Religiosity and Spirituality in the Lives of African Americans." *Journal of Community Psychology* 29, no. 5 (2001): 519–539.

McFadden, Susan H. "Religion and Well-Being in Aging Persons in an Aging Society." *Journal of Social Issues* 51 (2010): 161–175.

McGowan, Dale. *Atheism for Dummies*. Mississauga, Ont.: Wiley, 2013.

——. *Parenting Beyond Belief*. New York: Amacon, 2007.

McGowan, Dale, Molleen Matsumura, Amanda Metskas, and Jan Devor. *Raising Freethinkers: A Practical Guide for Parenting Beyond Belief*. N.p.: Amacon/American Management Association, 2009.

McGrath, Alister. *The Twilight of Atheism: The Rise and Fall of Disbelief in the Modern World*. N.p.: Galilee Trade, 2004.

Meyer, Ilan H. "Prejudice, Social Stress, and Mental Health in Lesbian, Gay, and Bisexual Populations: Conceptual Issues and Research Evidence." *Psychological Bulletin* 129 (2003): 674.

Miller, J. L., and R. M. House. "Counseling Gay, Lesbian, and Bisexual Clients." In *Introduction to the Counseling Profession*, ed. David Capuzzi and Douglas R. Gross, 386–414. Boston: Allyn & Bacon, 2001.

Newlin, Kelley, Kathleen Knafl, and Gail D'Eramo Melkus. "African-American Spirituality: A Concept Analysis." *Advances in Nursing Science* 25, no. 2 (2002).

O'Brien, Jodi. "Wrestling the Angel of Contradiction: Queer Christian Identities." *Culture and Religion* 5 (2004): 179–202.

Ozorak, E. "The Power, but Not the Glory: How Women Empower Themselves Through Religion." *Journal for the Scientific Study of Religion* 35 (1996): 17–29.

Pew Forum on Religion & Public Life. "U.S. Religious Landscape Survey: Religious Affiliation: Diverse and Dynamic. Pew Research Center." 2008.

Pinn, Anthony. *The End of God-Talk: An African American Humanist Theology*. New York: Oxford University Press, 2012.

Ray, Darrell. *Sex and God: How Religion Distorts Sexuality*. N.p.: IPC, 2012.

Ritchey, Jeff. "'One Nation Under God': Identity and Resistance in a Rural Atheist Organization." *Journal of Religion and Popular Culture* 21 (2009): 2.

Schnell, Tatjana, and William J. F. Keenan. "Meaning-Making in an Atheist World." *Archive for the Psychology of Religion* 33 (2011): 55–78.

Schopf, Josh. "Religious Activity and Proselytization in the Workplace: The Murky Line Between Healthy Expressions and Unlawful Harassment." *Columbia Journal of Law and Social Problems* 31 (1997): 39.

Schramm, David G., James P. Marshall, Victor W. Harris, and Thomas R. Lee. "Religiosity, Homogamy, and Marital Adjustment." *Journal of Family Issues* 33, no. 2 (2012): 246–268.

Seeman, Teresa E., Linda Fagan Dubin, and Melvin Seeman. "Religiosity/Spirituality and Health: A Critical Review of the Evidence for Biological Pathways." *American Psychologist* 58 (2003): 53.

Silverman, Dave. "Coming Out: The Other Closet." American Atheists (blog), http://atheists .org/content/coming-out-other-closet.

Siner, Samuel E. "A Theory of Atheist Student Identity Development." *Journal of the Indiana University Student Personnel Association* (2011): 14–21.

Sherkat, Darren E. "Beyond Belief: Atheism, Agnosticism, and Theistic Certainty in the United States." *Sociological Spectrum* 28 (2008): 438–459.

Smith, Jesse M. "Becoming an Atheist in America: Constructing Identity and Meaning from the Rejection of Theism." *Sociology of Religion* 72 (2011): 215–237.

Stenger, Victor J. *The New Atheism.* N.p.: Prometheus, 2009.

Streib, Heinz, Ralph Hood, Barbara Keller, Rosina-Martha Csoff, and Christopher Silver. *Deconversion: Qualitative and Quantitative Results from Cross-Cultural Research in Germany and the United States of America.* Göttingen: Vandenhoeck & Ruprecht, 2009.

Swan, Lawton K., and Martin Heesacker. "Anti-Atheist Bias in the United States: Testing Two Critical Assumptions." *Secularism and Nonreligion* 1 (2012): 32–42.

U.S. Census Bureau, U.S. Department of Commerce. The Asian Population in the United States. 2011. http://www.census.gov/population/race.

—— The Black Population in the United States. 2011. http://www.census.gov/population/race.

Unterrainer, H. F., Karl H. Ladenhauf, M. L. Moazedi, S. J. Wallner-Liebmann, and A. Fink. "Dimensions of Religious/Spiritual Well-Being and Their Relation to Personality and Psychological Well-Being." *Personality and Individual Differences* 49 (2010): 192–197.

Weinrach, Stephen G., and Kenneth R. Thomas. "The Counseling Profession's Commitment to Diversity-Sensitive Counseling: A Critical Reassessment." *Journal of Counseling & Development* 74 (1996): 472–477.

Whitley, Rob. "Atheism and Mental Health." *Harvard Review of Psychiatry* 18 (2010): 190–194.

Wilkinson, Peter J., and Peter G. Coleman. "Strong Beliefs and Coping in Old Age: A Case-Based Comparison of Atheism and Religious Faith." *Ageing and Society* 30 (2010): 337.

Winston, Kimberly. "At OKcupid, Being an Atheist Is a Date-Maker, Not a Deal-Breaker." 2012. http://archives.religionnews.com/culture/entertainment-and-pop-culture/At-OKcupid -being-an-atheist-is-a-date-maker-not-a-deal-breaker.

Zuckerman, Phil. "Atheism: Contemporary Numbers and Patterns." In *The Cambridge Companion to Atheism,* ed. Michael Martin, 47–65. New York: Cambridge University Press, 2007.

——. "Atheism, Secularity, and Well-Being: How the Findings of Social Science Counter Negative Stereotypes and Assumptions." *Sociology Compass* 3 (2009): 949–971.

Zuckerman, Phil. *Faith No More: Why People Reject Religion.* New York: Oxford University Press, 2012.